Healing Vegan Mac

SANAE SUZUKI

love,
sanae
my healing journey

Salli,
for your healing!

love,

Sanae

All photography by Sanae Suzuki and
Eric Lechasseur
Food preparation and photo styling by
Eric Lechasseur and Sanae Suzuki
English editing by Judy Lee, Carissa Burton,
Joel Klass and Christine Goodreau
Recipe editing by Christine Goodreau
Book design by Ellison / Goodreau, Los Angeles

love, sanae

my healing journey

This cookbook is dedicated to the three most important people in my life:

my father, Shin Takashima, and my mother, Toshiko Suzuki, who gave me life and raised me to prepare for my journey back to heaven; and my husband, lover, and best friend, Eric Lechasseur, who is teaching me to love, grow and thrive on this earth.

FOOD IS MEDICINE.

CONTENTS

ACKNOWLEDGMENTS

I would like to thank all the people and creatures I have met and encountered, from whom I have received knowledge, encouragement, strength and hope in order to heal myself. *Arigatou — Thank you!*

Words can't express my gratitude to my husband, Eric Lechasseur, for his love, support and partnership, through health, sickness, happiness and challenging times.

All of my macrobiotic teachers, starting with my first teacher, Cecile Tovah Levin, for her unflinchingly precise guidance toward healing. Michio Kushi and Aveline Kushi for their dedication to macrobiotics. Midori Hayashi for her kind assistance. Bill Dufty for his humor and encouraging me to accomplish more than I believe I can.

All the teachers who I have learned from since 1994: Cornellia Aihara, Herman Aihara, Noboru and Ida Muramoto, Kazuko and Junsei Yamazaki, Shizuko Yamamoto, Alex Jack, Charles Millman, Wendy Esko, Ed Esko, Carry Wolf, John Kozinski, Luchi Baranda, Bettina Zumdick, Warren Kramer, Clyde Motosue, Karin Stephan, Susan Krieger, Diane Avoli, Patricia Price, Verne Varona, Mina Dobic, David Briscoe, Madame Riviere, René Levis and Jacques Mittler for their commitment.

Macrobiotic friends, Ruška Porter, Mayumi Nishimura, Patricio Garcia de Paredes, John Saslow, Jessica Porter, Mark Hanna, Mark Berry, Christina Pirello, Carissa Burton, David Schmidt, Deco Nakajima, Marie Yamaguchi for fun times.

The Kushi Institute people, especially Olaf Fischer, Mirea Ellis, Judy and Larry MacKenney, Sandy Hall, Debora Wright, Hideki Kawai and Phiya Kushi for their help for all these years.

Meg Wolff and Dr. Neal D. Barnard, for their kind support.

Tobey Maguire for believing in me and giving me an opportunity.

My herbology teacher, David Crow, for his gentle soul.

Dr. Toby Hamilton, for saving my life in the ER after my car accident in Arizona.

My neighbor friend, Nancy Hamaluk, for her kindness.

Talented ceramists, Vladimira Zbori, Michiko Nakamura, Akemi Kotani, Frank Phillips, Ed Camhi, Ron Capri and Eric Lechasseur.

All my students and clients, who have helped me to practice and learn more in order to properly answer your questions and give appropriate advice.

All of my assistants who helped with cooking classes, worked at events and in the office of *mugen*, since 1995.

My good friends, Judy Lee, Christine Goodreau and Mike Ellison, without whose belief in me, and artistic support, this cookbook would not have been completed.

My golden girls, Kin, Dore, Kula, Oro, and my alley cats, Key-chain and Mai for their unlimited patience and unconditional love.

I thank all the people whose names are not mentioned who have touched and shaped me in some way, even for an instant.

love, sanae

FOREWORD

Macrobiotics was introduced in the United States in the early 1960's as a means to heal and prevent sickness, in part due to a typical American diet of hamburgers, hot dogs, TV dinners, and "junk foods." Fast foods today account for approximately half of all restaurant revenues in the U.S. This figure has tripled since three decades ago and continues to rise at an alarming rate, both here and in other countries around the world.

We are gravitating toward a fast-food-oriented lifestyle due to the impression that we are all so busy and in a hurry all the time. We feel as though there is not enough time in the day to accomplish what we set out to do. When mealtime comes, we do not think twice about food being anything but a way to stave off hunger, regardless of its lasting effect on our body and mind.

When the source of, and the process of preparing our meals are not taken into consideration, there is a price we have to pay. This price is in the eventual manifestation of diseases and illnesses. The body, mind and spirit, due to the lack of attention, break down and become unbalanced. When this occurs, we seek solutions in the form of surgery, medication, alternative treatment and therapy.

Sanae first came to understand macrobiotics when she was diagnosed with ovarian cancer. At the time, the doctors warned her that the cancer was very aggressive, and that she needed

treatment immediately. Despite the concerns of her family, friends and doctors, Sanae wanted to seek natural and holistic solutions that truly empowered her from within. She believed that true health is one in which you are freed from the fears, constraints and conditioning of your mind and are able to take charge of your life and live it by your own design. While searching for the "answer" to fighting her illness, Sanae discovered the macrobiotic way of recovering health.

I first met Sanae at the Kushi Summer Conference in 1994. I remember how impressed I was with her positive outlook despite the challenges she faced on her road to recovery. From that day forward, Sanae volunteered and worked diligently not only at conferences and events, but as my student and mentee. We had conversations about our life experiences, and she proved to be a "natural" and quick study in the pursuit of macrobiotics.

It is wonderful to see someone like Sanae heal herself and grow leaps and bounds while applying the philosophies and teachings of macrobiotics.

I remember the day she had her car accident and went into a coma. Her then partner Eric Lechasseur (they were later married in 2004) contacted me, and we had a conversation that further convinced Eric that the macrobiotic way of living is not just about food but is a life philosophy. I told him that Sanae will be fine because of her courage, strength and determination. Eric did not lose hope, and Sanae came out of the coma and started to make a remarkable recovery. Sanae and Eric's steadfast belief in the benefits of macrobiotics not only helped them overcome serious health issues, but elevated their relationship to a higher level of bonding, sharing and supporting.

I have always stressed the importance of not following any teaching or philosophy in blind faith, but to find one's own voice and path. Upon being introduced to macrobiotics, most people have the following impressions: the food is bland and aesthetically challenged; the ingredients are difficult to find; the regimen is too rigid; food preparation is difficult and time-consuming. Sanae has shattered these myths by breathing new life and color into traditional macrobiotic cooking and philosophy and creating a simple, relaxed, beautiful, varied, exciting and enjoyable macrobiotic style of cooking and living.

I call Sanae my excellent student. My only wish is that her story, life and cooking style will touch many more who are inspired toward the path to a life of health, happiness and peace.

Michio Kushi
The World leader of Macrobiotic education for health and peace, Brookline, MA

There are two ways to live your life.
One is as though nothing is a miracle.
The other is as though everything
is a miracle.
— Albert Einstein, 1879 - 1955

MY STORY

The Diagnosis

After the summer of 1993, I noticed that I felt tired all the time, nursing a low-grade fever for several weeks. Prior to this condition, I had been ill with some problems associated with my liver and had to take a few months off from work. After getting a checkup and blood test to find out if my liver had started acting up again, the doctor at the clinic said that my liver seemed to be fine, but my ovaries had a "serious problem." I fell into a deep shock, combined with a feeling of numbness, and much of what he said after that was a blur. I was diagnosed with ovarian cancer and advised to go to the hospital for more tests. At the hospital I was told that I had such an aggressive cancer that I had to have my left ovary removed right away. Since I did not have medical insurance the doctor recommended that I go back to Japan to have surgery and get treatment. Otherwise, he added, I wouldn't make it. Once again, I was stunned by the doctor's words, his voice barely audible as I sat there immobile and dazed.

The Turnaround

I lost my father to liver cancer in 1989. I saw how difficult it was for him to fight this cancer, and I was paralyzed by the daunting prospect of fighting for my own life without even knowing where to begin. I did not want to call my family in Japan for several reasons. My mother's health had been deteriorating since my father passed away, my sister had just suffered a miscarriage, and my brother was still too young to shoulder such bad news on top of everything else. I did not feel I would get the support I needed. Financially I was far from able to afford surgery or treatment. As hopeless as it seemed for me at the time, I now understand that my enlightenment and true life in macrobiotics would have its beginnings right then and there.

The Adventure

I had been frequenting a Japanese natural foods store called "Sogo" in the Little Tokyo region of Los Angeles, and the owner, Mr. Kikuchi, was always nice enough to talk to me about natural healing. When he first introduced me to the concept of macrobiotics, I recalled leafing through a macrobiotic cookbook (I think it was Aveline Kushi's *Complete Macrobiotic Cookbook*) at a yoga studio a few years prior. I remember thinking that the recipes were very much like traditional Japanese food, but since the name Kushi was not common in Japan, I thought the author might have been from somewhere else. I learned quite a lot from Mr. Kikuchi, but not enough to really understand how to heal myself. Since Sogo was near the hospital, I dropped in the day I was handed my "death sentence." Mr. Kikuchi noticed I had been crying and asked me what had happened. He explained that indeed macrobiotic food mirrored Japanese cuisine, but that it was more deeply focused on healing food. He referred me to a macrobiotic counselor in Los Angeles, Cecile Tovah Levin. He also told me about Aveline Kushi (who turned out to be Japanese) and her husband, Michio Kushi. With nothing to lose, I decided to embark on this road, at the gentle behest of the wise and kind Mr. Kikuchi.

The Breakthrough

All of my life I've felt that no matter what I want or don't want to do, I should at least give it a try first. Regrets are part of life and I decided that if I regretted anything, it would be from not having tried something rather than having tried it. I bought Michio Kushi's book *Cancer Prevention* and Aveline Kushi's *Complete Macrobiotic Cookbook* and started to try out the recipes. I also called Cecile Tovah Levin. Before I could see her, however, I was instructed to write down a great deal of information about myself, including a comprehensive list of the things I had been eating. This was not easy to do in a short time, especially while nursing myself. The process, ultimately, was an important step in learning about myself, about how I was brought up, and about the effects of my diet. She advised me on what to do, and I had to follow everything to a tee. At the time, I felt too weak to attend any of her classes since I was plagued with symptoms of a very bad flu; I couldn't even get out of bed. I needed someone to confirm what I was doing, but none of my friends knew anything about macrobiotics, and I felt alone and scared.

The Cleansing

The macrobiotic diet had triggered a detoxifying effect, and I soon realized I had been "sick" for several weeks with a fever and gooey discharge (from my eyes, nose, mouth and stool) associated with the detox process. During this time I stuck with my macrobiotic diet and remedy drinks, and the discharge continued for five long weeks. Following this episode it took me an entire year in order to not feel "sick," and to actually feel as though I was getting better. Looking back, after having studied macrobiotics for all of this time, I finally understand why it took an entire cycle of seasons to release the build-up of toxins accumulated over a lifetime, and now realize how we are indeed one with nature. My recovery from cancer took more than a full cycle of seasons, but it was a valuable time for me, helping to seal my resolve to work in macrobiotics. Sure enough, a job as a macrobiotic food consultant came along at the right time. This job kept me motivated to learn more and to take better care of myself.

The Test

On September 8, 2001, while driving back home to Los Angeles from the Kushi Institute in Becket, Massachusetts, having just completed my first Level IV study with Michio Kushi to become a macrobiotic counselor, I had a life-threatening automobile accident in the middle of the Arizona desert. Everyone thought I would not make it, except Dr. Hamilton, a young doctor at the ER trauma center. In the hospital, while my heart stopped for about 12 minutes, I had an out-of-body experience. Dr. Hamilton brought me back to life after making the decision to put a needle to my heart sac. When I came back to life, I experienced excruciating pain. I soon discovered that I had been tied to the bed railing because of my thrashing about. The doctor explained that he could not administer pain medication because it would have caused my heart to stop again. Many tubes ran through my mouth and into my lungs and abdomen. I had compound fractures in both knees, extending through the tibia and fibula, and the doctors considered amputating my left ankle, which was totally crushed. My heart and lungs were badly injured, and I suffered several broken ribs. My doctor told me I may never walk again, and advised me to eat meat to strengthen my bones. The hospital nutritionist thought I was stubborn and crazy for not eating the hospital food. As devastated as I was, I knew that this was no time to undo the healing effects of macrobiotics.

The Homecoming

After three weeks I felt I was not getting better in the hospital, where one could get no peace. The doctors and staff were doing their job, but the level of noise, commotion and disruption from constant checking, prodding and being awakened in the middle of the night was taking its toll. One time the nurses who started to change the bandages on my leg were called away, leaving me with my wounds open for over two hours. Another time I was happy to finally have my hair washed, except for the fact that it was three in the morning. I knew I should be grateful to be alive and in their care, but at the same time, I could not wait to be in a truly healing environment. Besides, I could not afford the hospital fees, having had an untimely lapse in my health insurance. I decided I just had to go home and see the sunlight, breathe the fresh ocean air, and feel the trees I had watched growing for years in my yard. I also knew that I had to be with my furry family, my beloved golden retrievers and cats. Two of my dogs had died in the accident and the surviving dog and cat that were traveling with me had been sent home to Los Angeles. I remember how happy I was to come home and take in my first breath of its familiar smells.

The Recovery

What followed was a long year of my bedridden life. My days and nights were filled with high doses of pain medication, and having my legs strapped to a machine 24-hours-a-day to keep them in constant motion and the blood flowing. I also suffered from intense bouts of Post-Traumatic Stress Disorder (PTSD). Words cannot adequately express my daily frustration and struggles. Many times I asked myself why I had come back to life. I cried and screamed until I eventually exhausted myself from crying and from re-evaluating my life over and over. Thinking back on how I lived during those challenging times gives me hope that I can prevail through any circumstance. It's still not easy for me to talk about those days, however, and someday it may help me to write more about it. During my recovery, I sought physical therapy for my legs, psychotherapy for my PTSD and emotional outbursts, meditation therapy for my spirit, and food therapy for my whole being. Gradually, I learned to move my body out of the bed and into a wheelchair. I adjusted to life in a wheelchair, to which I was bound during my second year of recovery, but I promised myself that no matter what happens — I would walk again.

The Miracle

In July of 2003, my long-time friend Eric Lechasseur asked me to marry him (this story will be written separately someday too). This gave me a wonderful opportunity to set a goal for myself: to walk on my wedding day, June 20, 2004. It was a difficult challenge, but with hard work and a little help from heaven, I managed to walk down the aisle along with my younger brother, who gave me away. As I walked toward Eric I noticed that everyone, including Eric, had tears in their eyes. Since then, my life has never been the same. I felt incredibly lucky to have the people that surrounded me in my life — and everything in life since then became a small miracle.

It has been over fifteen years since my first macrobiotic day, and I have never been healthier or happier. Preparing and eating delicious macrobiotic food gave me the basis of a healthy and natural lifestyle. I feel more satisfied, tranquil, equanimous and peaceful inside and out. Practicing the macrobiotic way is not always easy given that modern life is instant, artificial and yes, convenient. But I truly believe that choosing the easy way has never given me true happiness. I want to share what I know with people who have been seeking a healthier lifestyle, or who are lost, as I was, in the face of a seemingly hopeless situation. I also want to share, along the way, the gamut of feelings that beset me as I overcame the darkest periods of my life. I hope my story and recipes will provide you with a foundation of macrobiotics and help you heal and overcome the challenges in your life. Ultimately, I hope you will be inspired to find true macrobiotic happiness, as I have. Let us walk the path of macrobiotics together. Thank you for joining me.

love, sanae

INTRODUCTION

Welcome to love, sanae!

My healing journey of vegan macrobiotic recipes is divided into three sections: "Sanae's — Let's Get Started — Basics" (with fundamental information and basic recipes for preparing whole grains, soups, beans, vegetables, pickles, sea vegetables, fruits and beverages), "Five Seasons" (with each season corresponding to one of the five Oriental elements) and "Macrobiotic Essentials for Healing" (with information to enable you to understand the macrobiotic essentials in greater depth). The "Five Seasons" section also includes a "Holidays & Special Occasions" recipe section to show that even during times of stress and excess, people can share times of good healing.

Inside the "Five Seasons" section of this book, you will find recipes for each of the following categories:

Remedy Drinks

Sometimes the simplest things are the most important, and remedy drinks are a great example. When I was very ill, remedy drinks helped me daily, bringing me back gradually and gently to a more balanced center. As I got better, I forgot about them, not fully realizing their importance. It was only later that I realized how remedy drinks, in conjunction with the foods I already considered important to my health, help to keep me balanced.

Whenever I feel sick, my body needs a rest, which means not only taking time to rest physically, but also resting my digestive organs. When my beloved dogs and cats get sick, what do they do? They fast or eat less, lie in a warm or cool comfortable spot and rest quietly. They are indeed sometimes my best teachers. We need to learn

how to truly rest and take the proper remedy drinks with the confidence that we are going to get well, no matter what. In this section of the journey, I hope to introduce some of these remedy drinks, according to season, and share the related memories of my recovery.

I take these remedy drinks on an empty stomach before breakfast or between meals, drinking one to two cups a day for three to four days, or sometimes longer. Please remember that it is important to get proper advice from a professional macrobiotic counselor about the appropriate drinks to take for a specific condition.

Breakfast

When we experience and observe the dawning of a new day, the haze breaks slowly and the sun rises surely, giving us light, warmth and hope to our soul. We feel it as peaceful — yet powerful. We realize that our home on earth is moving, changing as we speak, everyday, in every moment, and we are a part of it. During sleep, our body is resting and re-charging our energy in a state of fasting. Breakfast is the essential food that lifts and opens up the body after this period of rest. I start the day with food that provides an uplifting quality, lightness, warmth and softness, like the person I want to wake up to, who will greet me with a kind, gentle embrace, and with gratitude.

I recommend avoiding the typical modern breakfast of bacon, sausage, eggs, coffee, donuts and pastries. Not only are these foods excessively high in cholesterol, saturated fat and sugar, they are also highly refined, oily and excessively sweet foods that can zap your energy. For many people, breakfast is a very challenging meal since they are often too busy racing out the door to take the time to prepare their own food. Additionally, there are few eating establishments that serve healthy, wholesome breakfasts. I highly recommend eating hot cereal, soup and vegetables for breakfast when we want to heal ourselves. These foods make for a nourishing and delicious breakfast to start your day feeling really good.

If you wish to cleanse or detox yourself, skipping breakfast is a suitable meal to miss since your body is already in a naturally cleansing state in the morning. Skipping breakfast and then eating a "regular" lunch would not be cleansing at all, however. When I go on a cleanse, instead of my usual breakfast fare, I'll have a remedy drink. For lunch, I'll have mild miso soup, a small portion of vegetables and light, soft whole grains. Dinner will also be light and consist of small portions.

Lunch

In the middle of the day we are the most active — so I eat something quick, vibrant and energetic. Preparing lunch should also be quick and energetic, not labored and time-consuming. Utilizing leftovers and organizing a menu plan is helpful.

Eating oily and heavy foods makes me feel sluggish and not well. I try to practice eating what my body needs — not what my eyes want. It is always important to maintain a good communication with the body, especially the intestines, and choose wisely according to your current condition.

I work from my home-office and I like to eat my lunch in the open air, in my garden or on the rooftop with the big blue sky. In this way, I feel connected to the earth and to the heavens. Everyone should find the time to go on a lunch picnic with family, friends and co-workers now and again. When you enjoy your lunch out in the open, in the fresh air, your taste buds are heightened, and foods taste exceptionally good!

Dinner

The dinner recipes included in this book are some of the soups and main dishes I have been using to heal myself since 1993. Some I still make and enjoy often, and others I make only as needed, but I love them all. These basic recipes are important to acquire a full understanding of macrobiotics and how to apply the principles to a more elaborate repertoire that you can enjoy for life. The dishes can be adapted very easily for family and friends to enjoy together.

Dinnertime is the closing of the day when I cook with more time and deliberation. I take equal care in eating at this time, in a grounded, enjoyable and calm manner, which helps aid my digestion. One important dinner principle I follow is not eating late at night, so that I can sleep better and my organs are free to rest and rejuvenate as well.

Desserts

I love sweets. They are probably the highlight of my day, if not my life. I am thrilled to have discovered vegan macrobiotic desserts, and am fortunate to have an amazing husband, Eric, who makes delightful, healthful desserts that I can enjoy without guilt. I am also grateful that vegan macrobiotic desserts don't make me worry about weight gain or high cholesterol, although I still have to be careful about overindulging. Too much of a good thing can still make one sick. Also, you should be cautious about eating commercial vegan "macrobiotic" sweets that may utilize inferior ingredients.

When I was healing, however, I did not eat desserts everyday, and I would advise you to do the same. At that time, I considered desserts more of a "reward" for myself about once every 1 or 2 weeks, and chose soft, unbaked recipes, like those featured in this cookbook.

Traditionally, sweets are best eaten at 3 o'clock in the afternoon, since that is the time our blood sugar levels tend to get low and may need to be balanced out. Eating a moderate amount of high quality vegan macrobiotic sweets at the right intervals makes for a satisfied, relaxed and happy existence.

Holidays

During the holidays, people tend to rationalize that just because it's "that time of year," they can overindulge in food and drink, and deal with the consequences later. Many of these holiday foods and drinks are far from the simple, basic diet we need for healing. The good news is that there are many vegan macrobiotic recipes that can be adapted into satisfying holiday recipes. Our first cookbook, *love, eric & sanae,* as well as the recipes in the book you are now holding, feature foods that many people love, and these recipes can be transformed from a more specific "healing" perspective to a healthful holiday dish to satisfy all palates by simply adjusting the quantity of oil, herbs and spices.

The holidays provide an opportunity to create healthier, yet attractive, tasty and enjoyable recipes for ourselves, our families and our friends. You just might surprise your guests with your deceptively healthy holiday spread!

These recipes are only to be taken as suggestions to guide you towards the benefits of a truly natural existence. (Note: If you are very sick, please contact a macrobiotic counselor to receive advice.)

sanae's "let's get started" basics

For Ruška...

After I was well along the path of writing this cookbook and the story of my healing journey, my new Apple computer crashed due to a defective hard drive and my "heart drive" to continue writing crashed right along with it. Shortly thereafter, I learned that my dear friend, beautiful Ruška Porter, who supported my macrobiotic recovery for over ten years, completed her life. At that point, I didn't feel like I could start all over. After wallowing in an emotional void, I started hearing Ruška's familiar voice saying, "Sanae, I love you, you can do it even better than before. Please write about your favorite dishes, and how you showed me the way to cook!" Indeed, we shared many moments, refreshing each other about the basic tools we learned at the Kushi Institute. Thank you, Ruška, my "nine fire" macrobiotic sister! I dedicate the following section of this book to you...

Basic principles provide a vital foundation when we are learning something new. Beginners on the path of healing need to know the importance of the fundamentals. Providing this information to you has allowed me the opportunity to reflect on how I first started; and my hope is that this section not only gives you a good start, but that it does so in the spirit of simplicity and adaptability to our modern contemporary lives. Knowing the basics brings me back to consider why I eat this way, and how I want to live; and my wish is that it does the same for you.

WHOLE GRAINS, SEEDS & NUTS

During my studies at the Kushi Institute, I once asked, "Why are whole grains so good?" As I listened, half expecting something technical about the advantages of their fiber and nutrient content, I was caught off guard by the answer I received. Instead of a nutritional lesson, I heard, "Whole grains are the ultimate marriage of the forces of Heaven and Earth, as they meet and merge in the grain, that is both fruit and seed, and become one. One seed of grain can bring us one thousand grains."

I had to stop and think for a moment, as this simple truth resonated very profoundly within me. Whole grains are often the seeds of grasses, and their beauty lies in the fact that they are self-sustaining. Whole, intact grains can grow if we plant them in soil — in fact, I have heard that whole grains can sprout after hundreds of years in storage. Whole grains are a living, vital, complete and natural food that provide us nourishment so that we may live.

In everyday Macrobiotic cooking, it is recommended that an average of 40 to 50 percent (by weight) of your diet consist of whole grains. There are many types of whole grains, such as brown rice, barley, and millet, as well as whole grains products, such as breads and noodles, all available in natural food markets.

Brown Rice

A good source of protein, phosphorus, and B vitamins, brown rice has all of its nutrients concentrated in the outer brown layers of the bran and germ. Brown rice, which only has the outer hull removed, is the most nutritious type of rice. Unfortunately, many consumers have been culturally indoctrinated to prefer white rice, which has undergone an extreme milling and polishing process which leaves practically no vitamin or nutrient content left in the grain. Replete with nutrients, brown rice is available in different sizes, textures and flavors. Each variety lends itself better to certain types of dishes, which can be observed in the diverse characteristics of foods, such as in paella, sushi, rice salad or pilaf. Categories of brown rice include:

Short-grain: Sweeter and glutinous
This generic size classification indicates a grain that is almost twice as long as it is wide. Some specific varieties of short-grain rice include: Sushi, Balinese Black or Purple, Forbidden Black Rice, CalRose, Mochi Gome, or Pearl. Very flavorful, short-grain rice yields a stickier, softer texture that works well in puddings, croquettes, rice balls, paella, or risotto.

Medium-grain: Soft and moist
This is the generic size classification for rice whose grain is almost three times as long as it is wide. Medium-grain rice is sometimes labeled short-grain, simply to distinguish it from long-grain rice. Some specific types of medium-grain rice include: Japonica, Turkish, Bhutanese Red, CalRiso, Arborio, Egyptian, Kalijira, Italian, Roma, Japanese, Spanish, Valencia, Thai sticky and Vietnamese Red. Medium-grain rice works well in pilafs, salads, risottos and desserts.

Long-grain: Light and fluffy

This is a generic classification for rice in which the milled grain is almost four times as long as it is wide. Some specific varieties of long-grain rice include: Basmati, Calmati, Himalayan Red, Jasmine, American, Persian, Texmati, Thai Black or Red and Wehani. Long-grain rice works well in pilafs and salads.

Sweet Brown Rice: Sticky and glutinous short-grain

Although called "glutinous," sweet brown rice, and all rice for that matter, is gluten-free. Glutinous rice contains high amounts of a starch, called amylopectin, that contributes to its sticky texture. Sweet brown rice contains more protein and fat compared to other types of rice. It is used for anemia, diabetes, strengthening weakened conditions in general, and as an aid for breast-feeding mothers in supplying abundant, high-quality milk. Sweet brown rice is a good choice for people who need to gain weight, as well as for active people. Mochi, often made from pounded sweet brown rice, is used in Japan as a healing food, and is incorporated into a traditional New Year's soup (see Ozoni Mochi Miso Soup recipe on page 51).

Other Grains

Barley: Chewy and easy to digest

Rich in fiber, niacin and minerals, like magnesium, copper and selenium, barley binds to fats in the blood and escorts them out of the body. There are several different types of barley available: whole barley, which has had only the outer, inedible hull removed; and pearled or pearl barley, which has been hulled, milled and polished to remove the bran. Hatomugi, also called "Job's Tears," is often misleadingly referred to as "pearl barley," when in fact, it is more closely related to corn than barley.

Millet: Very small and round compact grain

High in protein, magnesium, and B vitamins, this gluten-free and hypoallergenic grain is useful for treating stomach, spleen and pancreatic problems. Tasty when eaten as a porridge, added to soups, or incorporated into desserts, millet is fairly quick-cooking, but requires more water than most other grains during cooking, in order to achieve a creamy texture. The grain can be dry roasted prior to cooking for a nutty flavor.

Grain Combining

Brown rice can be deliciously combined and cooked with other grains, nuts, seeds and vegetables. Following are some examples:

- Brown rice combined with grains, such as: amaranth, pearled barley, whole barley, buckwheat, fresh sweet corn, hatomugi (Job's Tears), kamut, millet, whole oats, quinoa, spelt, sweet brown rice and whole wheat berries.
- Brown rice combined with dried beans, such as: Azuki, black soy, chickpea and kidney.
- Brown rice combined with seeds, such as: Lotus seeds, sesame seeds and pumpkin seeds.
- Brown rice combined with other ingredients, such as: sea vegetables, like hijiki and kombu, and ume plum.

How to Choose, Buy and Store Grains

Most of the dried grains available in California may look fresh, beautiful and clean, but when I examine them carefully, I sometimes see that they are not. Some are actually quite old and probably have been in storage for quite some time. When grains are new they are shiny and smooth and have a light greenish hue. Whenever possible, buy grains in bulk from a store with a high rate of turnover and only buy an amount that can be used up within 30 days. Transfer grains to airtight glass containers to prevent the natural oils from becoming rancid. Store the containers in a cool, dark place and not on the floor, to prevent moisture accumulation. Avoid placing containers near a radiator, stove, refrigerator or in direct sunlight.

How to Wash and Soak Whole Grains

Washing and soaking grains in the macrobiotic way is a deliberate, thoughtful process that allows one to control the type of energy that will inevitably be transferred to the end product. It is a process that may take extra time, but with a small amount of practice, effort and planning, these steps will soon become second nature. All grains should be washed prior to cooking in order to remove dirt and debris. Grains can be cooked without being soaked, but the process of soaking grains imparts a softer texture and increases their digestibility. I invite you to compare eating soaked and non-soaked grains, to see for yourself.

1. Place the whole grains on a tray or large dinner plate. Sort through and remove any visible hulls, stones, soil particles or heavy dust. Transfer grains to a fine mesh strainer.
2. Place the strainer into a larger bowl and fill with purified water. Wash grains gently, stirring with your hand in a counter-clockwise direction when you want to be more energetic, or in a clockwise direction when you want to be more relaxed.
3. Drain off the water (reserving it to water your plants later), and repeat the washing step 3 times or more, or until the water runs almost clear.
4. Give grains a final rinse to get rid of any small broken grains or dust still remaining. Pat the bottom of strainer with a clean dry cloth. Transfer grains to the cooking pot. Add the desired amount of water (amount specified in the recipe) and allow to soak for 4 to 8 hours, or overnight. (Note: in hot weather, grains can become mushy if soaked for too long.)
5. The soaked grains and water are now ready to cook (as per recipe instructions).

Cooking Whole Grains

All values listed below are based on 1 cup of dry grains.

Grain	Boiling		Pressure cooking		Porridge	
	Water	Cooking time**	Water	Cooking time**	Water	Cooking time**
Amaranth	1 ½ cups	30 min.	—	—	6 cups	45 min.
Barley						
Whole	3 cups	50 min.	2 ½ cups	40 min.	6 cups	90 min.
Pearled	2 ½ cups	45 min.	2 cups	35 min.	5 cups	60 min.
Hatomugi*	2 ½ cups	50 min.	2 cups	45 min.	8 cups	90 min.
Buckwheat, raw	2 cups	25 min.	1 ¼ cups	20 min.	5 cups	40 min.
Polenta	3 cups	30 min.	—	—	5 cup	40 min.
Couscous	1 ¼ cups	5 min.	—	—	—	—
Kamut	3 cups	50 min.	2 ½ cups	45 min.	—	—
Millet	2 ½ cups	30 min.	2 cups	25 min.	5 cups	45 min.
Oats, whole	3 cups	60 min.	2 cups	45 min.	5 cups	90 min.
Quinoa	1 ½ cups	20 min.	—	—	5 cups	30 min.
Brown Rice*						
Short-grain	2 cups	50 min.	1 ½ cups	45 min.	5 cups	90 min.
Medium-grain	2 cups	50 min.	1 ½ cups	45 min.	5 cups	90 min.
Long-grain	2 cups	45 min.	1 ½ cups	40 min.	4 cups	60 min.
Sweet	2 cups	50 min.	1 ½ cups	45 min.	5 cups	90 min.
Wild rice	2 ½ cups	45 min.	2 cups	40 min.	—	—
Rye berries	3 cups	70 min.	2 ½ cups	55 min.	—	—
Spelt	3 cups	45 min.	2 ½ cups	40 min.	—	—
Teff	3 cups	40 min.	2 ½ cups	35 min.	6 cups	50 min.
Wheat berries	3 ½ cups	80 min.	3 cups	60 min.	—	—

   * Hatomugi is also known as Job's Tears and pearl barley.
  ** Cooking times may vary depending on climate and season. This chart is only to be used as a general guide.
*** See also Basic & Simply Delicious Brown Rice recipe on page 32, as well as Rice & Water Ratios
     on page 34 for additional information.

How to Wash Seeds

Just like grains, washing seeds in the macrobiotic way is a deliberate, thoughtful process that allows one to control the type of energy that will inevitably be transferred to the end product. All seeds should be washed prior to cooking in order to remove dirt and debris. Seeds do not need to be soaked.

1. Place the seeds on a tray or large dinner plate. Sort through and remove any visible hulls, stones, soil particles or heavy dust. Transfer seeds to a fine mesh strainer.
2. Place the strainer into a larger bowl and fill with purified water. Wash seeds gently, stirring with your hand in a counter-clockwise direction when you want to be more energetic, or in a clockwise direction when you want to be more relaxed.
3. Drain off the water (reserving it to water your plants later), and repeat the washing step 3 times or more, or until the water runs almost clear.
4. Give seeds a final rinse to get rid of any small broken seeds or dust that still remains. Pat the bottom of the strainer with a clean dry cloth. The seeds are now ready to be dry roasted (as per next section) or incorporated into your recipe. (Note: if you intend to dry roast the seeds, do not allow seeds to drain for long after rinsing. If they lose too much moisture they run the risk of burning in the hot pan.)

How to Dry Roast Whole Grains or Seeds

Roasting grains reduces cooking times and produces a light and fluffy texture. The grains also become more digestible, which produces a more contracted and energetic result. I especially like roasting grains when it's a cold or rainy day, or when I particularly want grains to be dry. Roasting seeds brings out their nutty flavors and can be used as garnish on grains or vegetable dishes.

1. Wash and rinse the grains or seeds, according to the instructions in the previous sections. If washing grains, allow them to sit in a strainer for 2 to 3 minutes to thoroughly drain, then pat the bottom of the strainer.
2. Transfer the grains or seeds to a skillet that has been heated over a medium-high flame. Keeping the flame at this level until most of the water is evaporated, use a flat wooden rice paddle or wooden spoon, and gently but constantly move the grains/seeds back and forth in order to evenly roast. Move the paddle from a north to south, south to north, east to west and west to east direction. At this moment it is important to make purely deliberate movements with the wooden spoon to prevent burning. Reduce the flame to medium-low once the grains/seeds are dry.
3. For grains, continue roasting until they are golden-brown. If roasting seeds, continue roasting until they pop or are crushed easily between the thumb and index finger and produce a nutty fragrance (reduce the heat if you notice them starting to puff up). Be careful not to burn or scorch the grains/seeds. Scorched grains will have a bitter flavor when cooked. When roasting is complete,

immediately remove grains/seeds from the skillet. Grains are now ready to be cooked as per recipe, or can be used to make delicious teas. Seeds are now ready to eat, used as garnish, or incorporated into recipes. (See Gomashio recipe on page 127.)

How to Boil Seeds or Nuts

Seeds and nuts are a convenient snack for busy schedules. Consuming roasted seeds and nuts, however, can sometimes result in tight shoulders, neck pain, and even low back pain since roasting energy is very dry and may be too strong for certain conditions. In this case, I would suggest the simple technique of boiling seeds and nuts.

If you are boiling seeds, follow the instructions on the previous page for the proper procedure of washing seeds. If you are boiling nuts, a quick rinse is all that is necessary. Transfer nuts or seeds to a pan and add enough purified water to cover them. Over a medium-high flame, bring up to a boil, lower heat and simmer for 5 minutes. (Note: almond skins might come off, so depending on how you prefer your almonds, a more gentle boil may be necessary.)

When I'm having nuts or seeds that have been boiled, this usually means that my condition may become tight and I need to relax. In this case, I usually don't add sea salt, although occasionally I may choose to add one pinch of sea salt per one cup of seeds or nuts to the cooking water.

I recommend boiled nuts and seeds served over salads, grains or boiled vegetables. The flavor of boiled nuts and seeds is unique, but once you get used to the taste, you'll love 'em.

How to Dry Roast Nuts

Roasting nuts increases their digestibility and helps to prevent rancidity (oxidation). Nuts can be roasted either in an oven or on the stovetop. Oven roasting may be simpler, but I prefer the stove-top method described below, which infuses the nuts with more energy. With either method, the high oil content of nuts makes them easy to burn, so take extra care to not overroast.

To oven roast: Spread nuts on a parchment-lined baking sheet and roast for about 5 to 15 minutes (depending on size of nut), or until you begin to smell a nutty aroma, and they are lightly browned. To hand roast on the stovetop: in a heated skillet over a medium-high flame, pan roast the nuts, stirring gently but constantly using a flat wooden rice paddle or wooden spoon by moving the paddle from a north to south, south to north, east to west and back to east direction. It is important to make purely deliberate movements to prevent the nuts from burning and to ensure even roasting. Reduce the flame to medium-low once you begin to smell the nutty aroma. Allow nuts to cool and store in a glass jar for snacking or to use as garnish in salads or other dishes.

basic and simply delicious brown rice

Pressure-cooked Method

Pressure-cooking creates more energy, increases digestibility and brings out more of the natural sweetness of the brown rice. If you've never tasted delicious brown rice before, please try a pressure cooker. You'll soon discover that you can enjoy brown rice very much. I wouldn't cook brown rice this way all the time, however. During my first year of recovery, I cooked brown rice with a pressure-cooker everyday, and extended this a bit into my second year since I was still sick and very weak. But now, I only cook this way when the weather is cold and I feel that I need the extra energy. Remember, it's the balance we are after, besides nutrition.

Some people think that using a pressure cooker is too difficult, or they're afraid to use it. First and foremost, it's important to find a good quality pressure cooker. They have come a long way since the crude models from 50 years ago, and there are many good ones available now. You'll need to learn how to use it, just like anything else you need to learn. I do not recommend using an electric rice cooker, even if it has a mode for brown rice. If I am traveling and there is nothing else available but an electric cooker for my brown rice, then I'll use it, since I have little choice. (Or I may decide to fast.) It's really up to you to decide for yourself, especially after you've tasted the difference between electric vs. non-electric brown rice.

MAKES 4 SERVINGS

For the rice:
2 cups brown rice (short-grain)
3 to 4 cups purified water*
2 small pinches of sea salt

To make the rice:

1. Wash and soak the brown rice, according to the instructions listed in the section titled "How to Wash and Soak Whole Grains," found on page 27.
2. When soaking is complete, place the uncovered pressure cooker, filled with the soaked rice, over a medium-high flame until the water begins to boil. Add sea salt, secure lid on the pressure cooker and allow pot to come to pressure.
3. Place a flame deflector over the flame, reduce heat to low and simmer for 45 to 50 minutes.
4. Remove the cooker from heat and allow pot to sit until the pressure comes down naturally.
5. Wait an additional 5 to 10 minutes before removing the lid. Using a bamboo rice paddle or wooden spoon that has been moistened in water (to prevent sticking), gently stir the grains. This process allows rice to "breathe" and yields a light, fluffy texture.
6. The grains are ready to serve with the condiment of your choice. If not serving right away, cover the pot with a clean dishtowel or a bamboo sushi mat, instead of the lid, for better circulation of air.

Perfectly cooked rice will have small tunnels throughout the surface (as shown in photo).

Boiled Method

After I was eating pressure-cooked brown rice everyday I didn't feel the same satisfaction after eating boiled brown rice. What was I expecting? Of course different ways of cooking yield a different taste, energy, and satisfaction. As I started to enjoy boiled brown rice again, I noticed that it had an uplifting energy and tasted light and fluffy— perfect for warm weather. My favorite pots to use for the boiled method of cooking brown rice are made of ceramic, stainless steel, or sometimes, in winter, cast-iron. If you use a ceramic pot, which has a small hole on the lid, place a cooking chopstick (which is typically larger in diameter than regular chopsticks) to plug up the hole.

MAKES 4 SERVINGS

For the rice:
2 cups brown rice (short-grain)
3 to 4 cups purified water*
2 small pinches of sea salt

To make the rice:
1. Wash and soak the brown rice according to the instructions listed in the section titled "How to Wash and Soak Whole Grains," found on page 27.
2. When soaking is complete, place the pot filled with the soaking rice, uncovered, over a medium-high flame until the water begins to boil. Add sea salt, and cover with lid.
3. Place a flame deflector over the flame, reduce heat to low and simmer for 45 to 50 minutes.
4. Wait an additional 5 to 10 minutes before removing the lid. Using a bamboo rice paddle or wooden spoon that has been moistened in water (to prevent sticking), gently stir the grains. This process allows rice to "breathe" and yields a light, fluffy texture.
5. The grains are ready to serve with the condiment of your choice. If not serving right away, cover the pot with a clean dishtowel or a bamboo sushi mat, instead of the lid, for better circulation of air.

*The quantity of water is listed as a range since everyone has a different palate and texture preference. The higher quantity of water listed will yield a softer texture, and the lowest will yield a firmer texture. If you're not sure, you'll need to actually cook it both ways to find out for yourself how much water you prefer. When cooked properly, there should be small holes between the rice grains. (The rice should resemble sand that has been tunneled by small sand crabs, as shown in the photo.)

The Importance of Resisting the Urge to Peek Inside the Pot of Rice

Many people don't realize how important it is to resist the urge to peek inside a pot of cooking rice. By peeking inside, either during or immediately after the heat is turned off, you may end up with a pot of inedible grains. Those using a pressure cooker are most likely exempt, but if using a standard cooking pot, most people open the lid to check whether it's cooking or not. There is a saying in Japan, "Even if a baby is crying, never open the rice cooking pot until it is ready to open." By uncovering the pot while the rice is cooking or right after, you release great amounts of steam, and as a result, the temperature of the rice drops and the concentrated energy inside the pan and rice is disturbed. The reason most people peek inside is probably because they're not sure if it's cooking properly, or they don't trust the process, or they may lack intuitive cooking skills.

And don't think that just because you've turned off the flame, that your rice is "done!" The temperature and energy inside the pot is still quite high once the heat source has been removed, so it's equally important to resist the urge to uncover the pot for at least 5 to 10 more minutes. This allows the temperature to drop gradually and for the energy to be settled. Imagine that your grains are running at full speed inside the pot while they are cooking on the hot flame. The grains need to "catch their breath" and wind down, so that you can enjoy calmly relaxed grains.

During a cooking class, one of my students uncovered her pot of brown rice after it had finished cooking. We tasted the rice later, only to find that it was overly firm and tasted partially cooked. I asked her how much water she put in the pot, and how long she cooked the rice. Her answers were all perfect, and we scratched our heads, wondering what could have gone wrong. What I didn't realize is that she had uncovered the pot of rice immediately after she turned off the flame to peek inside. A few days later, we found out together what went wrong, and learned the importance of allowing the pot to sit, as is, for those vital 5 to 10 extra minutes.

Rice & Water Ratios

Water quantity changes as the brown rice quantity changes. I usually prefer the softer side of cooked rice and I use the following general ratios for all types of brown rice. Experiment with different ratios to find out which is your preference. Also see recipe on previous page, as well as the chart on page 28.

Brown rice : Purified water
1 cup : 1 ½ to 2 cups
2 cups : 3 cups
3 cups : 4 cups
4 cups : 5 cups
5 cups : 6 cups

brown rice cream
for Special Healing

This is the rice cream I made for my mom when she was very sick and couldn't eat much of anything. I remember when she put the cream in her mouth and was able to swallow it, she said, "So good, thank you." Later, she also remarked how she felt warm and better inside. To me, this experience exemplified what I believe "true healing" is all about.

MAKES 4 TO 6 SERVINGS

For the cream:
1 cup brown rice
10 cups purified water
pinch of sea salt
umeboshi plums, as garnish (optional)

To make the cream:
1. Wash and soak the brown rice, according to the instructions listed in the section titled "How to Wash and Soak Whole Grains," found on page 27.
2. When soaking is complete, transfer the rice to a cast-iron or stainless steel frying pan over medium-low heat. Using a wooden spatula, dry roast the rice until it is uniformly golden brown and the rice releases a nutty fragrance.
3. In a stainless steel or ceramic pot, combine the toasted rice and the water over a medium-high flame until the water begins to boil. Add sea salt, and cover with lid.
4. Place a flame deflector over the flame, reduce heat to low and simmer for 1 ½ to 2 hours, or until half the water has evaporated.
5. Wait an additional 5 to 10 minutes, remove lid, and allow to cool.
6. Transfer rice to an unbleached cheesecloth or a very fine mesh stainless strainer that is placed over a bowl. Squeeze or mash the rice cream to separate it from the pulp.
7. Transfer the cream back into the pot over a medium flame to reheat. Serve hot and garnish with an umeboshi plum or other garnish.

Variation: The umeboshi plum garnish can be substituted with nori, gomashio, scallions, chopped parsley, sunflower seeds, or pumpkin seeds.

brown rice congee
with Umeboshi Plum

Congee, also known as rice porridge, is a comforting dish typically eaten for breakfast in various parts of Asia. It can be made as a healing porridge for any time of day, or simply to keep you warm on a chilly day.

MAKES 4 SERVINGS

For the congee:
1 cup brown rice
5 cups purified water
pinch of sea salt
umeboshi plums, as garnish

To make the congee:
1. Wash and soak the brown rice, according to the instructions listed in the section titled "How to Wash and Soak Whole Grains," found on page 27.

2. When soaking is complete, transfer the rice to a cast-iron or stainless steel frying pan over medium-low heat. Using a wooden spatula, dry roast the rice until it is uniformly golden brown and the rice releases a nutty fragrance.

3. In a stainless steel or ceramic pot, combine the toasted rice and the water over a medium-high flame until the water begins to boil. Add sea salt, and cover with lid.

4. Place a flame deflector over the flame, reduce heat to low and simmer for 1 ½ to 2 hours, or until half the water has evaporated.

5. Wait an additional 5 to 10 minutes, remove lid. Note that not all the water will be absorbed. (The rice should be creamy, with some grains still visible.) Using a bamboo rice paddle or wooden spoon that has been moistened in water (to prevent sticking), transfer congee to individual serving bowls and garnish with the condiment of your choice.

Useful information:
Congee is a good remedy for weak intestines. Typical condiments served with congee include umeboshi plum (as shown in photo), tekka, shiso and nori.

azuki brown rice
with Black Gomashio

Whenever I visited my grandmother, she would serve me azuki rice, no matter what day it was. I always thought it was her special dish, until I later learned that azuki rice is symbolically served on happy occasions, and she was expressing how happy she was to see me.

MAKES 4 SERVINGS

For the rice with gomashio:
1 ½ cups brown rice
½ cup azuki beans
3 cups purified water
1-inch square piece of kombu
black gomashio (black sesame salt), as a
    condiment, (see recipe on page 127)

To make the rice with gomashio:
1. Wash and soak the brown rice and the azuki beans according to the instructions listed in the section titled, "How to Wash and Soak Whole Grains," found on page 27 and "How to Wash and Soak Beans," found on page 55.
2. In a pressure cooker over a high flame, combine the soaking rice and beans, water and kombu. Secure cover on pressure cooker and rapidly bring the pot to full pressure.
3. Place a flame deflector over the flame, reduce heat to low and simmer for 45 to 50 minutes.
4. Remove the cooker from heat and allow pan to sit until the pressure comes down naturally.
5. Wait an additional 5 to 10 minutes and remove lid. Using a bamboo rice paddle or wooden spoon that has been moistened in water (to prevent sticking), gently stir the rice and beans.
6. Serve garnished with black sesame salt. If not serving right away, cover the pot with a clean dishtowel or a bamboo sushi mat, instead of the lid, for better circulation of air.

Useful information:
Rice cooked with azuki beans is known as red rice. Traditionally, in the Far East, red is the color of happiness, and these tiny red beans have always been considered lucky. It is usually prepared for New Year celebrations, birthdays, graduations, and other joyful occasions. This dish is also served on the first and fifteenth of every month for Shinto festivities, and it is especially delicious made with sweet rice. Medicinally, azuki beans are strengthening for the kidneys.

Onigiri
Rice Balls

Onigiri are not only fun to make, but they're fun to eat too! They pack well for traveling, picnics or lunch.

MAKES 1 SERVING (2 BALLS)

For the rice balls:
sea salt
small bowl of purified water, for wetting hands
1 cup brown rice, cooked*
¼ to ½ umeboshi plum, or ½ to 1 teaspoon umeboshi paste, divided**

To make the rice balls:
1. Add a couple pinches of sea salt to the small bowl of water. Use this water to wet your hands while forming the onigiri. (This will prevent the rice from sticking to your hands.)
2. Place a pinch of sea salt on your wet hand. Prepare to form the onigiri in one of two ways:

Traditional Version:
After following steps 1 and 2, place about ¼ cup of the cooked rice in the palm of your cupped hand. Place one portion of the umeboshi plum or paste in the center of the rice in your hand. Scoop another ¼ cup of the rice and set it on top of the umeboshi. Now press the rice together so that the umeboshi is now hidden in the center. Using three or four firm squeezes, form the rice into the desired shape. Then lightly flip the ball between your hands a few times to smooth it out – these flips should be much lighter than the firm hands you used before.

Convenient American Version:
After following steps 1 and 2, take half of the rice and form it into a solid ball using three or four firm squeezes. Then lightly flip the ball between your hands a few times to smooth it out – these flips should be much lighter than the firm hands you used before. Press a small hole in the center with your thumb and place one portion of the umeboshi plum or paste inside. Close the hole and press the ball together again until it is solid.

3. Repeat procedure to form remaining rice into a second ball.
4. Arrange the onigiri on a platter garnished with pickles. Enjoy your rice balls and be happy!

*The ideal rice/water ratio for making rice balls is 1 cup uncooked rice to 2- to 2 ¼-cups of purified water, or for larger quantities, 2 cups of uncooked rice to 4 ⅛-cups of purified water. When cooked properly, there should be small holes between the rice grains. (The rice should resemble sand that has been tunneled by small sand crabs; see photo on page 33.) For making rice balls, it's best to use freshly cooked rice; leftover rice can often be too dry and may not hold its shape.

**Open the jar of umeboshi plums and remove what you plan to use with a wooden instrument (chopsticks or spoon). It is preferable to use wood over a metal instrument. Do not take the plum out of the jar with your fingers. The amount of ume plum or paste is listed as a range in this recipe, and depends on how much of a salty/sour taste you prefer.

Shapes for rice balls:
Balls, triangles, drums or cylinders, oval or egg-shaped

Rice ball varieties:
- Mixed with sea salt, gomashio, chopped vegetables, sea vegetables, or other condiments
- Coated with condiments such as gomashio, shiso powder, tekka, green nori flakes, kinako, nuts or other homemade condiments
- Stuffed with umeboshi plum or paste, shiso leaves, tofu, ginger, scallions, miso or combination of these
- Rice combined with grains or beans such as corn or azuki
- Wrapped with sheets of nori or shiso leaves
- Grilled

Ways to serve leftover rice balls:
- Pan-fried or deep-fried and served with grated daikon radish
- In soup
- In tea (ochazuke)

Ways to preserve rice balls for traveling:
- Cook with umeboshi
- Completely wrap in nori

Brief history of onigiri:
The simple act of shaping rice into balls and other shapes has been practiced for thousands of years. The first archaeological evidence of shaping rice comes from the fourth century BC in Japan, where villagers would soak grains of rice between layers of bamboo leaves before boiling and consuming them. By the fifth or sixth century AD, rice was being used not only as a food source throughout Asia, but also as a form of currency. As a result, rice was available only to the upper class. A couple hundred years later, around the eighth century AD, during the Heian period, the practice of forming rice into compact shapes so that it could be piled onto a plate and easily eaten began in earnest. Not until around 1500, during the Edo period, did rice become more readily available to the common people, with shaped rice becoming a standard part of the diet of Japanese farmers and soldiers.

As a result of the increase in industrialization and cross-cultural exchange happening in Japan during the Meiji period, from about 1895 to 1910, formative versions of "fast food" began to appear. It was during this time that the first lunch box containing rice balls was developed and sold to hungry travelers passing through Japanese train stations. Today, rice balls have become a Japanese staple and can be found in various permutations all over the world.

vegetable chirashi Sushi
Scattered Sushi

When I was growing up in Japan, my mom would bring a tasty rice salad, called "Chirashi Sushi," to an annual summer festival in my hometown. This cheerful dish can be sprinkled with many different varieties of vegetables.

MAKES 4 SERVINGS

For the chirashi sushi:
3 ounces fresh, firm tofu
4 shiitake mushrooms, dried
¾ cup purified water, for soaking the shiitake
1 pinch turmeric (optional)
sea salt, to taste
10 snow peas, stems removed
½ carrot, julienned, or thinly sliced and flower cut
3-inch long piece of daikon, thinly sliced into rectangles
½ cup lotus root, thinly sliced into half-moons*
2 to 3 cups cooked brown rice
1 cup purified water, for blanching vegetables
1 tablespoon soy sauce, to taste**
brown rice or umeboshi vinegar (optional)
2 red radishes, thinly sliced, for garnish
1 green onion, thinly sliced, for garnish
thin strips of nori, for garnish

To make the chirashi sushi:

1. In a small bowl, soak the shiitake mushrooms in the ¾ cup of soaking water for half an hour or more. Pour out and reserve the soaking water for later use. Chop the shiitake into thin strips and set aside.

2. Wrap the tofu in cheesecloth or a clean kitchen towel and sandwich it between two cutting boards. Press the moisture out of the tofu by weighing down the cutting boards with a bowl partially filled with water. Allow tofu to drain for half an hour or more.

3. In a skillet over a medium-high flame, crumble the tofu with 1/2 cup of the shiitake soaking water. Stir in the turmeric, bring to a boil, cover, reduce heat to low and simmer for 5 minutes. Add sea salt and stir the tofu like scrambled eggs until all of the liquid evaporates.

4. In a small saucepan, simmer the shiitake with the soy sauce and remaining soaking water, until there is almost no liquid.

5. In another small saucepan, bring the cup of blanching water to a boil. Quickly blanch the snow peas, carrots, daikon and lotus root, each separately, strain and set aside. (See useful information below for a variation on the lotus root.)

6. In a large, decorative bowl, combine the vinegar with the cooked brown rice to make sushi rice.

7. Spread the shiitake strips on top of the rice, followed by the tofu. Arrange the blanched vegetables all over the top. Sprinkle with garnishes, reserving the nori strips as garnish immediately prior to serving. Serve at room temperature for the best flavor.

Useful information:

The simplest, most popular home-style variety of sushi is called Chirashi Sushi (Scattered Sushi). This sushi has no raw ingredients (except for the red radish and green onion garnish), as the vegetables are either blanched or simmered with soy sauce or marinated in vinegar. This makes Scattered Sushi a convenient dish to be taken on outings, as it can be made ahead of time. Topped with all the multi-colored vegetables, this makes an eye-catching and festive party dish.

*Variation: You may also soak the lotus roots in vinegar for 15 to 20 minutes after blanching them for a tasty variation.

**See page 241 for important information about the various types of soy sauce.

hatomugi salad

I love hatomugi in the summer and the way its distinctive aroma and light texture perk up my taste buds. Also called Job's Tears or Coixseed, hatomugi is an unpolished cereal grass, similar to barley but more closely related to corn.

MAKES 4 SERVINGS

For the salad:
½ cup hatomugi (Job's Tears)
1 ¼ cup purified water, plus additional water, for soaking
1 pinch sea salt
1 cup onion, diced into ½-inch pieces
1 cup carrot, diced into ½-inch pieces
1 cup corn kernels
3 scallions, sliced into ½-inch pieces
¼ cup lemon juice (optional)
1 tablespoon soy sauce

To make the salad:
1. Wash the hatomugi according to the instructions listed in the section titled "How to Wash and Soak Whole Grains," found on page 27.
2. When soaking is complete, place the pot filled with the soaking hatomugi, uncovered, over a medium-high flame until the water begins to boil. Add sea salt, and cover with lid.
3. Place a flame deflector over the flame, reduce heat to low and simmer for 45 to 50 minutes.
4. Transfer cooked hatomugi to a large mixing bowl and allow to cool.
5. Fill a medium saucepan with about 2 inches of water and bring to a boil. Blanch the onion for a few seconds. Strain out the onion and set aside. Using the same water, continue to blanch each vegetable separately.
6. Add the blanched vegetables to the bowl of hatomugi. Add the soy sauce and lemon juice, stir to combine and serve.

Variation: 1 tablespoon of olive oil can be added during the summertime if your condition allows the use of oil.

Creamy millet
with Fresh Parsley Sauce

I never realized millet could be made so soft and creamy until I visited Switzerland during my healing journey.

MAKES 4 SERVINGS

For the millet:
1 cup millet
4 ½ to 5 cups purified water
pinch sea salt
Fresh Parsley Sauce (recipe at right)

To make the millet:

1. Wash the millet according to the instructions listed in the section titled "How to Wash and Soak Whole Grains," found on page 27, skipping the soaking step.

2. Lightly dry roast the millet according to the instructions listed in the section titled "How to Dry Roast Whole Grains and Seeds," found on page 29.
3. Meanwhile, in a large saucepan, bring the water to a boil. Add the dry roasted millet and sea salt. Reduce heat to low, cover and simmer for 30 minutes.
4. Remove from the flame and allow pan to sit undisturbed for another 5 to 10 minutes before removing cover.
5. Serve with Fresh Parsley Sauce.

For the parsley sauce:
2 tablespoons kuzu
1 cup purified water
¼ cup parsley, finely chopped and squeezed of excess water
sea salt

To make the parsley sauce:

1. In a small saucepan, combine the kuzu and water. Stir well until kuzu is completely dissolved.
2. Place the saucepan over a medium flame, bring the mixture to a boil, stirring constantly. Cook for about 1 to 2 minutes.
3. Add the chopped parsley and cook for another minute. Serve drizzled over the Creamy Millet.

Useful information:
See page 159 for information about millet.

Variation: The Parsley Sauce pairs well with the following recipes: Millet Cauliflower Mash, Brown Rice Lotus Patties, and Brown Rice Mochi Pancakes.

pan-fried mochi

Three Ways

Made from pounded rice, mochi makes a great snack, meal or dessert; and this Pan-Fried version is quick, easy and delicious. Served with a sweet or savory topping, this dish is sure to please everyone!

MAKES 4 SERVINGS

For the mochi:
8 to 10 slices of brown rice mochi, 3- by 2-inches
various toppings (three recipes following)

To make the mochi:
1. In a skillet over a medium-high flame, place the mochi slices about ½-inch apart.
2. Toast mochi on one side until golden brown. Turn slices over and lightly brown the other side. Keep the heat low, being careful not to burn the mochi.
3. Serve immediately with Grated Daikon with Nori Strips, Brown Rice Syrup with Lemon Topping, or with Sweet Amazake Dipping Sauce.

grated daikon
and nori strips topping

This topping works wonderfully with the Pan-Fried Mochi. I like to eat this as a meal or quick snack.

MAKES ½ CUP

For the topping:
½ cup daikon, finely grated
2 sheets toasted nori, quartered
soy sauce, to taste

To make the topping:
1. To toast the nori for general use, turn the flame on high and hold a sheet of nori 10 to 12 inches above the flame so that the inside fold faces downward. Rotate sheet above flame so that it toasts evenly.
2. Using scissors or a knife, slice the toasted nori into strips about 2 inches long.
3. Arrange 1 tablespoon of grated daikon on each serving plate. Place 1 or 2 drops of soy sauce on each daikon mound.
4. Garnish with several strips of toasted nori and serve with Pan-Fried Mochi.

brown rice syrup and lemon topping

When I'm in the mood for having mochi with a sweet taste, this is my favorite. Either lemon or tangerine juice can be used to give this dish a light freshness.

MAKES ½ CUP

For the topping:
½ cup brown rice syrup
2 to 3 tablespoons purified water
2 teaspoons lemon juice (or tangerine juice),
    freshly squeezed

To make the topping:
1. In a small saucepan over a medium flame, combine the brown rice syrup and water. Heat gently, and do not allow mixture to boil.
2. Reduce the flame to flow, add lemon or tangerine juice, and stir to combine. Remove from heat. Serve hot, drizzled over the Pan-Fried Mochi.

sweet amazake dipping sauce

When I'm pressed for time, I just heat up some store-bought amazake and use it as a sweet dip for the mochi. It's quick and simple, but oh so good. Try it out!

MAKES ½ CUP

For the topping:
½ cup plain/original flavor amazake, store bought
    or homemade (see recipe on page 79)
pinch sea salt

To make the topping:
1. In a small saucepan over a medium flame, combine the amazake and sea salt. Heat gently, and do not allow mixture to boil.
2. Transfer to a small bowl and serve as a dipping sauce for the Pan-Fried Mochi.

SOUPS

Soup is nourishing food. Elegantly representative of the ancient seas in which life began, soup at the beginning of a meal is relaxing and stimulating to the appetite. Soup is simple to make and easy to digest. In macrobiotic cooking we recommend having about 5 to 10% (by weight) of our daily food in the form of soup (1 to 2 cups, once or twice a day) made with sea vegetables (wakame or kombu), land vegetables, grains, and beans.

Miso soup is the staff of life. You may consider this an exaggerated statement — but it's not considered that way in my homeland. In Japan, miso soup is very traditional, and yet it is still considered a nutritionally important, modern staple food.

MAKES 4 SERVINGS

For the soup:

4 cups of kombu dashi (recipe on page 215)
1 cup onion, thinly sliced
½ cup carrots, sliced into rounds or julienned*
1 collard or kale leaf, cut into ½-inch pieces, stems chopped separately*
4 teaspoons barley miso*
2 tablespoons scallion, parsley, chives or watercress, chopped or minced, for garnish

To make the soup:

1. In a soup pot over medium-high heat, combine the kombu dashi and onions. Bring to a boil, reduce heat to low and add the carrots. Simmer until carrots and onions are tender, about 5 to 8 minutes.
2. Add the green stems and simmer for 1 minute. Add green leaves and simmer for another minute.
3. In a suribachi or bowl, combine the miso and ¼ cup of soup broth from the pot. Combine until creamy. Gently stir mixture into the soup and simmer for 2 minutes. Taste soup and add more miso if needed, but not so much that the soup becomes too salty. Miso should mingle with the flavor of the soup and enhance but not overpower it.
4. Reduce flame to very low so it does not boil. (Do not boil miso as the beneficial bacteria and enzymes will be destroyed by intense heat.)
5. Transfer to serving bowls and sprinkle with garnish.

recipe continued on the following page...

*It is recommended to change the vegetables and quantity of miso in the soup according to the season and weather:

Summer (hot): more greens or seasonal vegetables, like corn, and less miso.

Winter (cool/cold): more root vegetables and more miso.

Useful information:

Miso soup has been a traditional Japanese breakfast for many years until more recently, where it is becoming the soup of choice for lunch or dinner instead. Miso soup is generally eaten daily on a macrobiotic diet. Most miso soup served in Japanese restaurants is much too salty and is not recommended.

Miso paste is quite salty too, and for this reason I use it as more of a light seasoning for miso soup — to add flavor, aroma and depth to the vegetables and dashi. The paste is very savory and lends itself for use in other dishes besides soup. The paste is a fermented product made primarily with soybeans, some grains (such as barley or rice), sea salt and water. This enzyme-rich paste aids in digestion and assimilation, as well as alkalizing and strengthening the blood, and helps to discharge toxins. High in protein and rich in vitamins and minerals, miso is a very healthful addition to the diet.

When eating miso for medicinal purposes or as part of your morning soup, do not allow it to boil, as the beneficial bacteria and enzymes will be destroyed by intense heat. When the weather is cool, you can add more root vegetables and more miso to "yang-ize" the soup. You can also add tofu, natto (fermented soybeans), tempeh, or seitan, for more variety.

The extremely wide varieties of miso have been described as salty, sweet, earthy, fruity and savory. Deciding which one to choose all depends on the type of soup or dish you are making, the season, as well as your particular health condition.

Miso Varieties Available in The U.S. Include:

Barley (mugi) miso has a medium to dark brown color, medium flavor, and is most commonly used in macrobiotics. It has a yang quality and I use this miso frequently for soups, sauces, stews and dressings during all seasons. It is especially good for healing purposes.

White (shiro) miso has a light beige color and slightly sweet flavor. It is best used for mild flavor during spring and most of summer.

Fermented soybean (hat-cho or mame) miso has a dark reddish color, is aged (or smoked) and has the strongest flavor. It has a yang quality and is used very occasionally, due to its strong flavor. Best for use in the cold wintertime for making rich hearty stews or for special healing reasons.

Red (aka) miso has a reddish brown color and is most commonly used in Japan. This miso is often mixed with brown or white miso. I make my own mixture anytime I'm in the mood for a change.

Brown rice (genmai) miso has a light to medium brown color and slightly sweet flavor, similar to white miso. It is good for use during spring, summer and autumn.

Ozoni
Mochi Miso Soup

This soup is traditionally served in Japan at the beginning of a new year. Ozoni is a wonderfully hearty miso soup for autumn and winter.

MAKES 4 SERVINGS

For the soup:
1 quart Kombu and Dried Shiitake Dashi (see recipe on following page)
1 cup greens or Chinese cabbage, cut into 1-inch pieces
½ cup carrots, julienned, or
    ½ cup red radishes, quartered
½ cup cauliflower, flowerets
1 ¼ to 1 ½ tablespoons barley miso
several pieces Pan-Fried Mochi (see recipe on page 45)
1 sheet toasted nori, cut into 1-inch squares
1 cup scallions, thinly sliced

To make the soup:
1. In a pot over a medium-high heat, bring the kombu dashi to a boil. Add the greens or cabbage, then the carrots or radishes.
2. Lower the heat and simmer until cabbage and carrots are just about done, about 3 to 5 minutes.
3. In a suribachi or bowl, combine the miso and ¼ cup of soup broth from the pot. Stir until well combined. Gently stir the mixture into the soup and simmer for 2 minutes.
4. Add the Pan-Fried Mochi just before you turn off the flame. (See mochi variation, below.)
5. Serve soup hot, garnished with nori and scallions.

Variation: If a softer mochi texture is desired, add the mochi to the pot immediately after the diluted miso has been added. Feel free to add more vegetables if you like.

kombu and dried shiitake dashi

This is my basic recipe for soup stock. I sometimes use only kombu or a combination of kombu and dried shiitake.

For the dashi:
kombu (one ½-inch square piece per cup of water)
dried shiitake (one shiitake for every 1 to 2 cups of water), as an optional variation
purified water

To make the dashi:
1. Wipe the kombu and/or dried shiitake clean with a dry cloth.
2. To cook the dashi, use one of the following methods:

No-cook method: In a large pot or bowl, combine the kombu, shiitake and water, and soak for 2 to 3 hours.

Stovetop method: In a pot over a medium-high flame, combine the kombu, shiitake and water. Just before it comes to a boil, reduce heat, and simmer for 20 to 30 minutes.

3. Strain to remove the kombu and shiitake. Dashi will keep for 2 to 3 days in the refrigerator.

Useful information:
Kombu dashi is rich in minerals and is good to use for almost any soup base. It also adds wonderful flavor and nutrition to dressings and sauces. The optional dried shiitake adds additional flavor and can help dissolve animal fats, as well as promote relaxation.

Variation: For a lighter flavor and softer energy, I use 1" piece of wakame per cup of water instead of kombu.

millet and sweet vegetable soup

Many people only associate millet with bird food, and I did too before I began practicing macrobiotics. Now, millet is my favorite whole grain. It has a natural sweetness which helps satisfy my cravings.

MAKES 4 SERVINGS

For the soup:
½ cup millet
5 cups of Simple Kombu Dashi (see recipe on
  page 215)
¼ cup each of onion, green cabbage, winter
  squash, and carrot, cut into ½-inch cubes
⅛ teaspoon sea salt
snow peas, sliced diagonally, for garnish

To make the soup:
1. Wash the millet according to the instructions listed in the section titled "How to Wash and Soak Whole Grains," found on page 27, skipping the soaking step.
2. In a pot over a medium flame, combine the kombu dashi and the millet and bring to boil.
3. Add the onion, cabbage, squash, and carrots in a layered fashion, one on top of the other.
4. Bring to a boil, reduce the heat to low, cover and simmer for 30 minutes.
5. In a suribachi or bowl, combine the miso and ¼ cup of soup broth from the pot. Stir until well combined. Gently stir the mixture into the soup and simmer for 2 minutes.
6. Ladle soup into individual serving bowls and garnish with sliced snow peas.

Useful information:
See page 159 for information about millet.

BEANS

Beans are a great source of plant-based protein and are an important aspect to a wholesome, macrobiotic diet. In everyday macrobiotic cooking, beans usually make up about 5 to 10 percent (by weight) of the diet and consist primarily of beans such as azuki beans, lentils and chickpeas, which are smaller in size and contain less fat and oil than other beans. When we are trying to heal ourselves, however, only small amounts of legumes are recommended. During the healing process, we need to purge our system of the excessive amounts of animal proteins that we had been consuming throughout our lifetime before we begin consuming good quality, plant-based proteins. Even plant-based proteins can tend to stagnate us if we eat too much of it. The beauty and variety of beans are astounding, with each bean like a splendid bead or jewel.

In terms of energy, beans provide balance, and function as the perfect fulcrum between the rapid growth of vegetables and the calm, peaceful strength of whole grains. Beans are either cooked in a regular pot or in a pressure cooker (baked beans are not recommended for healing), and these methods are described in detail below. Regardless of the cooking method, do not add any seasonings, salt or miso (which is salty), until after the beans have been cooked, since adding these any sooner will make the beans tough and greatly increase their cooking time.

How to Choose and Buy Beans

Look for beans that have a natural shiny color, smooth skin and uniformly balanced shape. Beans that are chipped, broken, or have wrinkles and spots may be old and have lost their life force. Beans are best purchased in bulk from a store that has high turnover, to ensure maximum freshness.

How to Store Beans

It is best to store beans in airtight glass containers in a cool, dark place, away from direct sunlight. Do not store them near a heater, stove, refrigerator or on the floor where moisture might develop. Store each variety of bean separately since they have been dried by different methods and have different cooking times.

How to Wash and Soak Beans

Soaking beans makes them softer and more digestible. Lentils, split peas and azuki beans, and other small beans typically don't need to be soaked. Soaking is recommended for most other types of beans. Using hot water can reduce the required soaking time. Unsoaked or undercooked beans, as well as those cooked too quickly, can cause intestinal gas. Insufficient chewing and over-eating can also cause intestinal discomfort.

1. On a tray or dinner plate, spread out a small amount of dried beans and remove any visible hulls, stones, particles of soil or debris. Transfer sorted beans to a bowl and repeat the sorting process with any additional beans.
2. Add enough purified water to the beans to cover them. Rinse them by hand using a gentle, circular motion. Strain the beans in a colander. Repeat this process a couple more times, if necessary, until the water runs clear.
3. Transfer soaked beans to a pot and soak for 4 to 8 hours or overnight. I usually discard the soaking water, which can also contribute to intestinal gas.

How To Cook Beans

In macrobiotic cooking, it is recommended to cook beans along with a small strip of kombu. Kombu is a mineral-rich sea vegetable that speeds up cooking times and helps to balance the beans. There also must be sufficient liquid in your pot in order to keep the beans completely submerged for the entire duration of cooking. This will help to prevent any beans from drying out and becoming inedible. A "shock" method of cooking by adding water while the beans are cooking can also help beans to soften quickly.

When dried beans come to a boil, foam often forms on the top of the cooking liquid. This foam is a water-soluble protein released from the beans and will be absorbed back into the cooking liquid. It is not necessary to remove the foam.

If you are not following a strict healing diet, a small amount of oil can be added to the beans. Sea salt may be necessary to flavor the beans, but it is recommended to add the salt towards the end of the cooking time. Adding any sooner may increase the cooking time. Beans can be cooked on the stovetop by one of the following two methods described below. Baked beans are not recommended for healing purposes.

Boiled method:
Cooking beans using the boiled method is a slow process that allows the flavors of the beans and seasoning to intermingle, creating the hearty flavor you expect from bean dishes. The best cookware for boiling beans on the stovetop is a large heavy pot or saucepan made of stainless steel, ceramic or cast-iron.

Combine soaked dried beans and purified water (3 ½ to 4 cups water per cup of dried beans) in a saucepan or pot of appropriate size. Bring the beans to a boil, reduce the heat, then cover and simmer until beans are tender. The simmering process may take anywhere from 45 minutes to 2 hours, depending on the quantity and variety of your beans. Check the beans occasionally to see if they are submerged in the cooking liquid. If there is so much liquid absorption and evaporation that the top of the beans become exposed, add additional purified water to submerge the beans (the "shocking" method). When beans are about 80 percent done, uncover the pot and season with either ¼ teaspoon of sea salt, ½ tablespoon of miso, or 1 ½ teaspoons of soy sauce, per cup of uncooked beans. Cover the pot and continue simmering until the beans are soft. When done, remove cover, turn up the heat, and boil off any excess liquid.

Pressure-cooked method:
Using a pressure cooker is a much faster method of cooking beans as pressure cooking will infuse the pot with a strong energy. In a pressure cooker, most beans cook well with a ratio of two cups of water per cup of dried beans.

In a pressure cooker over a medium-high flame, combine the washed and soaked (if necessary) beans and secure the lid. Bring the pot to pressure, reduce heat to low, and cook until beans are nearly done (see time table chart below) and turn off the heat. Allow the pressure to come down naturally and remove cover. Season the beans with either ¼ teaspoon of salt, ½ tablespoon of miso, or 1 ½ teaspoons of soy sauce. Turn flame back on to low and continue to simmer the beans until all excess liquid has evaporated.

Cooking Beans

Except as noted, most beans should be soaked prior to cooking.

	Boiling	Pressure cooking
Bean	*Cooking time***	*Cooking time***
Azuki beans*	1 to 1 ½ hours	30 minutes
Black-eyed peas*	1 to 1 ½ hours	—
Black beans	1 to 1 ½ hours	30 minutes
Black soybeans	2 hours or more	60 minutes
Chickpeas	45 to 50 minutes	25 to 30 minutes
Great Northerns	1 to 1 ½ hours	30 minutes
Lentils*	30 to 45 minutes	—
Lima beans, large	45 to 60 minutes	20 minutes
Lima beans, baby	60 minutes	30 minutes
Navy or small white	1 to 1 ½ hours	30 minutes
Pinto beans	1 to 1 ½ hours	30 minutes
Red beans	1 to 1 ½ hours	30 minutes
Kidney beans	1 to 1 ½ hours	30 minutes
Soybeans	2 hours or more	60 minutes
Split peas, green*	45 to 50 minutes	20 to 30 minutes

*These beans generally do not need to be pre-soaked.
** Cooking times may vary depending on climate and season.
   This chart is only to be used as a general guide.

VEGETABLES

When I began my transition to eating vegan macrobiotic foods, I found that family, friends and others would invariably ask, "So what DO you eat?" They thought that once I stopped eating animal products, I would have little else to choose from. In fact, this couldn't be further from the truth. There are literally thousands of varieties of vegetables (as well as grains, beans, fruits and seeds), and so many different ways to prepare them! Vegetables support whole grains, and together they make quite a team. Vegetables create quick and active energy, while whole grains create a slower and calming energy. Vegetables provide beautiful color, crispness, and fresh taste to whole grains. It is recommended to prepare 3 to 5 fresh vegetable dishes every day.

Types of Vegetables for Healing

For healing purposes, there are three ways to categorize vegetable consumption in macrobiotic cooking: everyday, occasional, and to be avoided. These categories complement each other both in energy and nutrients, in order to help us achieve balance and greater health. Take collard greens, onions and carrots, as an example. The energy of collard greens nourish the upper part of the body and provides minerals like calcium and iron; onions nourish the middle of the body and provide biotin and B vitamins; and carrots nourish our root, or bottom part of the body and provide carotenes and potassium. The following list groups vegetables into their physical characteristics: leafy green, round, and root vegetables. Note that if your condition allows, it's okay to eat vegetables from the "to be avoided" list once in awhile, especially when they are in season.

Everyday use:

Leafy Greens
Bok choy
Carrot greens
Collard greens
Daikon greens
Dandelion greens
Kale
Leeks
Mustard greens
Parsley
Scallion
Turnip greens
Watercress

Round vegetables
Acorn squash
Broccoli
Brussels sprouts
Butternut squash
Cabbage, all types
Cauliflower
Hubbard squash
Kabocha squash
Onion
Pumpkin
Red cabbage
Rutabaga
Shiitake mushrooms
Turnips

Root vegetables
Burdock
Carrots
Daikon (fresh and
    dried)
Dandelion
Jinenjo
Lotus roots (fresh
    and dried)
Parsnips
Radish

Occasional use:

Celery
Chive
Cucumber
Endive
Escarole
Green beans
Green peas
Iceberg lettuce
Jerusalem artichoke
Kohlrabi
Lambsquarters
Mushrooms, white
Patty pan squash
Romaine lettuce
Salsify
Snap peas
Snow peas
Sprouts
Summer squash
Wax beans

To be avoided:

Artichoke
Avocado
Bamboo shoots
Beets
Curly dock
Eggplant
Fennel
Ferns
Ginseng
Green/red peppers
New Zealand spinach
Okra
Plantain
Potatoes
Purslane
Shepard's purse
Sorrel
Spinach
Sweet potatoes
Tomatoes
Taro
Yams
Zucchini

59

Raw or Cooked Vegetables?

Before I started eating macrobiotically, I was consuming lots of raw vegetables and salads and thought I was eating healthy. But I started to notice that I was frequently feeling cold, especially in my hands and feet, and I occasionally suffered from diarrhea. I learned, as I began to heal myself, that I needed to eat cooked vegetables for more warmth, balanced harmony, and better digestion. Since raw vegetables are cooling foods and can weaken digestion, unless you're chewing like a cow (have you seen how long a cow can chew?) - you may not be absorbing the nutrients you need. (Incidentally, thoroughly chewing our food is very important for optimal digestion, see pages 235 and 236 for more information.) I do eat raw salads on occasion, during hot summer days (after I had recovered from my illness), but I enjoy eating cooked vegetables the most, especially with so many different cooking styles to choose from.

Cooking Styles for Vegetables

Regular use:	Occasional use:
Boiling	Pressure cooking
Steaming	Sautéing
Waterless	Stir-frying
Soup	Raw
Pickling	Deep-frying
Pressing	Tempura
Water-sautéing	Baking
	Broiling

Organic Vegetables

More than 600 different pesticides are used in the United States, and many of these have the potential to cause cancer and other dangerous health effects. Why would we want to put substances in our body that are designed to kill living things? Studies have shown that many organic foods may contain higher levels of vitamins, minerals, and important phytonutrients, such as carotenes and flavonoids. Organic foods are better for you, the farmer and the planet. Many people do not realize that affordable organic foods are readily available by seeking out locally-grown and in-season foods from a farmer's market near you. Organic farming works with nature, rather than against it, and purchasing organic foods makes perfect sense in a macrobiotic lifestyle. (For more on organic produce, see page 246.) Organic vegetables are essential for healing as well as for everyday maintenance diets.

How to Wash Vegetables

Vegetables should be washed gently by hand under clean, running water to remove dirt and surface microorganisms immediately before you prepare and cook them, and not before. Washing or rinsing vegetables prior to storage can cause premature spoilage and promote mold growth. Plain simple, cool water works just fine. Do not use detergents, bleach or hot water. If you are purchasing your produce from a local farmers market, it is likely that the farmer just plucked the vegetables that same morning, and as a result, you may sometimes find particles of soil, as well as insects, such as lady bugs (after all, bugs love organic vegetables too!). Rather than rejecting this as distasteful, perceive the insects and fresh soil on your organic vegetables as a testament to their purity and just-picked freshness.

All natural vegetable brushes, made from palm fibers, called "tawashi" are very popular in Japan. Perfect for scrubbing root vegetables and ideal for cleaning the crevasses of suribachi bowls and sushi mats, a tawashi is a very handy and highly recommended kitchen tool available at Asian markets, online or in many natural foods stores. A tawashi is also very useful for scrubbing wooden cutting boards and utensils. A colander is another indispensable kitchen tool for washing vegetables.

Green leafy vegetables are washed gently by hand. Discard and compost the outer damaged leaves of leafy greens like cabbage, napa cabbage and bok choy before washing. Each leaf can be rinsed under running water. Gently pat dry with a soft cotton kitchen towel.

Leeks take a little more time to wash. Slice the leek in half length-wise and remove the fibrous root. Be sure to thoroughly wash each individual layer since soil particles often become trapped between the leaves.

Root vegetables can be gently scrubbed with a tawashi and water, taking care that you are not peeling the skin. Scrubbing gently is especially important for burdock root (also called "gobo"), since scrubbing moderately hard will remove the flavorful skin and you'll begin to see the white flesh beneath the skin. The skins of organic vegetables often contain the greatest concentration of nutrients and beneficial phytochemicals, and because of this, it is recommended to leave the thinner, edible skins on as often as possible.

Squash and pumpkins can also be washed by gently scrubbing with a tawashi and water.

How to Cut Vegetables

Cooking is a science, as well as an art, and the ways in which vegetables can be cut exemplify this truism. There are specific and precise—almost scientific—methods by which vegetables should be cut, and at the same time there is a seemingly unlimited variety of ways in which to do so. By simply changing the size, shape, width and thickness of the cuts, you are editorializing the dish – controlling the way the energy gets expressed, as well as how the dish gets presented. I have seen fantastically elaborate cutting techniques, but those take a lot of time and special skills. I think simple and classic methods of cutting can be very fresh and uncomplicated. Sometimes, however, you may want to take the extra time for fancy cuts, such as for special occasions. You are the artist, so enjoy different ways of cutting vegetables when you have time, and when you are busy with the day-to-day, simpler classic cuts are best.

Having a good, sharp knife is obviously very important, as is having good knife skills. I recommend that beginners use a lightweight vegetable knife. With practice, you can eventually graduate to a more heavy-handled knife. I also recommend a knife with a wide blade and sharp L-shaped corner near the handle. This sharp corner can be used to dig out any small blemishes or damaged areas of vegetables as well as the soil-filled areas around root tops.

If you scrutinize your vegetables carefully, observing their contours, ridges and shapes, they reveal their growth pattern. When cutting vegetables, I try to honor this pattern so that it follows the natural energy cycle. I also like to balance my cuts with the entire meal in mind. For instance, when I need to cut vegetables into small dice, say for a soup, I will use larger, rounder shapes for the other vegetable dishes I'm serving, in order to compensate.

I also change the vegetable selection and quantity, as well as the cutting techniques according to the season and weather:

Summer (hot): more vegetables; cut into smaller pieces; use of seasonal vegetables, like corn; less sea salt

Winter (cool/cold): fewer vegetables; cut into bigger chunks; use of seasonal vegetables, like parsnips and sweet root vegetables; more sea salt

63

Ways to cut vegetables for daily cooking:

1. *Matchsticks/julienne*— cut the vegetables on the diagonal. Then, slice each diagonal piece into thin matchsticks/julienne (千切り/sengiri).

2. *Quarters*— slice the vegetables lengthwise into halves. Then, cut each half down the center again. Thinly slice the quarters crosswise (銀杏切り/ichokiri).

3. *Flower shape*— cut 4 or 5 grooves around the vegetables lengthwise at equal distances. Then, slice into thin rounds (花形切り/hanagata giri).

4. *Rectangles*— cut the vegetables into large rounds 1- to 2-inches thick. Stand each round on its head and cut into 4 to 5 pieces, ¼- to ⅓-inch thick. Then, cut each section into thin rectangles (短冊切り/tanzakukiri).

5. *Half-flower shape*— cut 4 or 5 grooves around the vegetables lengthwise at equal distances. Cut vegetables lengthwise into halves. Then, thinly slice crosswise (半花形切り/han-hanagata giri).

6. *Dice*— first cut vegetables into 1- to 2-inch chunks. Stand each chunk on end and cut into ¼- to ½-inch cubes by cutting vertically, then, horizontally, then crosswise. When dicing onions, cut the onions in half horizontally, then cut thin parallel slices vertically, leaving the onion attached to the root base. Then, slice in the opposite direction towards the base. Finally, dice the root base into small pieces. (さいの目切り/sainomekiri).

7. *Rounds*— cut the vegetables into thin or thick coins or rounds (輪切り/wagiri).

8. *Rolling cut*— cut the vegetable on a diagonal, rotating vegetables towards you 80 degrees after each cut. The pieces will be the same size but irregularly shaped (乱切り/rangiri).

9. *Diagonal*— slice vegetables on the diagonal by holding the knife at an angle. The angle of the blade determines the length of the pieces (斜め切り/nanamekiri).

10. *Half-moons*— cut vegetables lengthwise through the middle into two halves. Then, cut each half crosswise into thin rounds (半月切り/hanngetsukiri).

11. *Slicing greens*— place 2 to 3 leaves on top of one another. Cut each leaf in half through the center and along the spine. Cut each leaf again, either straight or on the diagonal, into strips ⅛- to ¼-inch thick. Chop the spine very finely (青菜切り/aonakiri).

Opposite page:
Top row, left to right

1. Matchsticks
2. Quarters
3. Flower shape

Second row, left to right

4. Rectangles
5. Half-flower shape — flower shape cut in half
6. Dice
7. Rounds

Third row, left to right

8. Rolling cut
9. Diagonal
10. Half-moons

This page:

11. Slicing greens

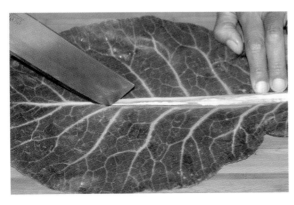

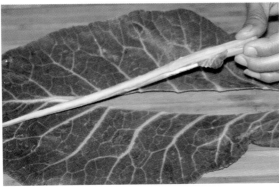

Extreme Yin

How to Select a Sweet-tasting Kabocha

Kabocha is one of my favorite round vegetables. It has a wonderfully natural sweet taste that everyone finds quite pleasing. As I started to use kabocha for remedies and various recipes, I discovered that its sweet taste was quite varied. It soon became my mission to determine the criteria for selecting a sweet-tasting kabocha squash.

Based on Yin & Yang energy, kabocha has a "low" character. A sweet-tasting kabocha is usually not too big, somewhat squat in height and is darker green in color, with a small-sized round "stem" at the bottom. Additionally, I noticed that if it's difficult to cut open, the kabocha is likely to be sweet. The kabocha should be mature, but certainly not old, since fresh is best. I encourage you to try tasting different types of kabocha and discover a sweet taste on your own. Good luck!

Extreme Yang

boiled salads

with Choice of Dressings

Boiled salad may not sound very exciting, but it's one of my favorites. When fresh, high-quality and organic vegetables are properly prepared, each vegetable's flavor, texture and taste are distinctly retained, and yet together they combine to provide a bouquet of delight on the taste buds. The simple, life-giving qualities of the vegetables are satisfyingly and deliciously apparent, which exemplifies why the simple things in life are often the best. My personal favorite combination of vegetables is carrots, cabbage, collard greens, and red radish. These salads work well with any of the dressings listed in the following section.

EACH RECIPE MAKES 4 SERVINGS

Boiled Salad: Version 1

For the salad:
4 to 6 cups purified water
1 small Romanescu cauliflower, whole with stem and core, or 1 cup cauliflower flowerets
8 baby carrots
4 red radishes, with tops
12 sugar snap peas, strings removed
½ cup young fresh fava beans, shelled
Miso Ginger Scallion Dressing, or other dressing, (see recipe on page 72)
fresh parsley, minced, for garnish (optional)

To make the salad:
1. In a large saucepan over medium-high heat, bring the water to a boil.
2. Add onions and boil for about 1 minute. Strain out the onions and transfer to a large mixing bowl.
3. Using the same water, continue to boil each vegetable separately, about 1 to 2 minutes each, strain and transfer to bowl.
4. Add dressing to the bowl and stir gently to combine.
5. Transfer vegetables to a single serving bowl, or to 4 individual serving bowls (dividing the vegetables evenly between each plate), and garnish with chopped parsley.

Boiled Salad: Version 2

For the salad:
2 cups purified water
2 large bok choy leaves, sliced into 1-inch diagonals, stems and leaves separated
1 cup red radishes, quartered

To make the salad:
1. In a large saucepan over medium-high heat, bring the water to a boil.
2. Add the white stems and boil for about 1 to 2 minutes. Strain out and transfer to a large mixing bowl.
3. Using the same water, boil the leafy portion for 1 minute, strain and transfer to bowl. Last, add the radishes and boil for 1 minute.
4. Add dressing to the bowl and stir gently to combine.
5. Transfer the vegetables to a single serving bowl or to individual serving dishes, and garnish with chopped parsley.

daikon salad
with Strawberry Ume Dressing

This salad is exquisitely refreshing and one of my personal favorites during spring and throughout the summer.

MAKES 4 SERVINGS

For the salad:
3-inch long daikon, about 2-inch diameter, thinly sliced into ⅛-inch rounds
4 cups purified water
Strawberry Ume Dressing, and garnish, (see recipe on page 74 and information on page 242)

To make the salad:
1. In a medium saucepan over medium-high heat, bring the water to a boil. Add the sliced daikon to the pot and blanch for 30 seconds or less. Drain and allow daikon to cool.
2. Transfer daikon to individual serving bowls, drizzle with Strawberry Ume Dressing, and garnish with mint or parsley.

Useful information:
It's important to decide which part of the daikon to use, since the taste of daikon is usually more pungent towards the bottom of the root, and sweeter towards the top. If you need to detox, use more of the bottom half of the daikon, and if you simply want to enjoy the daikon, then use more of the upper portion. After I got better, I also made this salad with raw soaked daikon, instead of boiled daikon. The soaking imparts a crispy texture to the daikon, for a crunchier salad. To make the soaked version, if your condition allows, first slice the root, then, briefly soak the slices in chilled purified kombu tea (made by soaking kombu in purified water).

salad dressings

Try these dressings atop the Boiled Salad, or to perk up any of your favorite vegetables.

EACH RECIPE MAKES 4 SERVINGS (ABOUT 1 CUP)

Miso Ginger Scallion Dressing

For the dressing:
4 teaspoons scallions, minced
1 to 1 ½ tablespoons barley miso
¾ cup purified water or kombu dashi
½ teaspoon grated fresh ginger juice, or to taste

To make the dressing:
1. In a suribachi, grind the scallions for several seconds.
2. Add the miso and puree into a smooth paste. Slowly add the water or dashi to obtain desired consistency.
3. Add ginger juice to taste.
4. Serve with Boiled Salad or other vegetables.

Useful information:
During the summertime, white miso is a very sweet and mild choice appropriate to the season, as is substituting orange juice for the water or dashi. If your condition does not allow fresh ginger, simply omit it from this recipe.

Ume Dressing

For the dressing:
1 ½ to 2 tablespoons umeboshi paste
1 cup purified water or kombu dashi
2 teaspoons scallions, finely chopped

To make the dressing:
1. In a suribachi, combine the umeboshi paste and water until well blended.
2. Serve with Boiled Salad or other vegetables.

Lemon Dressing

For the dressing:
¼ cup freshly-squeezed lemon juice
½ cup purified water or kombu dashi
4 teaspoons parsley, minced
2 teaspoons soy sauce
2 teaspoons sesame oil (optional)
1 teaspoon mustard (optional)

To make the dressing:
1. In a suribachi or bowl, stir all ingredients together until well combined.
2. Serve with Boiled Salad or other vegetables.

Sesame Dressing

For the dressing:
1 cup sesame seeds
2 tablespoons soy sauce
1 teaspoon freshly-squeezed lemon juice
½ to ¾ cup purified water

To make the dressing:
1. Wash and dry roast the sesame seeds according to the instructions listed in the sections titled "How to Wash Seeds," found on page 27, and "How to Dry Roast Whole Grains or Seeds," found on page 29. After roasting, transfer the seeds to a suribachi or blender.
2. Finely grind the sesame seeds. Stir or blend in the soy sauce, lemon juice and enough water to achieve desired consistency.
3. Serve with Boiled Salad or other vegetables.

Pumpkin Seed Dressing

For the dressing:
½ cup pumpkin seeds, hulled
1 umeboshi plum, or 1 ½ tablespoons umeboshi vinegar (umesu)
½ to ¾ cup purified water or kombu dashi
1 tablespoon scallions, parsley or chives, minced, for garnish

To make the dressing:
1. Wash and dry roast the pumpkin seeds according to the instructions listed in the sections titled "How to Wash Seeds," found on page 27, and "How to Dry Roast Whole Grains or Seeds," found on page 29. After roasting, transfer the seeds to a suribachi.
2. Grind the roasted pumpkin seeds into a paste.
3. Remove the pit of the umeboshi plum. Finely chop the plum and transfer to the suribachi (or add the umesu), and continue grinding until well combined.
4. Add a small amount of water or dashi until desired consistency is obtained.
5. Serve with Boiled Salad or other vegetables, sprinkled with garnish.

73

Tofu Scallion Dressing

For the dressing:
4 ounces soft tofu
2 cups purified water, for boiling
2 tablespoons scallions, chopped
1 cup kombu dashi
1 teaspoon chickpea miso

To make the dressing:
1. In a small saucepan over medium-high heat, bring the water to a boil. Add the tofu and boil for 3 minutes. Drain well and transfer to a suribachi.
2. Add the scallions to the suribachi and blend until smooth.
3. Add the dashi and miso and blend well.
4. Serve with Boiled Salad or other vegetables.

Walnut Dressing

For the dressing:
½ cup walnuts
2 tablespoons soy sauce
1 cup purified water or kombu dashi
yuzu vinegar, to taste

To make the dressing:
1. Dry roast the walnuts according to the instructions listed in the section titled "How to Dry Roast Nuts," found on page 30. Transfer roasted walnuts to a clean kitchen towel (or paper towel) and gently rub off any skins that may have loosened during roasting. (It is not necessary to remove all skins.) Transfer the walnuts to a suribachi or blender.
2. Add soy sauce and grind until smooth. Slowly add water or dashi until desired consistency is obtained.
3. Add yuzu and blend again.
4. In a bowl, combine the Boiled Salad or other vegetables with the dressing, stirring gently until well coated, and serve.

Strawberry Ume Dressing

For the dressing:
9 to 10 strawberries, chopped
2 to 3 teaspoons umeboshi paste
¾ cup purified water
1 to 2 teaspoons mint or parsley, chopped, for garnish

To make the dressing:
1. In a suribachi, mash the chopped strawberries using your clean hands, then use a surikogi to puree.
2. Add the ume paste and water and stir well to thoroughly combine.
3. Pour the dressing over daikon.
4. Drizzle over the Daikon Salad, Boiled Salad or other vegetables. Sprinkle with mint or parsley garnish.

refreshing sauerkraut and bean sprout salad

Sauerkraut isn't something I'm particularly fond of, but when it's mixed with other vegetables and the sweet taste of currants, I really enjoy it, and I think you will too. Its very light taste is good for spring and summer.

MAKES 4 SERVINGS

For the salad:
1 cup sauerkraut, juices reserved
¼ cup currants
purified water, for boiling
½ cup fresh bean sprouts
½ cup onion, thinly sliced, and soaking in purified water
fresh oregano sprigs, for garnish

To make the salad:
1. Gently squeeze the juices of the sauerkraut into a small bowl. Transfer sauerkraut to a large bowl.
2. Add the currants to the juice, and allow to soak for 5 to 10 minutes, or until currants soften.
3. In a small saucepan over medium-high heat, add about an inch or two of the purified water. Blanch the bean sprouts for about 30 seconds. Thoroughly drain and transfer to the bowl of sauerkraut.
4. Thoroughly drain the soaking onions, squeezing to remove excess water, and add to the sauerkraut bowl.
5. Add the currants, stir gently to combine and serve garnished with oregano sprigs.

PICKLES

I never liked pickles when I was a kid. I remember thinking that they tasted either too salty, too sour, or they just plain smelled funny! My mom often said, "Don't worry – you'll like them when you're grown up!" Usually my mom was right, but even after I turned 20 (the age when Japanese people are considered "all grown up") — I still didn't like pickles! When ordering a hamburger in a restaurant, I always had to say, "Please hold the pickles!" So, do I like pickles now? You bet! Most especially the ones we make at home. Ultimately, my mom's infinite wisdom rang true once again.

Although I didn't appreciate pickles growing up, the process of pickling allowed for the preservation of foods throughout history. Pickles are a staple food in various regions around the world that also provide health benefits. Naturally fermented pickles promote lactic acid bacteria, which is essential for the digestive process and assimilation of food. Pickles can also increase the appetite and strengthen our intestines. It is recommended to eat pickles towards the end of the meal as a digestive aid.

There are many different ways to make homemade pickles. Pickle presses made of plastic, readily available in Japanese markets, may be convenient but are not recommended for longer pickling times because of the toxic compounds that can be released from the plastic during fermentation. Here are some of my favorite ways of making pickles:

Pickling with Sea Salt

I like these pickles because as long as you have sea salt and vegetables, you can make them any time and almost any place. Since sea salt can be found just about anywhere in the world, I usually make these pickles when I am traveling, too. To begin, all you need is sea salt, vegetables, a glass bowl and a ceramic plate that fits the top of the bowl. Napa cabbage is my favorite vegetable for this type of pickle. The basic ratio is 1 to 3 teaspoons of salt per 2 cups of chopped vegetables, with root vegetables that are especially firm requiring the higher amount of salt (i.e. turnips usually need more salt than daikon).

Quick sea salt pickles can be prepared in the morning for eating at lunch and/or dinner, and generally require a bit more salt to hasten the pickling process. You can, of course, allow the vegetables to ferment for 2 to 3 days, but if you don't add enough sea salt for longer pickling times, the vegetables will spoil. Extra cold temperatures will halt the pickling process so don't put your pickles in the refrigerator until they are ready (or almost ready). Sea salt pickling and aging times can be extended for long periods, even as long as several weeks, right on your kitchen counter.

Pickling with Soy Sauce

When I first moved to the U.S. in the late 70's, it was not easy to find soy sauce. Now, however, this Asian seasoning sauce is ubiquitous. Soy sauce makes great tasting pickles. Try pickling broccoli, cauliflower, carrots, daikon, ginger, or any other vegetable that strikes your fancy. In a small saucepan, bring a 50/50 mixture of soy sauce and purified water to a light boil, remove from heat, allow to cool, and transfer liquid to a pickle container with a loose fitting lid. Using kombu dashi instead of water is another tasty variation that adds additional minerals to the pickles. Vegetables, either raw or blanched, should be submerged in the liquid and allowed to ferment from several hours to several days. After the desired length of time, remove pickles from the soy sauce and transfer them to a glass jar for storage in your refrigerator until ready to eat. The leftover soy sauce can be reused for another batch of pickles or used as seasoning in your cooking.

Pickling with Miso

Miso pickles boast a strong salty taste, but also a natural sweetness, which makes them a well-liked favorite. Plus, they're easy to make. Moisture and water can spoil miso pickles, and for this reason they are usually made with root vegetables, since leafy greens and other soft vegetables have a high water content and don't dry out well. My favorite choices are burdock, carrots, daikon, turnips, ginger, and lotus root. The beginning process is the same as making nuka pickles—drying the sliced root vegetables outside in a shady area on a bamboo tray for about a day, until they soften up and can bend; or I boil the vegetables for a few minutes instead. Next, fill a jar about halfway with miso. Completely submerge the sliced vegetables in the miso. The time required for aging pickles varies depending upon the type of vegetable used and the size of the cut. Thinly sliced vegetables will be ready in 1 to 3 days, and whole vegetables with slits cut into their skins and submerged in miso will usually pickle in 3 to 7 days. Vegetables cut into thick rounds will take 1 to 3 weeks. When ready, remove the vegetables, and wipe or rinse off the miso before serving. (See Burdock Miso Pickle recipe on page 215.) Only small amounts of miso pickles should be eaten at a time. (See page 50 for specific information about the various types and uses of miso.)

Pickling with Amazake

Sweet is an unlikely word you'd use to describe a pickle, but that's how I would describe amazake pickles. I may not have been fond of pickles growing up, but these amazake pickles were the only one's I would actually eat and enjoy. With a taste more akin to salad, amazake pickles are very easy and quick to make, especially with ready-made amazake available in natural food stores. Though store-bought amazake may be very convenient, please try making these pickles with my Homemade Amazake recipe (see recipe and amazake information on the next page), and I promise you won't be disappointed!

To make the pickles, simply submerge root vegetables such as daikon or turnips in amazake, along with a pinch of sea salt. Transfer to a pickle press and allow the mixture to sit for at least 1 hour, or up to 3 days, in a cool dry place (not the refrigerator). After pickling, store in a tightly sealed glass jar, and refrigerate for freshness. (See page 207 for Kabu Turnip & Green Top Amazake Pickle recipe.)

homemade amazake

Traditionally, amazake, which means "sweet sake" in Japanese, is a low-alcohol sweet beverage made from fermented rice that is often garnished with freshly grated ginger. Similar to the way eggnog is consumed here in America, amazake is served at family occasions, mostly during New Year's celebrations. Years ago, it was commonly sold by street vendors, and can still be found being served at inns and teahouses. The basic recipe for amazake is the same as it has been for hundreds of years: A starter culture called koji is added to cooked whole grain rice whereby enzymes break down the carbohydrates into simpler unrefined sugars. Ready-made amazake sold in most natural food stores contains no alcohol and is an organic, wholesome and nutritious beverage with no added sugars, and is available in a multitude of flavors. In addition to its use as a beverage or smoothie, amazake can also be used in desserts, as a natural sweetner, baby food, salad dressing, or pickling base.

For the amazake:
4 cups sweet brown rice
8 cups purified water
½ cup koji
pinch of sea salt
additional purified water
optional flavorings (fresh grated ginger, nuts, seeds, vanilla extract, etc.)

To make the amazake:

1. Prepare rice using the pressure cooker-method as described in the Basic and Simply Delicious Brown Rice recipe on page 32.
2. When rice is finished cooking, add the koji and thoroughly combine using your hands (if the rice isn't too hot; otherwise use a wooden spoon).
3. Transfer the rice and koji mixture to a glass jar or bowl, cover with a wet towel, and place near an oven or any other warm place in the kitchen. Allow mixture to sit for 6 to 10 hours.
4. Check the flavor of the amazake, stirring occasionally to melt the koji. If the mixture is very sweet, then it's ready; if not, continue allowing the mixture to ferment. Usually amazake is ready after about 12 hours at 140° F, or after 24 hours at 90° F.
5. After the fermentation process is complete, transfer the amazake into a pot and bring to a boil (to pasteurize). When bubbles start to show on the surface, turn off the heat.
6. Allow amazake to cool and purée in a blender if you like (adding any optional flavorings). Transfer to a container and store in your refrigerator.
7. When ready to serve, combine the amazake, sea salt and enough purified water to reach desired consistency in a large saucepan over a medium-high flame and bring to a boil. Remove from heat and serve hot, or allow to cool and serve as a cold drink. Amazake can be stored in the refrigerator for up to 2 weeks.

nuka pickles

Brown Rice Bran Pickles

The most common pickle found in Japan, made with a nuka (brown rice bran) pickling bed, has a satisfying crunchy texture and refreshing flavor that can vary from pleasantly tangy to very sour, salty and pungent. Though traditionally made with daikon, cabbage or cucumber, just about any type of vegetable can be fermented with the soft paste-like nuka bed. Though the traditional nuka bed is kept in a wooden crock, like my grandmother had, I use a decorative ceramic crock. Nuka pickles require stirring with the hands everyday. Due to varying methods, recipes, as well as the stirring energy introduced by your hands, the texture and flavor of the nuka paste will fluctuate, as will the flavor of your pickles.

For the nuka bed:

1 pound nuka doko
2 cups purified water
2 to 4 tablespoons sea salt
2-inch square piece of kombu
one cup "starter" vegetables (carrots, cabbage,
   daikon, etc.), coarsely chopped

To make the nuka bed:

1. The first batch of nuka doko is very important in making nuka pickles. In a large skillet over medium-high flame, dry roast the bran (nuka) until the color changes slightly and the smell of bran intensifies. When evenly roasted, turn off the heat and allow to cool.

2. In a small saucepan, boil the water. Add the sea salt and stir to combine. Add kombu, turn off the heat and allow to cool.

3. Transfer cooled off nuka to a ceramic crock or a wooden barrel (our crock is 6 inches in diameter and about 5 inches deep). Add the kombu water mixture. Using your hands, gently combine the ingredients to form the nuka doko, or basis of the brown rice bran pickle bed.

4. Add chopped starter vegetables. This helps to stimulate the fermentation process. Cover crock with a clean cotton cloth and allow to sit overnight.

5. Mix the nuka by hand once per day for the next 3 to 5 days. After this time, remove and discard the starter vegetables. The nuka doko is now ready to make pickles. (See the following recipes: Daikon Root and Green Top Nuka Pickles, page 151; Nuka Red Radish Pickles, page 203; and Carrot Nuka Pickles, page 228.)

Useful information:

The tips and ends of vegetables that are usually discarded can be used as the "starter" in this recipe. If nuka becomes too soft and the liquid rises, either drain it out or absorb it by adding fresh roasted nuka bran and a little sea salt. Be sure to add only a small amount at a time to avoid changing the flavor. Nuka doko will keep for a very long time if you mix it well on a daily basis and adjust the bran from time to time. In fact, some people have the same nuka doko for many years, as it's part of a family tradition. Nuka rice bran can be found at natural food stores or Japanese markets.

SEA VEGETABLES

The Japanese word for sea vegetables, kaisou, literally translates to "glass of the sea." When I first heard the term "seaweed" here in the U.S., I thought to myself, "Now that doesn't sound good... Who would eat 'weeds from the sea' unless they grew up eating it!" The texture and smell are already so foreign to American palates, that the addition of a terrible description is enough to frighten them off seaweed for good. Fortunately, someone came up with a better description: "sea vegetable." (To whoever first said this: thank you!) "Vegetables from the sea" is clearly a more accurate description, akin to vegetables grown on dry land. Nomenclature aside, there is no doubt that sea vegetables are highly nutritious. Rich in minerals, like iron, calcium and iodine, as well as high in protein and beta carotene, sea vegetables impart a relaxing energy, a reflection of their flowing movements underwater—strong yet flexible at the same time. Like the ocean, sea vegetables have a salty composition similar to human blood. They have cleansing properties too and are able to dissolve fatty deposits in the body. They are the perfect complement to whole grains, beans and land vegetables.

When you're sick and trying to heal yourself, it is so important to live by the old adage by Hippocrates: Let food be thy medicine. And sea vegetables clearly fit the bill. You've enjoyed your ice cream and your BBQ ribs for a while, so why not try something different? The healing and powerful qualities of sea vegetables provide us with the opportunity to eat in order to live, instead of living in order to eat.

Regular use:
Toasted nori
Wakame
Kombu
Arame
Hijiki
Sea palm
Agar
Green nori

Optional use:
Dulse
Irish moss
Mekabu

Sea vegetable recipes to try can be found on the following pages: 52, 99, 101, 113, 130, 131, 161, 177, 178, 197, and 212.

FRUITS

Many people are surprised to learn that fresh fruits are not a regular part of the macrobiotic diet. Those who consume either refined sugars or tropical fruits regularly often find that transitioning to a healing macrobiotic way of eating can be quite a challenge. I used to eat raw fruits as my desserts almost everyday, so when I started to learn macrobiotics I really missed having them. Studying and understanding why I don't need to eat a lot of raw fruits, especially tropical fruits, was a necessary process and helped me to overcome my desire to eat them regularly. In fact, at the beginning of my macrobiotic journey, I did not eat any fruits at all for over one month.

When we eat meat and animal products our core body temperature increases more than when we eat only plant-based foods. Fruits, especially raw tropical varieties, can actually help reduce body temperature. In tropical zones our body heat rises due to the higher humidity and overall atmospheric temperature, so eating tropical fruits actually makes sense because of their cooling effect. But if we are not living in a tropical zone and/or eating plant-based foods, tropical and raw fruits may cool off our body too much and weaken our overall condition. Everybody's needs and conditions are different so it is very important to seek advice from a macrobiotic counselor.

In the macrobiotic way, fruits can be eaten either cooked or dried, and on occasion, health permitting, also fresh. Fresh and cooked fruit can be garnished or seasoned with a pinch of sea salt. When eating fruits, choosing organic, seasonal and locally grown is key!

Tree fruits by season:
Early Summer – cherries
Summer – apricots, peaches, plums
Autumn – pears
Winter – apples, mandarin oranges, dried fruits
    (raisins, currants)

Ground fruits by season:
Spring – strawberries
Summer – cantaloupe, honeydew melon,
    watermelon
Summer through Late Summer – raspberries,
    blueberries, blackberries

Fruit recipes to try can be found on pages 73, 74, 140, 193, 217 and 231.

BEVERAGES

Besides remedy drinks, there are some beverages that I enjoy on a daily basis. The most important aspect about partaking in beverages is to drink them when you are actually thirsty, and not as a habit or simply because it's a routine of practicing macrobiotics. Whenever I go to a restaurant for dinner, the first thing the server will inevitably ask is what I want to drink. I used to habitually order a drink even though I wasn't thirsty. Then, later on, guess what? I had to get up in the middle of the night to go to the bathroom. I understand that when people are eating highly processed, non-natural foods, meats and animal products, they need to detoxify, and drinking water is one of many ways to do just that. However, when we are eating naturally balanced vegan macrobiotic foods, it is not necessary to drink in excess since the food is mild, not overly salty or spiced. Whole unprocessed foods naturally contain water, and this water is utilized by the body.

How much you drink should depend on what you're doing and what kind of weather you're doing it in. When I am teaching a cooking class and talking a lot, then I drink more. If, on the other hand, I am just staying at home and spending my day quietly, I may not drink much. When I go out to eat at a restaurant, I usually need to drink more because the food is heavily seasoned with oil and salt.

Below is a list of beverages that I use and recommend. Sometimes I find myself craving a sweet drink when it's a hot day or after eating salty food. And when I eat naturally sweetened desserts, I will enjoy a cup of tea, or a grain coffee on occasion. Personally, I never liked drinking milk, but anyone who had been drinking milk regularly may find soy or rice milk to be a good substitute; however, for healing, I don't recommend it very often. I also advise against drinking chilled or iced beverages, as well as those that are too hot.

Water:
Natural spring water, well water, purified water.
For healing, I do not recommend sparkling water.

Tea & coffee:
Kukicha (twig tea), see recipe on page 96
Barley tea
Dandelion tea, see recipe on page 97
Grain coffee

Occasional sweet drinks:
Amazake, homemade, see recipe on page 79
Carrot juice
Apple juice

Avoid:
Unfiltered tap or distilled water
Soft drinks
Alcoholic beverages
Caffeinated teas
Milk

the five seasons

SUMMER

(FIRE)

Noon
Red · Purple
Heat · Hot
Bitter

Odor
Colorful
More Liquid
9

Fresh
Light
Color
3 · 4

Afternoon
Yellow · Orange
Humid · Moisture
Sweet

Active
Expanding

Full
Moon

LATE SUMMER

(SOIL)

SPRING

(TREE)

Rising
Upward

Mars

South

Settling
Down

Increasing
Half-moon

Jupiter

East

Center

Earth

Obscured
Moon

Morning
Green
Windy · Warm
Sour

Intellectual
Taste
Reflection
2 · 5 · 8

North

West

Mercury

Venus

New
Moon

Decreasing
Half-moon

Floating
Will
Fluid
1

Quiet
Peaceful

Moving
Inside

Evening
White · Pale
Dry · Cool
Pungent

WINTER

(WATER)

Night
Black · Grey
Dry · Cool
Salty

Gathering
Strengthening
Voice
6 · 7

(METAL)

AUTUMN

Studying, learning and living the macrobiotic life style makes us sensitive to change. Just as we experience the cyclical changing of the moon, the seasons, climate and time of day, so too do we experience the transformation of our disposition, energy and temperament.

In order to best utilize the energy of these various transformations, it is helpful to make choices that exemplify the principles intrinsic to each season. The Transformations of the Five Elements, illustrated here, are very useful guidelines in the process of observing the yin/yang philosophy inherently linked to various foods, cooking and, ultimately, all aspects of life. I have been abiding by these principles myself for many years and hope that you find them useful too.

Food	Spring
Taste	sour
Cooking styles	blanching (quick boiling), steaming, quick pickling/pressing, lighter (less seasoning, less oil, less salt)
Grains	oats, barley, wheat, rye, hatomugi, spelt, kamut, fu, noodles
Vegetables	upward-growing leafy green vegetables, leeks, scallions, chives, baby carrots, sprouts, celery, mushrooms, snow peas, snap beans
Beans	split peas, navy beans, chickpeas, tofu, lentils
Sea Vegetables	wakame
Condiments	green nori flakes, wakame, umeboshi plum
Fruits	green apples (Pippins and Granny Smith)

Environment	
Color	green
Element	tree (wood)
Energy	rising, upward
Qualities	fresh, light
Time of month	increasing half-moon
Time of day	morning
Direction	east
Climate	windy
Temperature	warm
Planet	Jupiter
Numbers	3, 4

Body	
Internal organs	Solid: liver; Empty: gallbladder
Time of day meridian	11 pm to 1 am gallbladder 1 am to 3 am liver
Sense organs	eyes
Sense	sight
Gland	pituitary
Physical part/tissue	muscles
Physical branches	nails
Physical liquids	tears
Physical changes	gripping
Skin color	blue, gray
Odor	oily, greasy
Functions	color
Faculty	spiritual
Temperament	Balanced: patience/endurance/adventure/creativity Not balanced: cruelty/stubbornness/intolerance/rigidity/anger/short-tempered

Food	Summer	Late Summer
Taste	bitter	sweet (naturally sweet)
Cooking styles	simple, light boiling, short steaming, quick water-sauté, quick stir-fry, raw (salad), sushi	quick nabe, quick deep frying, grilling, raw, marinating
Grains	corn, polenta, grits, basmati, long-grain brown rice, quinoa	sweet rice, millet, oats, amaranth
Vegetables	bitter greens, large-leaf vegetables, shiso, carrot tops, parsley, garlic	round ground vegetables (cabbage, cauliflower etc.), lotus root, sweet corn
Beans	kidney beans, lima beans, broad beans, split peas, black beans	yellow soybeans, chickpeas, pinto beans
Sea Vegetables	nori, dulse, green nori flakes	arame, sea palm
Condiments	gomashio, sunflower seeds	pumpkin seeds
Fruits	berries, large melons (watermelon), figs	honeydew, cantaloupe

Environment		
Color	bright as the sun, red-purple	yellow-orange
Element	fire	soil (earth)
Energy	active, expanding	settling down
Qualities	colorful, more liquid	reflection, transition
Time of month	full moon	obscured moon
Time of day	noon	afternoon
Direction	south	center
Climate	heat	humid/moisture
Temperature	hot	cooling
Planet	Mars	Earth
Numbers	9	2, 5, 8

Body		
Internal organs	Solid: heart; Empty: small intestine	Solid: spleen/pancreas; Empty: stomach
Time of day meridian	11am to 1pm Heart; 1pm to 3pm small intestine; 7pm to 9pm pericardium; 9pm to 11pm triple heater	7 am to 9 am stomach; 9 am to 11 am spleen
Sense organs	tongue	mouth
Sense	speech	taste
Gland	thymus, heart governor/triple heater (circulatory and heart metabolism)	pancreas
Physical part/tissue	blood vessels	flesh
Physical branches	complexion	breast, lips
Physical liquids	sweat	saliva
Physical changes	anxious	sobbing
Skin color	red	yellow, milky
Odor	burning	fragrant
Functions	odor	taste
Faculty	inspirational	intellectual
Temperament	Balanced: tranquility/gentleness/cooperation/quietness/intuition/humor/joy/expression/spiritual union/happiness; Not balanced: separation/agitated/hysterical/excitement/excessive laughter and speaking	Balanced: sympathy/understanding/attractive/wisdom/consideration; Not balanced: irritability/critical/jealousy/envy/suspicion/worry

Food	Autumn	Winter
Taste	pungent (hot & spicy)	salty
Cooking styles	nishime (waterless cooking), medium boil, oil sauté, ohsawa pot, kimpira, pressing, oden	long nabe cooking, stewing, pressure-cooking, deep-frying, baking
Grains	brown rice, oats	buckwheat, dried chestnut
Vegetables	contracted small autumn vegetables, squash, ginger, daikon, fresh chestnut, round roots (turnip, radish, rutabaga, etc.)	long roots (burdock, carrot, parsnip, etc.), dried vegetables; sea vegetables: kombu
Beans	black soy beans, yellow soy beans, small white beans	azuki beans, black soybeans
Sea Vegetables	agar, hijiki	kombu
Condiments	miso, miso scallion, ginger, tekka	shio kombu, shio nori
Fruits	hard fruits	cranberry, dried chestnut, dried fruits

Environment		
Color	white & pale	black, grey & brown (blue)
Element	metal	water
Energy	gathering, strengthening, warming, moving	floating
Qualities	deep inside	quiet, peaceful
Time of month	harvesting, assembling	new moon
Time of day	decreasing half-moon	night
Direction	evening	north
Climate	west	cold
Temperature	dry/cool	cold
Planet	Venus	Mercury
Numbers	6, 7	1

Body		
Internal organs	Solid: lung; Empty: large intestine	Solid: kidney; Empty: bladder
Time of day meridian	3am to 5am lung; 5am to 7am large intestine	
Sense organs	nose	ears
Sense	smell	hearing
Gland	thyroid	adrenals, sexual organs
Physical part/tissue	skin	bones
Physical branches	breath	head hair
Physical liquids	mucus	urine
Physical changes	coughing	shivering
Skin color	pale	black, dark
Odor	fishy	putrefying
Functions	voice	fluid
Faculty	vital	will
Temperament	Balanced: happiness/security; Not balanced: defensiveness/lack of self-esteem/distance/despair/grief/sadness/depression/indecisive	Balanced: confidence/courage/inspiration; Not balanced: fear/hopelessness/shy/timid/distance/coldness

The Story of Spring

A Time to Start Anew

When I moved to the United States, it always struck me as odd that the school year started in September. I grew up in Japan where the academic school year begins in April, so to me, everything always feels like it's starting fresh with the advent of spring.

After the cold of winter it seems like everyone and everything can't wait to warm up and start to move again. I look around me in the spring and see life bursting forth in the hard, crusty trees. This is the true beauty of nature — life and energy flowing from the cold and still.

I fell sick just before the winter of 1993. It was truly a dark winter, and I felt totally lost within it. By the time I made it to the following spring I could finally see the light, as I was following wise advice, heading in a good direction, and starting down the path toward the beauty of nature. Having faith in the glory of spring and in myself gave me a new beginning. I appreciated being a part of nature.

TRANSFORMATION OF

spring

Remedy drinks:
Ume Sho Bancha
Kukicha, Twig Tea
Dandelion Tea with Brown Rice Syrup

Breakfast:
Miso Soup with Baby Spring and Sea Vegetables
Brown Rice and Whole Oats Porridge with Green Nori and
    Sesame Condiment
Steamed Baby Bok Choy

Lunch:
Couscous Salad with Lentils

Dinner:
Creamy Carrot Soup with Baby Spring Onion and Fried
    Carrot Tops
Brown Rice and Wheat Berries
Natto and Green Peas with Chives
Water-sautéed Chinese Broccoli
Green Apple and Cabbage with Wakame Condiment
Three-Hour Red Radish Pickles

Dessert:
Lemon Amazake Cream

ume sho bancha

Remedy Drink

This drink is easy to make. I find it to be a very effective drink to perk me up in the morning before breakfast, and the sourness of the umeboshi helps stimulate my appetite.

MAKES ONE SERVING

For the drink:
one-half or one umeboshi
a few drops soy sauce
1 cup Kukicha (twig tea), brewed
   (recipe on next page)

To make the drink:
1. Place the umeboshi in a tea cup with a few drops of soy sauce.
2. Pour in hot tea and stir well. Drink while hot and eat the plum.

Useful information:
The combination of umeboshi and twig tea is good for strengthening the blood and circulation through regulation of digestion. Umeboshi is a traditional pickled plum in Japan, usually round in shape, and varies from unwrinkled to very wrinkled. It has a salty and sour flavor, with a very alkaline composition, and contains citric acid, calcium, phosphorus, potassium and iron. The Japanese believe that eating umeboshi has a detoxifying effect on the body and can promote health. An old Japanese saying claims that umeboshi assists three detox actions: one for our food, a second for our water, and a third for our blood. In Japan, umeboshi is also added to okayu (Japanese congee) as a remedy for colds and flu. I use the umeboshi pit instead of sea salt or kombu when cooking whole grains, and I like to put the pit in my mouth when I go hiking to stimulate saliva flow so that I don't need to drink much water. Additionally, the seed inside the pit is edible and is believed to improve vision and assist intestinal function.

An umeboshi story: There is "God" in the umeboshi plum!
My mom told me that when I was four or five years old, I really loved eating umeboshi. After eating the umeboshi fruit, I kept the pit in my mouth for a few hours as though it was candy. When there was no more flavor, I asked my mom to crack it open so that I could eat the insides. My mom got tired of breaking open the pits for me and asked me why I liked eating the insides so much. My answer was "there is God inside the pit, and when I eat it, I feel God is helping me and making me feel good." I certainly remember eating umeboshi, but I don't recall expressing my rather profound statement. My mom just thought I was being a silly little girl, but as an adult, when I started to teach macrobiotics and explained to her how valuable and precious umeboshi plums and pits are, she remembered what I had said as a child. Perhaps my destiny in the universe was sealed right then and there — to follow the macrobiotic way.

95

kukicha

Twig Tea - Remedy Drink

This is a delicious, soothing and balancing tea with a rich flavor. It contains an abundance of natural tannins that aid digestion, and has the ability to neutralize both acidity and alkalinity in the foods we consume. It is much lower in caffeine than black and green teas, with no stimulants, making it an ideal beverage for everyone, including children, to enjoy.

MAKES 1 SERVING

For the tea:
1 ½ cups purified water
1 teaspoon kukicha/twig tea, dried

To make the twig tea:
1. In a small tea kettle, bring purified water to a boil. Add dried tea to the kettle.
2. Gently simmer for 5 minutes.
3. Strain and drink hot or warm.

dandelion tea

with Brown Rice Syrup - Remedy Drink

The bitter, sour taste of this tea reminds me of coffee, especially when I make it strong, but without the caffeine. I like to drink this in the afternoon with brown rice syrup to relax, and at the same time be strengthened.

MAKES 1 SERVING

For the tea:
1 ½ cups purified water
1 to 2 teaspoons dried dandelion root
1 to 2 teaspoons brown rice syrup

To make the tea:
1. In a pot, combine water and dandelion root over a medium flame.
2. Bring to a boil and simmer for 5 to 10 minutes.
3. Strain, add rice syrup and serve.

Useful information:
This tea strengthens the stomach and intestines, as well as increases vitality. Strong dandelion tea looks almost like coffee, and is useful for those who want to quit drinking coffee. Try blending this tea with green tea, which contains caffeine.

Dried dandelion root as a tea is available at natural foods markets. You can also make your own from fresh roots if you happen to have mature dandelion growing in your garden: Dig up the dandelion roots. About 2 or 3 roots with a minimum length of 2 inches is usually sufficient to yield 1 or 2 cups of tea. Thoroughly wash and dry the roots. Cut the roots into small pieces and roast them in a skillet with a little sesame oil. Grind them to a powder in a coffee grinder. The powder is now ready to make tea as described above.

miso Soup

with Baby Spring Vegetables & Wakame

Baby spring vegetables, found in abundance at my local farmers' market, are always calling out to me, "we are little jewels from the field ready to be discovered!" Having baby spring vegetables in my morning miso soup is a great luxury to me. I can taste each vegetable separately, and at the same time, together they create a perfect harmony.

MAKES 4 SERVINGS

For the soup:
4 to 5 cups purified water
1 to 2 inches wakame (¼- to ½ -inch per cup
    of water)
2 baby carrots, julienned
2 baby turnips, cut into quarters, including some
    green tops
1 cup baby broccoli, cut into flowerets
4 teaspoons barley miso

To make the soup:

1. In a large saucepan over a medium-high flame, combine the water and wakame. Cover and bring to a boil. Reduce the flame to medium-low.
2. Add the carrot and simmer one minute. Add the turnip and simmer for one to two minutes. Add the broccoli and simmer for another minute.
3. Reduce the flame to very low. Once the liquid has stopped boiling, place a few tablespoons of the broth in a cup or small bowl. Add miso and stir with a spoon or chopstick. Gently stir the diluted miso into the pot of soup.
4. Cover and simmer (do not let it boil) for one more minute and remove from flame.
5. Transfer the soup into individual bowls with the vegetables invitingly and decoratively arranged and serve while hot.

Useful information:

As the weather changes, the amount of miso changes. The spring weather can be fickle, changing quickly from warm to cool and windy. If it's cool, try adding a little bit more miso. Experiment with different vegetables and enjoy the variety. A garnish of chopped scallion, parsley or chives can also be added for more raw vegetable freshness.

99

brown rice and whole oats porridge

with Green Nori & Sesame Condiment

As hibernation is complete and the gentle spring light shines though the window, I find that I have a good appetite. During this time, I love eating something comforting, yet strengthening. This porridge is soft and at the same time packed with solid goodness.

MAKES 4 SERVINGS

For the grains:
1 ½ cups short-grain brown rice
½ cup whole oats
4 ½ cups purified water
1 small pinch of sea salt
Green Nori and Sesame Condiment
   (recipe on next page)

To make the grains:

1. Wash the brown rice and whole oats separately, according to the instructions listed in the section titled "How to Wash and Soak Whole Grains," found on page 27.
2. Combine rice and oats in pressure cooker, add the purified water and soak for 4 to 8 hours or overnight.
3. When soaking is complete, place pan, uncovered, over a medium-high flame until the water begins to boil. Add sea salt, secure lid on the pressure cooker and allow pan to come to pressure.
4. Place a flame deflector over the flame, reduce heat to low and simmer for 45 to 50 minutes.
5. Remove the cooker from heat and allow pan to sit until the pressure comes down naturally.
6. Wait an additional 5 to 10 minutes and remove lid. Using a bamboo rice paddle or wooden spoon that has been moistened in water (to prevent sticking), gently stir the grains.
7. Serve grains with Green Nori and Sesame condiment.

Useful information:

When the weather gets very warm, or when I want to release tightness from my body, I make this porridge without using a pressure cooker. In this case, I add an additional ½ cup of water. If I want to be even more relaxed, I add an additional cup of water to make a softer, creamier porridge.

green nori and Sesame

Condiment

When I was in high school I loved nori flakes on my vegetable pancakes, also known as "okonomiyaki." The combination of sesame seeds and sea vegetables is a tasty variation for people who are only accustomed to eating plain sesame seed condiment (gomashio).

MAKES 4 SERVINGS

For the condiment:

4 teaspoons sesame seeds, dry-roasted, (see section titled "How to Dry Roast Whole Grains or Seeds," found on page 29)
4 teaspoons green nori flakes

To make the condiment:

1. In a small bowl, combine sesame seeds and nori flakes thoroughly. Serve with cooked grains (about 2 teaspoons per serving).

Useful information:

Green nori flakes are a good way to introduce people to sea vegetables if they are not accustomed to eating them. Mixed with roasted sesame seeds, nori enhances the pleasure of eating grains. It is a good source of calcium and iron. Nori flakes are available by mail order or over the Internet from macrobiotic food suppliers, as well as at Japanese and natural foods markets.

Steamed baby bok choy

When I first discovered the naturally sweet flavor of baby bok choy, I wanted to eat it as a dish in itself — just as simple, morning greens.

MAKES 4 SERVINGS

For the bok choy:

4 cups purified water
one small pinch sea salt
2 bunches of baby bok choy

To make the bok choy:

1. Cut each bunch of bok choy into verticle halves in order to wash away grit from the insides of the leaves. (Otherwise, cut each leaf from the stalk and wash one by one.)
2. In a large saucepan over medium-high flame, bring water to a boil.
3. Add the sea salt and bok choy placing the white parts of the plant in the water first.
4. Boil the bok choy for 1 to 2 minutes (do not overcook). Strain the water in a colander placed over a bowl or sink.
5. When greens are cool enough to handle, slice white part diagonally with a sharp knife and arrange like a flower (as shown in photo).

Useful information:

Bok choy is a variety of the Chinese cabbage and is a good source of calcium and vitamin C. Bok choy makes a great addition to wok-fried tofu and vegetables.

couscous Salad

with Lentils

This makes a quick and easy grain salad for lunch. So delicious, simple and fun that you forget you're eating healing food.

MAKES 4 SERVINGS

For the lentils:
½ cup French lentils
1 ½ cups purified water
1 one-inch piece of kombu
¼ onion, chopped
1 to 2 teaspoons soy sauce

To make the lentils:
1. Place the lentils in a fine mesh colander, rinse under running water and drain.
2. In a small saucepan, combine the purified water, lentils, kombu and onion.
3. Bring to a boil over medium-high flame. Place a flame deflector over flame and reduce heat to low. Cover and simmer for 40 to 45 minutes, or until lentils are tender.
4. Turn off the flame and allow pan to sit, covered, for 2 minutes.
5. Stir in the soy sauce, cover for another 2 minutes and set aside. Lentils are ready to combine with couscous salad, or can be eaten separately as a lentil dish.

For the salad:
1 ⅓ cups purified water, plus additional water for blanching
1 tablespoon olive oil (optional)
2 pinches sea salt
3 baby carrots, washed and diced
1 cup whole wheat couscous*
2 cups sugar snap peas, washed, halved, with ends of pods trimmed off

To make the salad:
1. In a medium saucepan over high heat, bring water to a boil. Quickly blanch snap peas for about 45 seconds and drain. Transfer snap peas to a bowl and set aside.
2. In the same pan over medium-high heat, combine the purified water, oil, sea salt and carrots. Bring to a boil.
3. Add couscous, stir well to combine and cover. Turn off the flame and allow pan to sit for 10 minutes.
4. Using a wooden spoon moistened with water, stir in the blanched snap peas and cooked lentils.

Variation: The couscous in this recipe can be replaced with millet, quinoa or amaranth.

Creamy Carrot Soup

with Baby Spring Onion & Fried Carrot Tops

Spring carrots are vibrant and sweet. The pastel orange color is appealing, fun and perfect for celebrating the season's bounty. The carrot's strength, sweet taste and color help stimulate the appetite, and the creamy texture is especially soothing and relaxing.

MAKES 4 SERVINGS

For the soup:
3 cups carrot, diced
1 cup onion, diced
½ cup cooked brown rice
4 to 5 cups kombu dashi (recipe on page 215)
1 cup baby spring onions, peeled
   (or substitute regular onion, finely minced)
⅛ teaspoon sea salt
3 tablespoons white miso
Fried Carrot Tops, as garnish
   (recipe on next page)
Tofu Sour Cream, as garnish
   (recipe on next page)

To make the soup:

1. In a large pot over medium-high flame, add a portion of the kombu dashi to a depth of about ½- to ¼-inch.
2. Add onion and sea salt. Water-sauté until onions become translucent.
3. Add carrots and remaining kombu dashi. Bring to a boil, add rice, cover and simmer 30 to 40 minutes.
4. Gently stir in the miso and allow pan to simmer for two minutes and turn off flame.
5. Transfer mixture to a food mill and purée until smooth and creamy.
6. Transfer soup to individual serving bowls and garnish with Fried Carrot Tops and Tofu Sour Cream. Serve hot.

Useful information:

Carrots come in many sizes and colors (orange, yellow, red and white). The bright orange color signifies beta-carotene, which is metabolized into vitamin A in humans when bile salts are present in the intestines.

fried carrot tops

MAKES 4 SERVINGS

For the garnish:
4 to 5 small branches fresh, green carrot tops
safflower oil (for deep frying)

To make the garnish:
1. Remove carrot tops from roots and wash very well. Wipe with a clean, dry cloth to remove moisture.
2. Deep fry the carrot tops in oil (2 to 3 inches deep) at 325° F. Drain on paper towels.

Useful information:
For medicinal cooking, instead of frying the carrot tops, try blanching them first and chop very finely. Chopped scallions also make a suitable medicinal garnish.

tofu sour cream

MAKES ABOUT 1 CUP

For the sour cream:
6 ounces silken tofu, medium-firm
juice from 1 lemon
2 pinches sea salt
2 tablespoons olive oil

To make sour cream:
1. In a small saucepan, blanch the tofu in boiling water for one minute. Drain thoroughly and transfer to a blender.
2. Add remaining ingredients and blend until creamy.
3. Transfer to a container and refrigerate until well chilled.
4. Serve as shown in photo, or create your own design.

Useful information:
The addition of Tofu Sour Cream makes for an attractive dish and provides more smoothness to the soup, but for medicinal purposes, use gomashio instead. Tofu Sour Cream will keep for up to 2 or 3 days in the refrigerator. Be sure to use "silken" tofu for best results.

brown rice and wheat berries

Wheat berries lend a delightfully nutty texture to the rice, which gets richer the more you chew.

MAKES 4 SERVINGS

For the grains:
1 ½ cups brown rice, washed
½ cup soft spring wheat berries, washed*
3 cups purified water
1 small pinch sea salt

To make the grains:

1. Wash the brown rice and wheat berries separately, according to the instructions listed in the section titled "How to Wash and Soak Whole Grains," found on page 27.
2. Transfer the grains to a pressure cooker, add purified water and soak for 4 to 8 hours, or overnight.
3. When soaking is complete, place pressure cooker, uncovered, over a medium-high flame until the water begins to boil. Add sea salt, secure lid on the pressure cooker and allow it to come to pressure.
4. Place a flame deflector over the flame, reduce heat to low and simmer for 45 to 50 minutes.
5. Remove the cooker from heat and allow pan to sit until the pressure comes down naturally.
6. Wait an additional 5 to 10 minutes and remove lid. Using a bamboo rice paddle or wooden spoon that has been moistened in water (to prevent sticking), gently stir the grains. The grains are ready to serve.

Useful information:

I make this grain combination when I feel like having a nutty, chewy texture. It can be made without a pressure cooker by adding ½ cup more water.

Variation: Try combining the brown rice with barley or whole rye, for variety.

natto and green peas
with Chives

Natto is an acquired taste due to its powerful smell, strong flavor and sticky consistency. As a child, even I couldn't be persuaded to eat it! I created this recipe for the novice natto eater and hope you'll learn to love it as I now do. The many health benefits of natto are worth expanding your taste buds for!

MAKES 4 SERVINGS

For the Natto and Green Peas:

2 tablespoons soy sauce
4 to 6 tablespoons purified water,
  plus additional water for blanching
5 ounces green peas
5 ounces natto beans, packaged or homemade
  (recipe on next page)
1 bunch chives, chopped

To make the Natto and Green Peas:

1. In a small saucepan over a medium flame, combine the soy sauce and purified water. Cook for 30 to 60 seconds (do not allow to boil). Set aside.
2. In a medium saucepan filled halfway with water, blanch the green peas (about 1 to 3 minutes). Drain thoroughly.
3. Stir in the natto and chives. Add soy sauce mixture a little at a time until desired taste is achieved.
4. Serve Natto and Green Peas over the cooked grains.

Useful information:

Popular in Japan, natto is fermented soybeans commonly eaten for breakfast with rice and miso soup. High in protein and vitamin K, natto is an excellent digestive aid and may help reduce the likelihood of blood clotting, heart attacks, pulmonary embolism, or strokes. In fact, recent studies show that natto may also have a cholesterol-lowering effect. Be sure to buy organic natto, which is ready to eat "as is."

homemade natto

MAKES ABOUT 2 ½ POUNDS

For the natto:
2 cups soybeans (smaller soybeans are better, about 250g)
purified water, for soaking
about one pinch Bacillus natto bacteria (about 0.1g), mixed with 3 tablespoons of purified water

To make the natto:

1. Wash the soybeans thoroughly, and soak in three times the amount of purified water (by volume) for 12 to 24 hours at room temperature.
2. When the soybeans have swollen to twice their dry size, steam them in a pressure cooker (put the steaming rack in the pressure cooker with enough water to almost touch the steaming rack) for about 45 minutes, or steam in a bamboo steamer for about 6 hours or until the beans can be easily mashed between two fingers.
3. Transfer the steamed soybeans to a flat casserole dish. Using a wooden spatula, stir in the diluted natto bacillus mixture, being careful not to break the soybeans.
4. Tear off a sheet of parchment paper large enough to cover the casserole dish. Poke air holes across the parchment paper every couple of inches or so, and cover the dish.
5. Cover the dish in a thick towel. Transfer the dish to a warm, dry area, about 40 to 42C (104 to 108F); a gas oven that has a pilot light is ideal. Allow to sit for 14 to 15 hours. Important note: Natto fermentation requires sufficient oxygen, so you may need to open the cover a little bit. Without enough air circulation, natto may become bitter; with too much, its surface may become dry.
6. Natto is ready when soybeans have a sticky texture and have turned whitish in color. Allow natto to cool and transfer into small containers for storage in the refrigerator until ready to serve.

Note: Cultured natto bacillus is very sensitive to high and low temperatures. Adjusting the temperature is key to making a successful batch of natto. If it doesn't work, you can always add a little more cultured natto bacillus. Just try it out, making adjustments as you go along. Once you get the hang of it, and with a little time and practice, you'll soon discover that making homemade natto is easy, healthful and very delicious.

water-sautéed chinese broccoli

Water-sautéing is a method of sautéing vegetables without oil. When I first heard of this I didn't think it would work, but it brings out the natural sweetness of vegetables, and it's now my favorite way to sauté.

MAKES 4 SERVINGS

For the Chinese broccoli:
purified water
1 bunch Chinese broccoli
pinch of sea salt

To make the Chinese broccoli:

1. Wash broccoli. With a sharp knife, cut flowerets (including some stem) to a length of about 2 inches and set aside. Slice remaining stems into 2-inch long lengths.
2. In a large sauté pan over a medium flame, add about 1/4-inch of water.
3. Add sea salt and broccoli stems. Allow stems to cook for one minute (do not stir).
4. Add flowerets, additional water (only if needed), cover and cook for another minute, being careful not to overcook.
5. Strain and serve.

Useful information:
Chinese broccoli is widely available in California. It is a slightly bitter leaf vegetable with a small number of tiny flowering heads similar to broccoli. It is high in vitamins A and C, as well as calcium and iron.

green apple and cabbage
with Wakame Condiment

This recipe is great for early spring, just before the apples are all gone from the last harvest's storage. The sourness of green apples blended with the natural sweetness of cabbage, make for a winning combination, hands down!

MAKES 4 SERVINGS

For the apple and cabbage:
4 cups purified water for blanching
8 leaves green cabbage, sliced into 1- to 2-inch
   strips
½ green apple (Pippin or Granny Smith),
   julienned
1 teaspoon umeboshi paste
1 teaspoon purified water for seasoning
Wakame Condiment (recipe below)

To make the apple and cabbage:
1. In a large pot over a high flame, bring water to a boil. Blanch cabbage and apple quickly, about 1 minute or less. Drain thoroughly in a colander and transfer to a medium-sized bowl. Set aside.
2. In a small bowl, thoroughly combine umeboshi paste and water to make the seasoning.
3. Add umeboshi seasoning to cabbage mixture and gently stir to combine.
4. Squeeze cabbage mixture to drain any excess liquid and serve with a sprinkling of Wakame Condiment.

Useful information:
Cabbage contains potent anticancer phytochemicals, and has been shown to benefit the stomach and gastrointestinal tract. Apples are a rich source of potassium, soluble fiber and vitamin C.

wakame condiment

A spring sea vegetable, wakame can be made as a delicious condiment to enjoy with vegetables and grains.

MAKES ABOUT 1 CUP

For the condiment:
1 cup wakame, soaked and chopped
2 tablespoons soy sauce
2 tablespoons purified water

To make the condiment:
1. In a medium saucepan over a medium-high flame, combine the wakame, soy sauce and water.
2. Bring to a boil, cover, reduce heat to low. Place a flame deflector over the flame and simmer until almost all liquid has evaporated, about 5 to 10 minutes.

Useful information:
Wakame is recommended for blood purification, intestinal strength, skin, hair, reproductive organs and menstrual regularity.

113

three hour red radish pickles

I enjoy making 3-hour pickles in the afternoon so that they're ready in time for dinner. Pickles are best eaten toward the end of the meal to help settle the stomach in the evening.

MAKES 4 SERVINGS

For the pickles:
8 red radishes sliced into thin rounds
1 teaspoon lemon juice
1 teaspoon sea salt

To make the pickles:

1. In a medium bowl, thoroughly combine all the ingredients by hand. Transfer mixture to a pickle press. Press for 3 hours. (Note: If you don't have a pickle press, lay a plate over the radish mixture and place a heavy weight on top of the plate.)
2. Remove pickles, squeeze out excess liquid, and taste. If it's too salty, rinse pickles in a strainer under running water. Squeeze again and transfer to a serving dish.

Useful information:
Pickles help to increase the appetite, aid digestion, and strengthen the intestinal flora due to their high enzyme content. Using our hands is an important process of making pickles in order to complement our natural oils with the sea salt, as in yin and yang, to contribute natural enzymes to the process. Pickles are best enjoyed in small amounts only.

lemon amazake cream

When the Meyer lemons in my backyard are ready to pick, I know spring is here. Their sour, yet sweet flavor, similar to mandarin oranges, is refreshing on the palate.

MAKES 4 SERVINGS

For the cream:
3 to 4 tablespoons kuzu
¼ cup purified water
1 pint (2 cups) Amazake, original flavor
¼ cup meyer lemon juice*
1 tablespoon brown rice syrup
1 teaspoon agar powder
fresh lemon zest** (optional)

To make the cream:
1. In a small bowl, thoroughly dissolve kuzu in the purified water and set aside.
2. In a medium saucepan over medium-high flame, combine the amazake and the kuzu mixture. Continue stirring until mixture thickens. Using a wire whisk, beat briskly to dissolve any lumps.
3. Add the lemon juice, rice syrup and agar to the pan. Stir well to combine and continue cooking until agar is dissolved.
4. Pour mixture into four small ramekins. Allow to cool. Serve sprinkled with lemon zest on top.

 *Variation: If you don't have Meyer lemons you can substitute with different varieties of lemon. However, you may need to add additional rice syrup, since Meyer lemons are more naturally sweet than other varieties.

 **Be sure to only use the outermost part of the lemon (the rind) for best flavor. The white pulpy part beneath the rind has a bitter flavor. If you don't have a zester to remove the rind, a vegetable peeler can also be used.

The Story of Summer

A Time To Be Active And Mobile

Imagine the color red, as brightly and purely as you can. I see this color when I close my eyes and look toward the sun. I believe that summer and the brightness of the sun give us our greatest source of energy. The sun is always there, even on a cloudy or rainy day, ever patiently waiting to come out to warm us. I want to be like the sun — constant, energetic and patient. Feel the heat and active energy this season provides. Feel your heart beat faster. Feel the urge to move forward. And then, remember to take a nap so you don't burn out!

TRANSFORMATION OF

summer

Remedy drinks:
Dried Daikon-Shiitake Tea
Corn Silk Tea

Breakfast:
Summer Miso Soup with Quinoa and Vegetables
Water-sautéed Kale with Gomashio

Lunch:
Cool Noodles with Daikon Oroshi
    and Shiitake-Kombu Dipping Broth
Pressed Napa Cabbage Salad with Dulse Flakes

Dinner:
Chilled Cucumber Soup
Long-grain Brown Rice and Fresh Corn
    with Nori and Shiso Garnish
Blanched Arugula Greens
Summer Kimpira with Carrot Tops
Quick-Marinated Tofu with Sesame Sauce
Green & Yellow String Bean Pickles

Dessert:
Watermelon Kanten with Blueberries and Amazake Cream

dried daikon-shiitake tea

Remedy Drink

I have learned to use this tea for dissolving all fatty substances. It helps to relax my stiff shoulders and reduce fever/excess body heat from eating too many animal products, baked goods or salty foods.

MAKES 1+ SERVING

For the tea:
¼ cup dried daikon
1 dried shiitake mushroom (1- to ½-inch diameter)
2 cups purified water

To make the tea:
1. In a bowl, combine the water, daikon and shiitake, and allow to soak until soft, for 15 to 30 minutes or more, depending on the thickness of the shiitake.
2. Pour the soaking water out into a saucepan, and squeeze excess water out of daikon and shiitake into the pan. Using a sharp knife, chop the vegetables finely and add back to the pan.
3. Over medium-high heat, bring mixture to a boil, reduce heat to low and simmer for 15 to 20 minutes.
4. Strain and drink hot or warm. Extra tea can be stored in the refrigerator for up to 2 or 3 days and reheated as needed.

Useful information:
Dried daikon, also known as "kiriboshidaikon," is a very popular radish in Japan. The giant, sun-dried white radish is available in many Asian markets in the U.S. The traditional way of making dried daikon is by shredding the fresh root, laying it out in the sun to dry on rice or bamboo mats for several weeks during clear, dry days. Drying daikon imparts an especially sweet, mellow flavor. Be sure to only purchase unbleached, dried daikon.

Dried shiitake mushrooms have many health benefits, including potent immune strengthening properties. For remedy drinks, I recommend dried, instead of fresh, shiitake, whenever possible.

120

corn silk tea

Remedy Drink

The first time I saw corn silk as a remedy drink was when I had just started studying macrobiotics. It was fascinating to me that a simple thing like corn silk can heal us. Corn silk is the beautiful, shiny yellowish thread-like strands found inside the husk of corn. It tastes very mild, while at the same time soothing and relaxing.

MAKES 2 SERVINGS

For the tea:
Corn silk strands from 2 to 3 ears of fresh corn
2 to 3 cups purified water

To make the tea:

1. In a medium saucepan over medium-high flame, combine the corn silk and water.
2. Bring to a boil, reduce heat to low and simmer about 10 minutes.
3. Strain and drink hot or warm.

Useful information:

For more than a century, corn silk has been a remedy for all types of urinary conditions, including inflamed bladders and painful urination. Corn silk is also used to treat such diverse conditions as: enlarged prostate, gonorrhea, kidney disorders, heart trouble, jaundice, hepatitis, malaria and obesity. It is rich in vitamin K, making it effective in controlling bleeding during childbirth. Corn silk tea can also be used as an enema. Fresh corn silk strands can be dried and stored for use in winter. Simply allow them to dehydrate naturally, either outside in a shady area or indoors. This process takes anywhere from a few days to a week, depending on humidity levels.

123

Summer miso Soup
with Quinoa & Vegetables

Having soup on a hot summer day may not sound enticing, but having light miso soup actually builds vitality to better enjoy the long days of summer. Quinoa is a light, slightly crunchy and subtly-flavored grain that is high in protein. This is our favorite miso soup in the summer.

MAKES 4 SERVINGS

For the soup:
¼ cup quinoa
4 to 5 cups Kombu Shiitake Dashi
   (recipe on page 52)
¼ cup onion, diced (about ¼ of an onion)
2 to 3 ounces yellow beans, sliced slivered (about 10 to 12 string beans)
2 to 3 ounces green beans, cut into ½-inch lengths
4 teaspoons white barley miso

To make the soup:
1. Wash the quinoa according to the instructions listed in the section titled "How to Wash and Soak Whole Grains," found on page 27.
2. In a large soup pot over medium-high flame, combine quinoa and dashi. Bring it to a boil and cook, about 5 to 10 minutes.
3. Add the onion and bring to a boil again. Reduce the flame to low and simmer for 15 minutes.
4. Add the yellow beans and simmer for 1 minute. Add green beans and simmer an additional minute.
5. In a cup, small bowl or a suribachi, add the miso and a small amount of soup broth. Using a spoon, chopstick or surikogi, thoroughly combine and dilute the miso with the broth.
6. Stir the diluted miso into the pot of soup, cover and simmer (do not boil) for 1 minute. Remove pot from heat and serve hot.

Useful information:
Aged barley miso is fermented for 2 to 3 years. White barley miso is fermented and aged six months to one year, so it has a light, sweet taste and smooth texture. It is good for creamy sauces, dips and salad dressings, and delicate enough to be refreshing in the summer. Since miso is a fermented food, it is rich in living, beneficial enzymes. For this reason, it is important to not overcook the miso. (See page 50 for more information about miso.)

Quinoa is gluten-free, easy to digest and full of high-quality complete protein that contains all 8 essential amino acids. Over 5000 years ago the Peruvian Incas cultivated quinoa as one of their staple crops.

Water-Sautéed Kale
with Gomashio

Having greens in the morning makes me feel very clean. It's a pure and simple feeling. Water-sautéing is a very quick, fresh and easy cooking style to make greens for your morning meal.

MAKES 4 SERVINGS

For the kale:
4 to 5 kale leaves,* washed thoroughly
1 to 2 cups purified water
1 to 2 teaspoons Gomashio
   (recipe on next page)

To make the kale:
1. Using a sharp knife, destem the leaves. Slice stems diagonally into very thin 1- to 2-inch long slices and set aside. Chop the leaves into 1 to 2-inch pieces and set aside separately.
2. In a large stainless steel skillet over a medium-high flame, add enough water to just cover the bottom of the pan (about ¼ to ½ inch high) and bring to a boil.
3. Spread the sliced stems in the skillet. Using wooden chopsticks or a wooden spoon, cook evenly for 1 minute. Add chopped leaves and cook for about 30 to 45 seconds.
4. Reduce the flame to medium-low and simmer for 30 seconds, or until the greens are tender, but still bright green.
5. Strain, transfer to a serving dish and garnish with Gomashio.

Useful information:
Kale is considered to be a highly nutritious vegetable with powerful antioxidant and anti-inflammatory properties. Kale is a rich source of calcium, beta carotene, and vitamins K and C.

Variation: There are many other varieties of greens that work well with the water-sauté method, including: collard greens, Chinese napa cabbage, watercress, mustard greens, dandelion greens, daikon tops and turnip tops.

gomashio
Sesame Salt

This is the classic and basic sesame salt condiment that is used daily on macrobiotic foods. Until you've made your own, you will never know how incredibly delicious it tastes. Whenever I make this at home, I enjoy the aroma of sesame so much that I feel like I'm meditating.

MAKES ABOUT 1 ½ CUPS

For the Gomashio:
1 tablespoon sea salt
18 tablespoons sesame seeds (1 cup plus 2 tablespoons)

To make the Gomashio:

1. In a large skillet over medium-high flame, add the sea salt. Stirring with a wooden spatula, dry roast the sea salt until its color turns slightly gray. Transfer salt to a suribachi. Using a surikogi, grind salt until it becomes a fine powder with no lumps. Set aside.

2. Wash and roast the sesame seeds according to the instructions listed in the sections titled "How to Wash Seeds," and "How to Dry Roast Whole Grains or Seeds," found on page 29.

3. Transfer the hot, roasted sesame seeds to the suribachi. Using a surikogi, slowly grind the seeds in an even, circular motion. Continue grinding until seeds are 50% to 80% crushed and thoroughly coated with salt. Do not grind seeds into a powder.

4. Allow mixture to cool. Store in an airtight glass or ceramic container.

Useful information:

The ratio of sea salt to sesame seeds can be adjusted to individual needs, seasons and change of environment. Normally, I use a 1 : 18 - 22 ratio of sea salt to sesame seeds. This ratio can change depending on your health condition with regards to salt intake. Black sesame seeds are more medicinal, strengthening and healing, but not necessary if difficult to find. Roasting the sea salt helps release the strong chlorine from the salt. Roasted sesame seeds may also be used as a condiment or garnish without salt. Sesame seeds are rich in manganese, copper, and calcium, and contain vitamins B1 (thiamin) and E. They also contain phytosterols associated with reduced levels of blood cholesterol. The nutrients of sesame seeds are better absorbed if they are ground or pulverized before consumption. Buy only natural, unhulled sesame seeds and do not use hulled white sesame seeds. Also, be careful when purchasing black sesame seeds, since some of them are colored by using black dye.

cool noodles

with Daikon Oroshi & Shiitake Kombu Dipping Broth

How soothing it is to have cool noodles on a hot day! This is our favorite lunch in the summer, in a shady spot under the trees. The wide variety of garnishes brings out different flavors, and we can be creative and make our own combinations.

MAKES 4 SERVINGS

For the noodles:
8 ounce package udon noodles
purified water, for boiling
3 cups broth, chilled* (recipe following)

For the garnish:
4 tablespoons fresh daikon, finely grated
4 fresh green shiso leaves
shiitake mushrooms, reserved from broth recipe
   (see below)
2 tablespoons carrot, finely shredded
1 tablespoon scallion, thinly sliced
1 tablespoon dry roasted sesame seeds

Noodle cooking tips:
- 98° C is the best temperature for boiling noodles.
- Use at least 10 times the quantity of water to noodles.
- In order to not reduce the temperature of the boiling water, add noodles gradually.
- Gently stir noodles with cooking chopsticks or a wooden spoon to prevent sticking.
- Adjust flame periodically to prevent the pot from boiling over.

To make the noodles with garnish:

1. Cook noodles according to the directions on the package. Note: thinner udon noodles made of whole wheat cook faster than thicker ones. Drain noodles and rinse thoroughly with cool water to prevent them from cooking further and from clumping together. (See noodle cooking tips, below.)

2. Ladle the broth into 4 individual serving bowls. Divide noodles onto 4 plates. Noodles and broth are served separately, using the broth as a dip.

3. Arrange garnishings (daikon, shiso, sesame seeds, mushrooms, carrot and scallions) on individual plates, or decoratively arrange them with the noodles.

4. Garnishes are typically eaten by adding them to the dipping broth first, then dipping noodles into broth—though this depends on personal preference.

Useful information:
Did you know there are more than 50 different kinds of udon noodles in Japan? You can substitute buckwheat noodles (soba) instead of udon in this recipe. Soba noodles cook faster than udon. Noodles are easy to digest and make for a satisfying, quick lunch.

129

shiitake kombu dipping broth

While sleeping over at my grandparents' country home when I was about 3 or 4 years old, I remember watching intently as my grandmother cooked all day over an old-fashioned stove. She would often tell me, "You know, Sanae, if you can make a good dashi, you can make all food taste delicious. Remember that!" At the time, I didn't know, of course, why dashi was so important, but I recall her using the broth not only in soups, but also to make vegetables, dressings, sauces and stews. Well, sure enough, I now use dashi in all sorts of dishes.

For the broth:

2 dried shiitake mushrooms
1 cup purified water for soaking shiitake
    mushrooms
1 piece kombu, 2 to 3 inches long
4 cups purified water
2 to 3 tablespoons soy sauce

To make the broth:

1. Soak the shiitake mushrooms with 1 cup of water for 15 to 20 minutes or until soft. Remove shiitake from soaking water, reserving the water for later use.
2. Using a sharp knife, slice off and discard the hard end of the stems. Slice the mushrooms into thin strips.
3. In a soup pot over a medium-high flame, combine the kombu, purified water, soy sauce and sliced shiitake, along with the reserved soaking water. Bring to just before a boil, reduce heat to low and simmer for 20 minutes.
4. Remove the kombu and reserve it for other dishes. Strain out the shiitake and serve it along with the other garnishes listed on the previous page.

pressed napa cabbage salad

with Dulse Flakes

I used to love fresh raw salad before I studied macrobiotics, and when I heard of "pressed salad," I was curious. Pressed salad is a pickling method that's a simple way to make raw vegetables more digestible. The freshness and natural sweet taste of napa cabbage along with the slightly bitter dandelion greens combine to give "salad" a new meaning.

MAKES 4 SERVINGS

For the salad:

4 cups napa cabbage, thinly-sliced into 1-inch strips
¼ bunch dandelion greens, finely chopped
1 teaspoon sea salt (or to taste)*
½ ounce Maine coast dulse, soaked and coarsely chopped into ½-inch pieces

To make the salad:

1. In a large bowl, combine the cabbage and greens. Sprinkle with the salt and dulse.
2. Using your hands, thoroughly combine the mixture, massaging the vegetables until they get shiny, wet and begin to wilt.
3. Transfer mixture to a pickle press and apply pressure. If you don't have a pickle press, lay a plate over the cabbage mixture and place a heavy weight on top of the plate.
4. Allow mixture to sit about 1 hour or more (the longer you leave it, the stronger the pickled flavor).
5. Transfer pickles back to bowl (or remove weight and plate). Using your hands, squeeze out the excess liquid. Rinse with purified water if pickles taste too salty. Arrange attractively in a serving dish.

Useful information:

I heard that pressed salad was the origin of coleslaw, but without all the mayonnaise and sugar. Coleslaw is often served with meat dishes or fried foods, which makes sense because pickled foods aid in the digestion of foods with a high fat content. In addition to aiding digestion, pressed salads, like pickles, strengthen the intestines and increase the appetite. Pressed salad is a form of cooking without using fire, but mixing sea salt with our hands, which give their own natural oils, combined with pressure and time. You can also use daikon, cucumber or your favorite vegetables. Pressed salad will keep about one week if stored in the refrigerator.

Napa cabbage is rich in vitamin C and is a good souce of fiber. Dandelion greens are rich in calcium, iron and vitamins A and K. Dandelion greens also support digestion, reduce swelling and inflammation, and treat viruses, jaundice, edema, gout, eczema and acne.

*Note: When making pressed salad, it is almost impossible to measure the perfect amount of sea salt since all vegetables contain differing water contents. For this reason, it may be necessary to adjust the amount of sea salt accordingly. After pressing, pickles can be rinsed if they taste too salty.

131

chilled cucumber soup

This soup has a refreshing melon-like taste and can be dressed up like a martini at a hot summer's eve party.

MAKES 4 SERVINGS

For the soup:
4 cucumbers
½ to 1 teaspoon sea salt, for rubbing cucumber ends
3 cups Kombu Shiitake Dashi Broth, (see recipe on page 52)
1 teaspoon sea salt
2 tablespoons dill, finely minced (optional)
black sesame seeds and sage flowers, for garnish

To make the soup:

1. To get rid of the bitterness of the cucumber, cut off the tips, rub the ends with a little sea salt, and peel off the skin. Slice open cucumbers, deseed and coarsely chop. You should have about 2 cups chopped.
2. In a medium saucepan over a medium-high flame, combine the cucumbers, dashi and sea salt. Bring to a boil, cover and simmer for 5 to 7 minutes.
3. Transfer to a food mill or blender and purée until smooth.
4. Add dill if desired, blend again and refrigerate for 2 to 3 hours, or overnight.
5. Serve in attractive long-stemmed glassware and garnish with a sprinkling of black sesame seeds and sage flower petals.

Useful information:
Cucumber is a plant native to India and other tropical regions, and for this reason it is recommended during the summer and late summer seasons when the temperature is warm. It is a popular fresh vegetable in a variety of salads and sandwiches, but if a person has poor blood circulation and often feels cold, eating too much cucumber can aggravate these conditions. Cucumber is used for its diuretic, cooling and cleansing properties, and can naturally reduce your temperature. It is also used to detox after eating excessive animal foods and to control constipation.

long-grain brown rice and fresh corn

with Nori & Shiso Garnish

Corn season is for celebrating a bright golden summer. I love how corn lends a sweet and light texture to the brown rice.

MAKES 4 SERVINGS

For the grains:
2 cups long-grain brown rice
3 to 3 ½ cups purified water
1 cup corn kernels, freshly cut from the cob
pinch of sea salt or 1-inch piece of kombu
nori and shiso powder, for garnish

To make the grains:

1. Wash the brown rice according to the instructions listed in the section titled "How to Wash and Soak Whole Grains," found on page 27.
2. After soaking, add corn to the rice/water mixture. Place pot over a medium-high flame and bring to a boil.
3. Add sea salt or kombu and cover. Place a flame deflector over the flame, reduce heat to low and cook for 45 to 50 minutes.
4. Remove pot from the stove and allow to sit for 5 to 10 minutes. Remove cover. Using a bamboo rice paddle or wooden spoon that has been moistened in water (to prevent sticking), gently stir the grains, fluffing them by lifting grains from the bottom of the pot and turning them over.
5. Serve with garnish of nori and shiso powder. If you are not eating grains right away, cover the pot with a clean dish towel or a bamboo sushi mat, instead of a lid.

Useful information:

Corn is good for boosting the nervous system, preventing macular degeneration, aiding digestion, and protecting against heart disease. Be sure to buy organic corn. Conventionally-grown corn has often been genetically modified. Choose fresh corn with bright green, tight and fresh-looking husks. Pull the husk open to make sure that the ear contains tightly packed rows of plump kernels. The kernels should be smaller at the tip of each ear. Large kernels at the tip are a sign of over-maturity. If you pinch a kernel, milky juice should spurt out. To maintain the natural sweetness of corn, purchase as fresh as possible and store ears in the refrigerator, as warmth causes the sugar content to be converted into a bland-tasting starch. The core can be used for soup stock after the kernels are removed. It makes a very sweet soup stock.

blanched arugula greens

Arugula, also called "rocket," typically grows on dry, disturbed ground and is easily grown in my garden here in Santa Monica, California. It has a flavor almost like that of sesame seeds. Most people use arugula as a raw salad ingredient, but I find it very delicious to eat as lightly blanched greens.

MAKES 4 SERVINGS

For the greens:
3 to 4 cups purified water
3 cups arugula greens, thoroughly washed
pinch of sea salt or 2 to 3 drops of soy sauce

To make the greens:
1. In a large pan over a medium-high flame, add the purified water and bring to a boil.
2. Add greens to the pan. Using wooden chopsticks or a wooden spoon, gently stir the greens to ensure they are evenly cooking for about 45 seconds to 1 minute.
3. Reduce the flame to medium-low. Add sea salt or soy sauce and simmer for another 30 seconds or until the greens are tender, but still brightly colored.
4. Drain off the water and spread greens out on a large plate to cool.
5. Transfer cooled greens to a cutting board and cut into 1 to 2-inch long pieces.
6. Transfer greens to a serving dish.

Useful information:
Arugula, native to the Mediterranean region of Morocco, is rich in minerals, including calcium and iron, as well as vitamins A and C. Arugula has potent detoxifying and anticancer properties. Water-sautéing is a very easy, simple and pure method of preparing arugula and other greens.

quick-marinated tofu
with Sesame Sauce

In Japan, there is a popular summer dish featuring fresh tofu called "hiyayakko." The quality of most tofu in the U.S. is different and not as tasty to eat fresh, so I created this recipe to enjoy tofu with more flavor, yet in the hiyayakko style.

MAKES 4 SERVINGS

For the tofu:
1 pound firm or soft tofu
purified water
½ pound white miso
Sesame Sauce (recipe on next page)

Note: I titled this recipe "quick-marinated" because the traditional method involves marinating for up to 2 to 3 days, instead of several hours. Longer marinating times will produce a type of tofu "cheese" with a sharper flavor.

To make the tofu:
1. In a medium saucepan over a medium-high flame, add the block of tofu and enough purified water to cover tofu. Bring to a boil, reduce heat to low and simmer for 5 minutes.
2. Turn off heat, drain water and press tofu to remove as much water as possible. Wrap tofu with a clean cotton dishtowel and transfer wrapped tofu to a plate. Place a heavy weight on top of tofu and allow to sit for ½ hour.
3. Unwrap and coat the entire block of tofu with the miso paste. Wrap tofu in parchment paper or cheesecloth. Allow tofu to sit at room temperature for 4 to 6 hours, or overnight.
4. Unwrap tofu and scrape miso off into a storage container. Save miso for use in soups or stews.
5. Slice tofu into rectangles or cubes and serve with Sesame Sauce.

Useful information:
Tofu is now popular in many countries as a versatile and high-quality vegetable protein. Tofu is low in calories and has no cholesterol. I do not recommend eating tofu too often for healing purposes because of its cooling energy.

Sesame Sauce

The soy sauce in this recipe can be substituted with umeboshi paste for a unique variation.

MAKES ABOUT ⅔ CUP

For the sauce:
½ cup sesame seeds
1 tablespoon soy sauce
½ cup purified water
1 teaspoon lemon or orange juice (optional)

To make the sauce:
1. Wash and roast the sesame seeds according to the instructions listed in the sections titled "How to Wash and Soak Whole Grains," found on page 27, and "How to Dry Roast Whole Grains or Seeds," found on page 29.
2. Transfer the hot, roasted sesame seeds to a suribachi. Using a surikogi, slowly grind the seeds in an even, circular motion. Continue grinding until seeds are almost powder-like in consistency.
3. Add the soy sauce, water, and if desired, lemon or orange juice and stir to combine thoroughly. Serve with marinated tofu.

Useful information:
This sauce is also delicious when served with steamed, boiled or blanched vegetables. Sesame seeds are rich in minerals like manganese, copper, and calcium, and also contain thiamin and vitamin E.

Summer Kimpira
with Carrot Tops

Kimpira (alternately kinpira) is a very strengthening dish traditionally using root vegetables, but this recipe introduces an equally strengthening, yet lighter version that's perfect for the long warm days of summer.

MAKES 4 SERVINGS

For the kimpira:
1 tablespoon sesame oil or ¼ cup purified water (water-sauté recipes: see page 112, 126, 154, and 203)
3 cups celery (about 4 stalks celery)
3 cups yellow summer squash (about 2 yellow squash)
3 teaspoons soy sauce
¼ cup carrot tops, chopped

To make the kimpira:
1. In a large skillet over a medium flame, heat the oil or water.
2. Add the celery and sauté for 1 to 2 minutes. Add squash and sauté for another minute.
3. Add the soy sauce and cook for 30 seconds more, stirring gently.
4. Stir in the carrot tops, remove from heat and serve.

Useful information:
Kimpira is a Japanese cooking style of "sauté and simmer" that is commonly used to cook root vegetables, such as carrots, burdock and lotus root. Usually this dish features the use of sesame oil, soy sauce, mirin, and slivered chili peppers, but for summer kimpira, chili peppers are omitted. Sauté this dish quickly so the vegetables maintain freshness and are not overcooked. Carrot tops are a very good source of vitamins and calcium. Please see page 180 for a root vegetable-style kimpira recipe.

green and yellow string bean pickles

I wanted to create a pickle recipe with a fresh and crispy quality and have found this one to be a hit at our home. Try it yourself, and you'll soon see that you can't get enough!

MAKES 4 SERVINGS

For the pickles:
4 green string beans, washed and stems removed
4 yellow string beans, washed and stems removed
2 cups purified water, for blanching string beans
1 cup purified water, for pickling
1 ½ teaspoons sea salt

To make the pickles:

1. In a medium saucepan over a medium-high flame, add two cups of the water and bring to a boil.
2. Quickly blanch the string beans for 1 minute, drain water and then plunge them in cool water.
3. In the same pan over a medium-high flame, combine sea salt with 1 cup of the water. Bring to a boil, turn off flame and allow salted water to cool off naturally.
4. Fill a small glass jar (that is large enough to fit all the string beans) halfway with the cooling salted water. Add blanched string beans. If water does not reach all the way to the top of the jar, add additional salted water.
5. Cover top of jar with cheesecloth or cotton cloth and secure with a string or rubber band. Allow jar to sit at room temperature, undisturbed, for 12 to 24 hours. For a stronger pickling, allow jar to sit longer than one day.
6. When pickling process is completed, remove the cloth and serve sliced or as shown in photo. If not serving pickles right away, secure jar with a lid and store in the refrigerator.

Useful information:
Quick, salted pickles can be made in the morning and eaten that evening, or allowed to ferment for 2 to 3 days. Pickles are very good for the digestive system (see page 77 for more information). Green and yellow string beans are low in calories and high in vitamins A and C, as well as an excellent source of vitamin K, dietary fiber, potassium and iron. Green beans are also a good source of protein, magnesium, thiamin, riboflavin, copper, calcium, phosphorus, omega-3 fatty acids and niacin.

watermelon kanten

with Blueberries & Amazake Cream

Ever since I was a child, I have loved to eat watermelon in the summertime. The color is so lively, vivid and refreshing. I still remember spending summer vacations in my mom's countryside home, where we often bought watermelon from a local farmer. We placed it in a big bucket of cold well water and devoured it later that afternoon, after a long hot day at the beach. What a happy taste to grow up with! When I was advised to not consume raw fruits during my recovery, I came up with this recipe so that I could continue to relive this delightful childhood memory.

MAKES 4 SERVINGS

For the kanten:
½ of a small (1½- to 2-pound) watermelon
2 to 3 tablespoons agar flakes
pinch of sea salt
16 to 32 blueberries (about 2½ to 4 ounces)
1 to 3 teaspoons brown rice syrup (optional, depending on natural sweetness of watermelon)
Amazake Cream (recipe on next page)

To make the kanten:
1. In a blender or food mill, purée the watermelon. You should end up with about 2 cups of melon purée.
2. In a large saucepan over a medium-high flame, combine watermelon purée, agar and sea salt.

3. Gently stir constantly until agar has completely dissolved and mixture begins to thicken, about 5 to 8 minutes (do not allow mixture to boil). Stir in rice syrup if additional sweetening is desired.
4. Transfer mixture into either a 6- by 9-inch or 8- by 8-inch glass baking dish, or into several small molds.
5. Sprinkle kanten with blueberries, cover and refrigerate until jelled, or leave in a cool area of the room until firm.
6. Cut into 1-inch cubes and serve with Amazake Cream.

Useful information:
Kanten is a delightful, all-natural, plant-based gelatin made with fruit, beans, nuts, or seeds set in a seaweed gel made from agar-agar. The quantity of agar determines how soft (2 tablespoons per 2 cups of liquid) or firm (3 tablespoons) you want your kanten to be. If your kanten is not firming up properly, it may be that you did not stir and cook it enough, the kanten flakes are too old, your energy is too weak, you are tired, or any combination of the above. If your kanten is overly firm, it may be that you used too much kanten flakes, or that your mental and physical condition is very tight and not relaxed.

Agar is approximately 80% fiber so it helps regulate your digestive system. Agar has a neutral flavor and can be used with sweet or savory flavorings.

amazake Cream

MAKES ABOUT 2 CUPS

This cream sauce adds a delightful softness and naturally-sweet taste to kanten and other desserts. It's versatile and easy to make.

For the cream:
2 cups plain/original flavor amazake, store bought or homemade (see recipe on page 79)
1 tablespoon of kuzu, dissolved in 2 tablespoons of purified water

To make the cream:
1. In a medium saucepan over a medium flame, combine amazake and kuzu mixture. Stir and cook until mixture thickens and is creamy in texture.
2. Serve the cream either under or poured over the Watermelon Kanten cubes (recipe at left).

Variation: This cream is also delicious when served with fresh fruits and berries, or cooked apples. This cream also combines well with Azuki Glaze (see recipe on page 218) as a simple yet satisfying bean dessert.

Story of Late Summer

A Time to Reflect on Change

This period is the forgotten season, separated and lost from the traditional four. In Japan, my home country, late summer usually runs from the end of August through the end of September. During this time, the polar air slowly reaches into the country and the first typhoons arrive, signaling the end of summer.

It's a short season, but I feel its impact is significant. I get the sense of this time when I've arrived home after a day of bustling activity and social contact. I not only feel tired, but also lonely. Late summer is a time to reflect on the changing moods within and around us, and to prepare ourselves for the upcoming autumn season.

TRANSFORMATION OF

late

summer

Remedy drinks:
Sweet Ame Kuzu
Sweet Vegetable Drink

Breakfast:
Heart-Lifting Miso Soup
Brown Rice Mochi Pancakes with Kabocha Sauce
Daikon Root and Green Top Nuka Pickles

Lunch:
Brown Rice and Lotus Patties
Water-sautéed Watercress
Corn-on-the-cob with Ume Paste

Dinner:
Sweet Vegetable Chickpea Soup
Millet Cauliflower Mash with Shiitake Gravy
Quick Nabe with Roasted Pumpkin Seeds
Arame with Sweet Corn
Red Radish and Ume Plum Vinegar Pickles

Dessert:
Kabocha Millet Cake

 Sweet ame kuzu
Remedy Drink

This drink helps me to relax my mind and body. It has especially helped ease tension headaches in the back of my head.

MAKES 1 SERVING

For the drink:

1 teaspoon kuzu
2 to 3 tablespoons purified water
1 cup purified water
1 to 2 teaspoons brown rice syrup (or substitute with barley malt)

To make the drink:

1. In a small bowl, dissolve kuzu in two or three tablespoons of cool water.
2. In a small saucepan over a medium flame, add the dissolved kuzu. Stir in the 1 cup of water, and rice syrup.
3. Bring to a boil over medium flame. Cook, stirring constantly to prevent lumps from forming, until the mixture becomes translucent. Reduce flame to low and simmer for 5 minutes.
4. Drink while hot or warm.

Useful information:

Kuzu is the world's premier root cooking starch — a versatile thickener that dissolves quickly in any cold liquid and has no perceptible taste. It binds more strongly than arrowroot. Very low in calories, kuzu contains no fat and is an easily digestible source of complex carbohydrates.
This drink is great for any time of day when you're feeling particularly stressed. In fact, monks have been known to drink ame kuzu after a hard day of begging, to ease off the tension and make themselves more mellow and relaxed for study. The kuzu root is also the traditional medicine of choice for a host of digestive disorders, as well as for treating hypoglycemia, PMS and tension caused by intake of too many yang foods (such as chips, crackers, and other hard, baked goods). Kuzu is also useful in reducing fever in children, who may take a fancy to the sweetness and actually enjoy drinking their medicine!

145

Sweet Vegetable drink

Remedy Drink

Until I began practicing macrobiotics in 1993, I was a sugar junkie, regularly loading up on simple sugars and sweets. This drink helped me curb my excessive craving for sugar. It's very useful for softening tightness caused by excessive intake of animal or salty foods, and for relaxing the body and muscles.

MAKES 1 SERVING

For the drink:
¼ cup onion, minced
¼ cup cabbage, minced
¼ cup winter squash, minced
¼ cup carrots, minced
3 to 4 cups purified water

To make the drink:

1. In a medium saucepan, layer the minced vegetables in the following order: onion, cabbage, winter squash, and carrots. Add the water.
2. Bring to a boil over medium-high flame, reduce heat to low and simmer for 20 minutes.
3. Strain the vegetables and reserve them for another use*. Drink only the liquid portion while hot or warm.

Useful information:

In macrobiotic cooking, the ingredients rarely come prepped, so one will acquire a lot of practice chopping and cutting vegetables. This recipe presents a perfect opportunity to hone your knife skills. The more finely you chop the vegetables in this recipe, the sweeter the remedy drink will become. This drink is good to take in a small cup every day or every other day in the mid to late afternoon (3 to 4 pm). In this way, it can help reduce cravings for simple sugars and other strong sweets. The natural sweetness of this drink is very mild, so you might not feel satisfied in the beginning, but that may be due to the fact that your taste bud sensitivity is diminished from regular simple sugar consumption. Depending on the individual, it may take 3 to 10 days of abstaining from refined simple sugars in order to regain the natural sensitivity of your taste buds, and enjoy a taste of what nature has so beautifully provided.

*The reserved vegetables may be used with the Sweet Vegetable Chickpea Soup recipe found on page 157.

heart lifting miso soup

During my healing process, I experienced many difficult times, especially when the end of summer and the sensation of cold air converged. In those dark moments I used two different kinds of leafy greens to open up my melancholy heart and lull my overactive liver.

MAKES 4 SERVINGS

For the soup:

½ cup carrot, sliced diagonally
½ cup collard greens, sliced
(separate the tough stems, slice them diagonally, and slice the leaves into 2-inch squares)
1 cup napa cabbage, sliced into 2-inch squares
1 cup scallions, sliced diagonally
4 to 5 cups dashi (recipe on page 215)
4 teaspoons barley miso

To make the soup:

1. In a large pot over a medium-high flame, bring the dashi to a boil. Add carrots, reduce heat to low and simmer for 1 to 2 minutes, or until carrots are tender, but still crisp. Add collard green stems first and simmer for 1 minute. Add collard green leaves and cabbage and simmer for 1 minute. Add scallions and simmer for 30 seconds.

2. Reduce heat to very low. Place miso in a suribachi or bowl and add ¼ cup of the soup broth from the pot. Using a chopstick or surikogi, blend until miso is thoroughly dissolved. Add mixture to soup and gently stir to combine. Taste and add more miso if needed, taking care not to over-salt the soup. (The miso should just mingle with the flavor of the soup and enhance but not overpower it.)

3. Turn off flame and serve hot. Garnish can be added if desired. (In accompanying photo we did not add garnish, opting to keep it simple, instead.)

Useful information:

Miso soup is generally eaten daily on a macrobiotic diet, to help alkalize and strengthen the blood, aid digestion and assimilation, and to discharge toxins. Serve this soup for breakfast to awaken and prepare the stomach for digestion. Both collards and napa cabbage are wide and large leafy greens that provide more openness and soft energy to the soup. If you are feeling tight and tense, use only napa cabbage to help you relax. Collard greens and napa cabbage, both members of the cruciferous or cabbage family, are rich in calcium, beta-carotene and vitamin C, and exhibit strong anticancer properties.

brown rice mochi pancakes
with Kabocha Sauce

Whoever said healing food is dull and boring? These mochi pancakes are just as fun to make as they are to eat. They're guaranteed to bring your sunny side up!

MAKES 4 SERVINGS

For the mochi pancakes:
12 ½ ounces (354g) brown rice mochi, plain and unflavored
sesame oil
Kabocha Sauce (recipe following)

To make the mochi:
1. Using a sharp knife, cut mochi blocks into 4 smaller pieces. Using a cheese grater, coarsely grate the mochi.
2. In a large stainless or cast-iron skillet over medium heat, warm the oil. Place about ¼ cup of grated mochi per pancake in small flat mounds, about 3 inches in diameter. Keep each mound separated so pancakes do not stick together.
3. Using a spatula, cook each side until they are slightly melted, about 1 to 1 ½ minutes per side.
4. Remove mochi cakes from pan and place on serving plates. Repeat process until any remaining mochi is used up.
5. Drizzle pancakes with Kabocha Sauce and serve immediately.

Useful information:
Used for centuries as a healing food in Japan, mochi is made from pounded sweet brown rice. This easy-to-digest food is good for anemia, strengthening weakened conditions in general, and to aid breast-feeding mothers in supplying abundant, high-quality milk. It lends a chewy goodness to soups, and is used to make Ozoni (see recipe on page 51), a traditional New Year's dish. Be sure to purchase brown rice mochi (rather than white rice), which is most readily found in the refrigerated section of natural foods stores.

Variation: These pancakes are also tasty when served with the Fresh Parsley Sauce recipe on page 43 and Azuki Glaze recipe found on page 218.

kabocha Sauce

MAKES ABOUT 1 CUP

For the sauce:
1 ½ cups kabocha squash, peeled and diced
1 cup purified water
pinch of sea salt

To make the sauce:
1. In a medium saucepan over a medium-high flame, bring water to a boil. Add kabocha, bring to a boil, and add the sea salt.
2. Reduce flame to low, cover and simmer for 10 to15 minutes, or until kabocha is soft enough to purée. Drain.
3. Transfer squash to a food mill or blender and process until smooth. Serve with mochi pancakes, or other dishes.

Variation: When kabocha is unavailable, you can substitute with another hard winter squash. This sauce is also delicious when served as a soft spread for steamed, natural yeast-free bread, or rice cakes.

daikon root and green top nuka pickles

Brown Rice Bran Pickles

Nuka (brown rice bran) pickles are one of the best pickles recommended in macrobiotics. I never knew why or how good they truly were until the first time I made them at home. Most store-bought pickles have sugar and artificial preservatives. One taste and you'll agree: Making homemade pickles is well worth the effort!

MAKES 4 SERVINGS

For the pickles:

nuka doko, (brown rice bran pickling bed)*
1 daikon root,** with green tops

To make the pickles:

1. Using a sharp knife, cut the daikon and green tops into pieces that will fit into your pickle crock, or leave the root whole, if it will fit. (The smaller you cut the vegetables, the sooner they will pickle.) Transfer them to a bamboo tray and dry them outside, in a secluded shady spot, for about 12 to 24 hours.
2. Transfer the dried daikon and greens onto the prepared nuka doko, evenly laying them down, like they are going to sleep. They should be ready after 2 to 3 days to one week, depending on how large you cut the daikon.
3. When the pickles are ready, cover the mixture with a plate. Place a heavy weight on top of the plate. Cover crock with cotton cloth. Store crock in a dark, cool, dry area.
4. Mix the nuka daily by hand, or whenever you remove a pickle, to help blend the flavors and prevent mold. When removing the daikon and greens, get as much of the bran back into the crock. Rinse daikon and greens under cool water and slice them before serving. Only one to three pieces of pickles are sufficient per meal.

Useful information:

Naturally fermented pickles promote lactic acid bacteria, which is essential for the digestive process and assimilation of food.

If nuka becomes too soft and the liquid rises, either drain it out or absorb it by adding fresh roasted nuka bran and a little sea salt. Add only a small amount to avoid changing the taste. Nuka doko will keep for a very long time if you mix it well on a daily basis and adjust the bran from time to time. In fact, some people have the same nuka doko for many years, as it's part of the family tradition.

See page 81 for instructions on how to prepare, store and maintain a nuka doko.

**Variation: Try using pickling cucumbers, baby carrots, red radishes, cabbage leaves, cauliflower flowerets, or other seasonal vegetables in this recipe.*

brown rice and lotus patties

I love lotus root and this happens to be my favorite way to eat it. The unique texture and flavor of the grated lotus in my mouth makes me feel happy and satisfied.

MAKES 4 SERVINGS

For the patties:

1 lotus root, about 6 to 7 inches long, grated, plus 4 pieces lotus, very thinly sliced, for making lotus chips
¼ onion, chopped
¼ carrot, chopped
2 cups cooked brown rice
2 to 3 tablespoons brown rice flour
1 teaspoon sea salt
sesame oil

To make the patties:

1. Using a ceramic grater, grate the lotus root. Squeeze out juices and reserve in a small bowl.
2. Transfer grated lotus into a medium bowl. Add chopped onion, chopped carrot, cooked brown rice, brown rice flour and sea salt. Stir to thoroughly combine. If the mixture seems too dry, add some of the reserved lotus juice.
3. Form mixture into 4 patties, about 2 to 3 inches in diameter.
4. In a skillet over a medium-high flame, heat the oil. Sauté patties on one side first in a covered pan for 1 to 2 minutes or until light brown. Flip patties over, cover pan, reduce flame to medium-low, and sauté until light brown. Turn off the heat, remove patties from pan and set aside.
5. To make the lotus chips, scrape out any bits of patty remaining in the skillet. Add a small amount of oil to the skillet and warm over a medium flame. Add sliced lotus and fry for about 30 seconds on each side, or until crispy. Drain on paper towel.
6. Serve patties drizzled with lotus sauce and garnished with a lotus chip and sprinkling of chives.

For the lotus sauce:

½ cup lotus juice
sea salt
¼ cup+ Simple Kombu Dashi (see recipe on page 215), or purified water
2 tablespoons chives, chopped

To make the lotus sauce:

1. In a medium saucepan over a medium flame, add the lotus juice and sea salt. Using a wooden spatula, stir to combine.
2. When mixture begins to thicken, stir in the dashi or water (adjusting the amount to achieve desired sauce thickness), and simmer for an additional 2 minutes.
3. Turn off the heat and stir in the chives. Serve sauce over lotus patties.

Useful information:

Lotus root has played a prominent role as a healing food for many centuries throughout Asia. It is rich in fiber, vitamin C, potassium, thiamin, riboflavin, vitamin B6, phosphorus and copper. It is recommended as a remedy for the throat and for quelling coughs.

153

Water-Sautéed Watercress

I like to use watercress when I need to prepare greens quickly. It has a slightly sweet, bitter and pungent taste, creating a sense of perfect balance.

MAKES 4 SERVINGS

For the greens:

purified water

3 cups watercress, thoroughly washed and ends trimmed

pinch of sea salt

To make the greens:

1. Cover the bottom of a stainless steel skillet with about ¼ to ½ inch of water. Over a medium-high flame, bring the water to a boil.
2. Add the watercress. Using a wooden spoon or chopsticks, evenly cook the greens for 30 seconds to 1 minute, adding additional water if necessary.
3. Reduce the flame to medium-low. Add sea salt and simmer for another 30 seconds, or until the watercress is tender, but still brightly colored. (If watercress is very mature with large stems, cover the pan with a lid for about 30 seconds, taking care not to overcook.)
4. Remove greens from skillet, rinse with cold water. Drain, squeezing gently to remove excess water and transfer greens to a cutting board.
5. Using a sharp knife, cut greens into 1 to 2 inch lengths. (Or arrange in a spiral on serving dish, as shown in photo.)

Useful information:

Watercress is high in iron, calcium and folic acid, in addition to vitamins A and C. It readily grows as an aquatic vegetable or herb near stream banks. Watercress acts as a mild stimulant, and its pungent taste stimulates the lungs and prepares the body to receive the autumn season. There are many other varieties of greens that work well with the water-sauté method, including: collard greens, Chinese napa cabbage, watercress, mustard greens, dandelion greens, daikon tops and turnip tops.

corn on the cob

with Ume Paste

Most of my non-macrobiotic friends eat corn on the cob with butter or margarine and are initially taken aback when I serve corn on the cob with ume paste. But after trying it, they're hooked!

MAKES 4 SERVINGS

For the corn:

4 cups purified water
4 ears fresh sweet yellow corn, with husks
2 to 4 teaspoons ume paste

To make the corn:

1. In a pot large enough for all 4 ears of corn, add water. Over a medium-high flame, bring water to a boil.
2. In the meantime, wash the corn without removing husks.
3. Place the corn with husks in the boiling water, cover and cook for 5 minutes or more.
4. Remove corn from the pot and set aside to cool.
5. When husks are cool enough to handle, remove husks and arrange corn on a serving platter with ume paste on the side, or spread on top of corn, as shown in the photo. Note: Ume paste is salty, so use sparingly.

Useful information:

See pages 95, 245 and 298 for useful information about ume paste. If you can't find ume in paste form, you can make your own with whole umeboshi plums: Remove pit from the plum and purée it in a suribachi with a little water to a paste-like consistency.

Variation: The corn can also be steamed instead of boiled.

Sweet Vegetable Chickpea Soup

This is a light yet satisfying soup with a naturally sweet taste. I enjoy reflecting on the late summer season by sipping this soup while beholding the beauty of the sunset.

MAKES 4 SERVINGS

For the soup:

4 to 5 cups Simple Kombu Dashi Broth
   (recipe on page 215)
1 cup each of various sweet vegetables (onion,
   carrot, cabbage, winter squash), chopped*
½ cup cooked chickpeas, or about ¼ cup dried
   chickpeas
¼ teaspoon sea salt
parsley, chopped, for garnish

*Note: You can also use the leftover chopped vegetables from the Sweet Vegetable Remedy Drink recipe found on page 146.

For the chickpeas:

¼ cup chickpeas, sorted to remove debris and
   washed
 purified water, for soaking
 2 cups water, for cooking
 1-inch strip of kombu

To make the soup:

1. If using dried beans, wash, sort and soak the beans according to the instructions listed in the section titled "How to Wash and Soak Beans," found on page 55.
2. In a large pot over a medium flame, bring dashi to a boil.
3. Add the onion, and cook for about 1 minute. Add the remaining vegetables in the following order: carrot, cabbage, squash — by simmering each vegetable individually for about 1 minute before adding the next vegetable.
4. Add the cooked chickpeas, reduce the flame to low and simmer for 20 minutes. Add sea salt to taste, stir gently and turn off heat.
5. Ladle soup into individual serving bowls and garnish with a sprinkling of chopped parsley.

Useful information:

Chickpeas, one of the earliest cultivated land vegetables, are high in protein and calcium, yet low in fat. The high fiber content of legumes make them an excellent food choice for those with heart disease, as well as a healthy source of complex carbohydrates for persons with insulin sensitivity or diabetes. Legumes contain phytochemicals that exhibit anticancer properties.

millet cauliflower mash

with Shiitake Gravy

My favorite whole grain, besides brown rice, is millet. Our friends always enjoy this dish, which resembles mashed potatoes, whenever we serve it. I made this dish many times during my healing process, to combat my cravings for sugar and to aide in cleansing my body of animal proteins.

MAKES 4 SERVINGS

For the mash:
1 cup millet
3 to 3 ½ cups purified water
2 cups cauliflower, diced
⅛ teaspoon sea salt
Shiitake Gravy (recipe following)
fresh parsley sprigs, as garnish

To make the mash:
1. Wash the millet according to the instructions listed in the section titled "How to Wash and Soak Whole Grains," found on page 27, except eliminate the soaking step.
2. In a skillet over medium heat, lightly dry roast the washed millet, stirring constantly, until it smells toasty.
3. Meanwhile, in a large saucepan over medium-high heat, bring the water to a boil. Add millet, cauliflower and sea salt, reduce heat to low, cover and simmer for 20 minutes.
4. Transfer to a food mill or blender and purée until smooth and fluffy, adding a little water if necessary.
5. Serve with Shiitake Mushroom Gravy and garnish with a sprig of fresh parsley.

Useful information:
Millet is a gluten-free grain that is high in protein and rich in B vitamins. Cauliflower contains compounds that help to inhibit the growth of cancer.

shiitake gravy

with Onion

MAKES 4 SERVINGS

For the gravy:
2 shiitake mushrooms, dried
2 cups purified water, for soaking
¼ cup chopped onion
1 heaping tablespoon kuzu, dissolved in 2 tablespoons water
1 teaspoon soy sauce, to taste

To make the gravy:
1. In a medium bowl, combine the shiitake mushrooms and water. Allow to soak for 30 minutes.
2. Remove shiitake, reserving soaking water and coarsely chop. Set aside.
3. In a medium saucepan over medium heat, combine ¼ cup of the shiitake mushroom soaking water and the onion. Sauté onions for 1 minute.
4. Add remaining soaking water and chopped shiitake mushrooms, cover and simmer for 15 minutes.
5. Add the dissolved kuzu and stir constantly until sauce thickens.
6. Flavor with soy sauce and serve with Millet Cauliflower Mash.

Useful information:
This gravy also pairs well with the Brown Rice Lotus Patties recipe found on page 153.

quick nabe
with Roasted Pumpkin Seeds

When I was growing up in Japan, nabe dishes were the most social way to eat with friends, workmates or family. Here is a quick nabe-style dish for everybody to enjoy.

MAKES 4 SERVINGS

For the nabe:

1 to 1 ½ tablespoons pumpkin seeds, hulled
2 to 4 cups purified water (depending on how
    much liquid you want at the end of cooking)
2 to 4 inch strip kombu
¼ cup burdock, sliced in ½-inch rolling cut
1 cup carrot, sliced in ½-inch rolling cut
½ cup cauliflower stems or other leafy green
    stems, sliced in ½-inch pieces
½ cup jinenjo potato, peeled and sliced in ¼-inch
    diagonal cuts
soy sauce, to taste

To make the nabe:

1. Wash and dry roast the pumpkin seeds according to the instructions in the sections titled "How to Wash Seeds" and "How to Dry-roast Whole Grains or Seeds" on page 27. Set aside.
2. In a large pot (preferably ceramic) over a medium-high flame, combine the water and kombu and bring to a boil.
3. Add the sliced burdock and simmer for 2 to 3 minutes. Add carrot and simmer 1 minute. Add cauliflower stems, reduce heat to low, cover and simmer 1 minute. Add jinenjo potato and soy sauce, to taste. Cover, continue to simmer for another minute.
4. Turn off heat, remove cover and gently stir vegetables.
5. Arrange vegetables in individual serving bowls, ladle in a small amount of broth and garnish with pumpkin seeds (as shown in photo). Or, if you've used a decorative ceramic pot, transfer the nabe to the center of the table and serve "family-style," as described below, with the pumpkin seeds on the side.

Useful information:

Nabe is simply the Japanese word for "pot." Nabe dishes in Japan are all one-pot stews cooked and served in a special, often decorative, ceramic pot. The pots are filled with stock and vegetables that bubble away over a gas burner in the center of the table, where diners help themselves in a shared, casual and festive atmosphere. There are many regional and personal varieties of nabe, some served with dipping sauces and others made with a tamari- or miso-based broth.

Arame
with Sweet Corn

Arame is a good introduction to sea vegetables because of its mild taste and soft texture. It blends well with other flavors, especially with fresh, in-season corn.

MAKES 4 SERVINGS

For the arame:

½ cup arame, dried
½ to 1 cup purified water
½ cup onion, sliced into half-moons
½ cup carrot, thinly sliced into matchsticks
1 cup fresh corn kernels
½ to 1 tablespoon soy sauce
¼ cup very thinly sliced carrot and scallion for garnish

To make the arame:

1. In a medium bowl, add the arame and enough water to submerge it. Wash gently, swirling with your hand to loosen any sand. Drain.
2. In a medium sauté pan over medium heat, combine the onion and enough of the purified water to cover bottom of pan to a depth of about ½ inch.
3. Cook the onion for 1 to 2 minutes, stirring to cook evenly. Layer the carrots on top of the onion and do not stir. Layer arame on top of the carrots. Pour enough water to cover onions and carrots.
4. Bring to a boil, cover, reduce heat to medium-low and simmer for 20 minutes.
5. Season to taste with soy sauce. Layer the corn on top, cover and simmer for 5 more minutes.
6. Turn off the heat, gently stir vegetables to evenly mix the vegetables. Serve warm or at room temperature.

Useful information:

Arame comes in brown strands and can be steamed, sautéed, added to soup, or eaten in salads. This healthful sea vegetable is high in calcium and iron, and is also harvested for alginate and iodine. This dish can be refrigerated for up to 3 days. Add a small amount of water to reheat on the stovetop, or simply allow it to sit until it reaches room temperature.

Variation: You can also substitute with hijiki instead of arame in this recipe.

161

red radish and ume plum vinegar pickles

The plum vinegar imparts a beautiful pastel pink color, enhancing the beauty of this dish. It is quite salty and slightly fruity in flavor, the perfect blend for a pickle.

MAKES 4 SERVINGS

For the pickles:

1 cup red radishes, thinly sliced
2 to 2 ½ tablespoons umeboshi vinegar
1 or 2 red shiso leaves, thinly sliced (optional)

To make the pickles:

1. In a pickle press or medium-sized bowl, combine the radishes, vinegar and shiso leaves. Stir well.
2. Cover pickle press and apply pressure. If using a bowl, place a smaller plate (which fits inside the bowl) over the top of the radishes. Place a heavy weight on top of the plate to provide pressure.
3. Allow radishes to sit under pressure for at least one hour.
4. Remove pickles from press and rinse if they taste too salty. Squeeze out excess liquid by hand, place on a serving dish or serve with a grain dish, as shown in photo.

Useful information:

Pickles contain beneficial enzymes, which increase the appetite, aid digestion, and strengthen the intestines and immune system. For additional fermentation, allow pickles to sit for 1 to 2 days without refrigeration. When fully fermented, these pickles will keep for about 1 to 2 weeks when stored in the refrigerator. Red radishes are a good source of vitamin C, folic acid and potassium.

Ume plum vinegar is made from the natural juices left over from the traditional process of pickling the umeboshi plums with sea salt and red shiso (beefsteak) leaves. This ruby red, tangy condiment found in Japanese markets and natural food stores is sold under many different names, which may be confusing. These names include: umeboshi vinegar, umeboshi plum vinegar, ume vinegar, ume plum vinegar, pickled plum vinegar, and plum vinegar. Whichever names you prefer, just remember that this vinegar is very salty, so use in moderation. Sprinkle over cooked or steamed vegetables, add to salad dressings and dips and use for pickling.

kabocha millet cake

I was advised to avoid baked goods during my healing process, so my husband Eric and I came up with this "cake." Kabocha's sweet taste and cheerful color gave me hope during my recovery.

MAKES 9 TO 12 SERVINGS

For the cake:

1 cup millet
2 cups purified water
1 cup apple juice
1 pinch sea salt

For the topping:

1 pound kabocha squash, thinly sliced ⅛-inch thick
1 teaspoon agar flakes
⅓ cup purified water
4 tablespoons apricot jam,* fruit-sweetened
1 pinch sea salt

To make the cake:

1. Wash and roast the millet according to the instructions listed in the sections titled "How to Wash and Soak Whole Grains," found on page 27, and "How to Dry-roast Whole Grains or Seeds," found on page 29, skipping the soaking step.
2. In a saucepan over a medium-high flame, combine the millet, water and apple juice and bring to a boil. Add sea salt, reduce heat to low, cover and simmer for 30 minutes.
3. Transfer cooked millet to a 9-inch square pan or round pie pan. Evenly spread the millet along the bottom of the pan, pressing firmly to form a flat surface, or "crust." Set aside and allow to cool.

To make the topping and assemble the cake:

1. In a large pot fitted with a steamer basket, steam the sliced kabocha for 3 to 4 minutes.
2. Gently spread the steamed kabocha slices decoratively, in a fan arrangement over the millet.
3. In a small saucepan over medium-high flame, combine the agar and water. Cook until the agar dissolves and becomes clear in color. Add the apricot jam and sea salt, and stir to combine.
4. Strain mixture and pour over the kabocha slices.
5. Transfer pan to the refrigerator until agar has set.
6. Slice into 9 to 12 pieces and serve.

Useful information:

Kabocha is a Japanese variety of winter squash, also called Japanese pumpkin. It is rich in beta-carotene and is a good source of vitamin C, potassium and folic acid. See millet information on pages 43 and 159.

Variation: Apricot jam can be substituted with steamed carrot, apple, or strawberries for topping. Strawberries should only be steamed for 30 seconds or less.

The Story of Autumn

A Time To Harvest

With the changing of the seasons, our bodies and minds are also changing. This was the time I was diagnosed with cancer in 1993. I could feel that my body was shifting from the active summer mode to the sedate winter mode. When I observed nature at this time, I saw the deciduous trees shed their leaves, which had already changed to a reddish or brownish hue. The sight of a first leaf falling with a peaceful motion made me realize why autumn is also called fall. But autumn is also the season of the harvest, reaping the benefits of a long and fruitful year. In the beginning my illness kept me away from such ruminations, but I knew in my heart that my harvesting time would come, and even in suffering I needed to choose the right soil and seeds for myself.

TRANSFORMATION OF

autumn

Remedy drinks:
Lotus Root Tea
Carrot Daikon Drink

Breakfast:
Kabocha Ojiya, Porridge
Daikon Greens Ohitashi
Lotus Pickles

Lunch:
Onigiri with Hijiki
Simple Leafy Greens
Kimpira Gobo

Dinner:
Black Soybean Soup
Brown Rice with Chestnuts
Furofuki Daikon with Miso Sauce
Three-colored Layered Vegetables
Ginger Pickles
Negi Hige, Fried Scallion Root

Dessert:
Poached Pear Flowers with Persimmon and Ginger

lotus root tea

Remedy Drink

I made this drink many, many times in the beginning of my healing journey. It helped to clear up my sinuses and relieve congestion in my lungs from all the excess animal protein and dairy foods that I had been eating. Now I use this drink from time to time, whenever I feel mucus forming in my lungs and sinuses, or if I start coughing. It works gently, but surely, and can be made with fresh or dried lotus root (in whole or powdered form).

MAKES 1 SERVING

For the tea (using fresh lotus root):
½ cup fresh lotus root, grated
½ to 1 cup purified water
pinch of sea salt

To make the tea (using fresh lotus root):

1. Place the grated lotus pulp in a piece of cheesecloth and squeeze out the juice into a measuring cup. The amount of juice you get will vary depending on the quality and freshness of the lotus. The pulp may be saved and added to other dishes, like miso soup.
2. In a small saucepan over a medium-high flame, combine the juice with an equal amount of the purified water. Add a pinch of sea salt or a few drops of soy sauce.
3. Bring juice mixture to a boil, reduce heat to low and simmer for 2 to 3 minutes.
4. The tea should be thick and creamy. Serve hot.

For the tea (using dried whole lotus root):
⅓ ounce (about 10g) dried whole lotus root
1 cup purified water
pinch of sea salt

To make the tea (using dried whole lotus root):

1. In a small bowl, combine dried lotus root and the purified water, and allow to sit for about 5 to 10 minutes until soft. Remove lotus root and reserve soaking water.
2. With a sharp knife, finely chop the reconstituted lotus. Or, for a creamier texture, mash the lotus in a suribachi.
3. Transfer the lotus root back to the soaking water. Add a pinch of sea salt or a few drops of soy sauce.
4. In a small saucepan over a medium-high flame, combine the reconstituted lotus, the soaking water and the sea salt, or a few drops of soy sauce.
5. Bring juice mixture to a boil, reduce heat to low and simmer for about 15 minutes.
6. Strain the liquid, reserving the pulp for some other dishes, like miso soup. Serve hot.

continued on next page…

For the tea (using lotus root powder):
1 teaspoon lotus root powder
1 cup purified water
pinch of sea salt

To make the tea (using lotus root powder):
1. In a small saucepan over a medium-low flame, combine the water and lotus root powder, and stir to dissolve.
2. Add a pinch of sea salt or a few drops of soy sauce.
3. Reduce heat to low and simmer for 2 to 3 minutes. Do not boil. Drink while hot.

Useful information:
This tea is most effective when prepared from fresh lotus root. However, if unavailable, like when you are traveling, you may use dried lotus root or lotus root powder which may take effect more slowly. I usually opt for sea salt instead of soy sauce to season this drink because the tea's primary purpose is to neutralize excessive protein. Although many prefer the taste of soy sauce, I don't use it in this tea because of its higher protein content. I also prefer the sweeter taste when prepared with sea salt. If your present health condition allows, you may also try stirring in a few drops of freshly grated ginger juice, just before serving, to open up your sinuses.

carrot daikon drink

Remedy Drink

This drink helps to detoxify excess fat and protein in the body. I needed this drink to detox my body, especially the intestines, from the excessive consumption of one of my favorite foods — eggs. This drink also helps me when I go out to eat at restaurants, even vegan macrobiotic ones, that serve oily, salty foods.

MAKES 1 SERVING

For the drink:
¼ cup fresh daikon, finely grated*
¼ cup fresh carrot, finely grated*
1 cup purified water
½ umeboshi plum, finely chopped
soy sauce (optional)
¼ to ½ sheet of nori, shredded

To make the drink:
1. In a small saucepan over a medium-high flame, combine the grated daikon, carrots and purified water, and bring to a boil.
2. Add chopped umeboshi and a few drops of soy sauce (if desired), reduce heat to low and simmer for 2 to 3 minutes.
3. Transfer into a serving cup, add shredded nori, and drink hot.

Useful information:
This preparation is helpful in dissolving fat deposits within the body and quickly reducing high cholesterol. Note, however, that consuming this healing beverage in excessive quantities or with too great a frequency may weaken your condition, as this drink can drain the body of minerals.

*Grating with a flat, ceramic grater is recommended for a better effect.

Kabocha Ojiya

Porridge

Having ojiya in the morning helps us to receive uplifting energy softly and helps our mind and body to relax when the weather is cooling down. It has a very nurturing effect, and I remember as a child my mother serving ojiya when I was feeling ill or exhausted from being overly active. Adding Kabocha lends a sweet taste.

MAKES 4 SERVINGS

For the porridge (using uncooked rice):
1 cup brown rice
1 cup kabocha, cubed into bite-sized pieces*
4 to 5 cups purified water (depending on desired consistency)
pinch of sea salt
black gomashio, as garnish

To make the porridge (using uncooked rice):

1. Wash and soak the rice according to the instructions listed in the sections titled "How to Wash and Soak Whole Grains," found on page 27.
2. In a medium stainless steel or ceramic pot over a medium-high flame, combine the rice and the water, and bring to a boil.
3. Add kabocha and bring to a boil again. Add sea salt. Reduce heat to low, place a flame deflector over the flame, cover and simmer for 45 to 50 minutes.
4. Remove the pot from the stove and allow to sit undisturbed for 5 to 10 minutes, before removing cover.
5. Using a bamboo rice paddle or a large wooden spoon, gently stir to harmonize rice and kabocha together.
6. Serve garnished with gomashio.

For the porridge (using cooked brown rice):
2 cups cooked brown rice
3 to 4 cups purified water (depending on desired consistency)
1 cup kabocha, cubed into bite-size pieces
pinch of sea salt

To make the porridge (using cooked brown rice):

1. In a medium stainless steel or ceramic pot over a medium-high flame, combine the cooked rice and the water, and bring to a boil.
2. Add kabocha and bring to a boil again. Add sea salt, reduce heat to low, cover and simmer for 20 to 30 minutes.
3. Serve garnished with gomashio.

Useful information:
Ojiya is simply any cereal grain that has been boiled with ample water to achieve a softer, unified porridge-like texture. In many cultures, it is commonly served for breakfast with condiments. In some cases, those condiments—notably sugar, milk, cream and/or butter—render an otherwise wholesome food into an unhealthful and unbalanced start to your day.

See section titled "How to Select a Sweet-tasting Kabocha," found on page 66.

daikon greens ohitashi

Many people don't know that daikon greens are edible and actually quite scrumptious. In fact, daikon tops are one of our favorite greens. Simply blanching these greens brings out their natural stimulating pungency and warm flavor in the prime of autumn.

MAKES 4 SERVINGS

For the greens:

3 to 4 cups purified water
2 bunches daikon greens, thoroughly washed
1 pinch sea salt or 2 to 3 drops of soy sauce

To make the greens:

1. In a large pot over a medium-high flame, add the purified water and bring to a boil.
2. Add the greens stalk-side first, and arrange them in a spiral around the inside of the pot. Using a wooden spoon or chopsticks, gently stir and evenly cook the greens for about 1 to 2 minutes (depending on desired crispness).
3. Reduce the heat to medium-low. Add sea salt or soy sauce and simmer for 30 seconds or until the greens are tender, but still brightly colored.
4. Drain, gently squeezing the water out and spread greens out on a plate to cool. Note: As with all vegetables that I parboil, after draining I do not cool them by rinsing them or putting them in ice water. Instead, I use the traditional Japanese method of fanning them for a minute or two with an uchiwa (paper fan), which prevents them from becoming water-logged and flavorless.
5. After they have cooled, cut greens into 1- to 2-inch long pieces and serve.

Useful information:

In Japanese "ohitashi" means "dip into" and in this case dip into hot water (or blanch), resulting in greens with a lovely deep color and fresh taste. Ohitashi is usually made with spinach, but almost any type of leafy greens will do. Daikon greens are the leafy tops of the mildly spicy, giant white Japanese radish with a pungent, slightly bittersweet flavor. Many people unknowingly discard the green tops of many root vegetables without realizing that not only are they edible, but are a very healthful addition to the diet. Daikon greens are high in calcium, iron, and vitamin C. Chopped ohitashi greens taste great served with brown rice or sautéed with other vegetables, or simply by themselves with miso dressing or sesame sauce.

lotus pickles

Lotus is an extremely versatile ingredient. As a pickle it is visually beautiful and imparts a rare sensation on the palate. As a child I used to cut it into pieces to use as a stamp to dip into paint and create artwork.

MAKES 4 TO 6 SERVINGS

For the pickles:
1 cup purified water, for pickling
1 fresh lotus root, about 3 to 4 inches
purified water, for cooking
sea salt
½ cup ume plum vinegar

To make the pickles:

1. In a small saucepan over a medium-high flame, bring the pickling water to a boil, turn off the heat and allow it to cool.
2. Wash the lotus root and peel off any dark, soft, or damaged spots and skin, if any. Slice lotus root into ⅛-inch rounds.
3. In a medium saucepan over a medium-high flame, combine the sliced lotus and enough purified water to cover the roots.
4. Bring to a boil and add sea salt. Reduce heat to low and simmer for 15 to 20 minutes.
5. Strain cooked lotus roots and set aside to cool.
6. Layer cooled lotus in a glass jar large enough to just fit all the sliced roots.
7. Fill the jar with half of the cooled-off pickling water. Add the ume plum vinegar. Add additional pickling water (if needed to fill the jar completely).
8. Secure a cotton cloth, cheesecloth or paper towel over mouth of jar and allow to sit at room temperature for 12 to 24 hours.
9. Before serving, rinse pickles with water if too salty and decoratively arrange on a plate.
10. Pickles will keep in the refrigerator for about two weeks.

Useful information:
You can reuse the pickling liquid to make another batch of pickles. Pickles increase the appetite, aid digestion, and strengthen the intestines.

Variation: Carrots, daikon, turnips, broccoli stems, and many other vegetables can be substituted in this recipe.

onigiri with hijiki
Hijiki Rice Balls

Onigiri brings back pleasurable memories of my mom. When I was a child, she often made delicious onigiri for my snack or lunch, or for picnics and field trips. I sometimes wished my mom would make sandwiches instead, like the other trendy, Americanized moms, but she always said that in time I would learn the balancing essence of onigiri. Sure enough, I have learned to appreciate her efforts after studying macrobiotics.

MAKES 1 SERVING (2 RICE BALLS)

For the onigiri:
sea salt
small bowl of purified water
1 cup brown rice, cooked*
¼ cup hijiki, cooked (plain cooked or as leftovers from the recipe on the next page)

To make the onigiri:

1. Add a couple pinches of sea salt to the bowl of water. Use this water to wet your hands while you are forming the onigiri. (This will prevent the rice from sticking to your hands.)
2. In a medium bowl, thoroughly combine the rice and hijiki with a wooden spoon or by hand.
3. Divide the rice mixture in half. With one half of the mixture, form a solid ball. Using three or four firm squeezes, form the rice into the desired shape (balls, ovals, triangles, cylinders). Lightly flip the ball between your hands a few times to smooth outer texture. (Note: these flips should be much lighter than the firm hands you used before.)
4. Form the remaining rice into another solid ball and repeat shaping process. Serve onigiri with pickles.

Useful information:
"Onigiri" comes from the word "nigiru" in Japanese, which means grip, grasp, or hold. Our hands have "ki" energy that makes holding, grasping and gripping very yang motions which gather energy, especially in the digestive area. Rice balls come in many sizes and are all-purpose, easy to make and satisfying. A meal in itself, they are convenient for school, office, outdoor lunches and traveling. A perfect dish for any occasion, the best part is you can eat them with your hands! Leftover onigiri can be enjoyed pan fried, deep fried, or added into soup or tea (ochazuke). To preserve onigiri for a few days, stuff them with charcoal-cooked umeboshi, or wrap completely with nori. See pages 38 and 39 for detailed information regarding various shapes, varieties, techniques, and serving suggestions for onigiri.

The ideal rice/water ratio for making rice balls is 1 cup uncooked rice to 2- to 2-¼ cups of purified water.

177

hijiki
Sea Vegetable

Hijiki is a very easy dish to make and quite convenient since it keeps well in the refrigerator for several days. I mix hijiki with rice, salads, sandwiches or wraps. When we make hijiki at home, I say to Eric, "Do you feel like eating gorilla hairs tonight?" (Don't you think it looks like gorilla hairs?!)

MAKES 4 SERVINGS

For the hijiki:
½ cup hijiki, dried
purified water, for washing and soaking, plus
     ½ to 1 cup purified water, for cooking
½ cup onion, sliced into half-moons
½ cup carrot, sliced into matchsticks
½ to 1 tablespoon soy sauce

To make the hijiki:
1. In a small bowl combine the hijiki and enough purified water to submerge. Wash gently, swirling to loosen any sand. Drain off and discard water.
2. Add additional fresh water to the bowl of hijiki and soak for 10 to 15 minutes.
3. In a medium sauté pan over medium-high heat, add purified water to a depth of ½ inch.
4. Add the onion and sauté for 1 to 2 minutes, stirring to cook evenly. Carefully layer the sliced carrots on top and do not stir. Layer hijiki on top of the carrots. Add additional water, if necessary (just enough to cover onion and carrot layers).
5. Bring to a boil, reduce heat to medium-low, cover and simmer 20 to 25 minutes.
6. Season to taste with soy sauce and simmer 5 minutes.
7. Turn off heat and stir vegetables gently to evenly combine. Transfer to a serving bowl, or incorporate into onigiri, as described on the previous page.

Useful information:
There are usually two kinds of hijiki available in the U.S. The common type is the sprouted tips of the hijiki which are small in length and soft in texture. The other type is the stem portion, which boasts a stronger flavor and a tougher, almost crispy texture.

simple leafy greens

I miss simple leafy greens whenever I eat out. So many types of fresh leafy greens are available at natural food stores and farmers markets, but restaurants rarely make use of them, whether in simple or elaborate dishes. We eat leafy greens at home every day. It's an excellent way to cleanse the very foundation of health — our blood.

MAKES 4 SERVINGS

For the greens:
purified water
3 to 4 cups leafy greens*
1 pinch sea salt

To make the greens:

1. In a large sauté pan over medium-high heat, pour enough of the purified water to fill pan to a depth of about 2 inches. Bring to a boil.
2. Add greens and sea salt. Cook for about 45 seconds to 1 minute.
3. Drain and transfer to a serving plate.

Useful information:

For larger portions, use 5 cups of greens to about 4 to 5 inches of water in a large pot. For a more concentrated and stronger effect, cover pot with lid during boiling. For a lighter effect, uncover the pot during boiling. Boiling vegetables, depending on the method, can create quick energy (with a high flame/short cooking time) or slow, steady energy (with a medium flame/longer cooking time).

*There are many varieties of greens that work well with this recipe, including: kale, collard greens, Chinese napa cabbage, watercress, mustard greens, dandelion greens, daikon tops, and turnip tops.

kimpira gobo
Simmered Burdock Root

This dish surprises most people who try it for the first time. Burdock (gobo), a dark, woody and distinctly unsavory-looking root, boasts a sweet, nutty taste and a delicate, yet crunchy texture. You have to be either Japanese, macrobiotic, or a foodie to know this dish, but almost everyone who tries it likes it and, hopefully, feels the bounty and healing power of the earth.

MAKES 4 SERVINGS

For the gobo:
1 tablespoon sesame oil
1 cup gobo (burdock root), julienned*
1 cup carrot, julienned
purified water
1 cup lotus root, sliced in quarter moons
black sesame seeds, dry roasted, for garnish
   (see sections titled "How to Dry-roast
   Whole Grains or Seeds," found on page 29,
   and "Condiments & Garnishes," found on
   page 242)

*Burdock root has a brown-colored, tissue-paper-thin skin that can easily be scrubbed away revealing the white flesh underneath. Be extra gentle when scrubbing burdock root with the tawashi vegetable brush (see page 62 for more information) so as to retain as much of the skin as possible.

To make the gobo:
1. In a cast-iron or stainless steel pan over medium-high heat, warm the oil.
2. Add the gobo. Using a wooden spatula, sauté the gobo for about 2 to 3 minutes, or until you begin to smell an earthy aroma.
3. Add carrots and sauté for 1 to 2 minutes.
4. Add just enough of the purified water to cover the vegetables and bring to a boil.
5. Add lotus root and stir quickly. Reduce flame to low, cover and simmer for 20 to 25 minutes.
6. When burdock is tender and water is down to about ½ inch, add soy sauce to taste and cook another 5 minutes or until there is almost no liquid.
7. Serve garnished with sesame seeds.

Useful information:
The name "kimpira" comes from a fictional legendary hero, Kimpira Sakata, who embodied strength and vitality. Kimpira in Chinese characters (金平) means golden peace, for a strong and peaceful balance.

Gobo root definitely falls into the "can't judge a book..." category of vegetables that tastes like a cross between celery and an artichoke. It is not easy to find good gobo, but if possible, find roots that are firm and plump and smell freshly-dug with a sweet, earthy aroma. Avoid those that look limp or dried out. If you can only find limp gobo, the roots can be revived if you soak the slices in cold water. Gobo is high in fiber and low in calories. It is also a source of iron, calcium, vitamins B6 and C, as well as the prebiotic, inulin. Refrigerate in the vegetable compartment for up to three to four days.

180

black soybean soup

Black soybeans have a rich, smoky and sweet flavor brought out by slow cooking. This soup is an excellent source of protein and produces a relaxed, warm and nurtured feeling.

MAKES 4 SERVINGS

For the soup:
4 cups purified water
1 cup black soybeans
½ cup onion, chopped
1- to 2-inch strip of kombu
1 tablespoon miso
parsley, chopped, for garnish

To make the soup:
1. Wash, sort and soak the beans according to the instructions listed in the section titled "How to Wash and Soak Beans," found on page 55.
2. Combine soybeans, onion and kombu in a pot or pressure cooker and cook according to instructions listed in the section titled "How to Cook Beans," found on page 56.
3. When beans are finished cooking, add the miso and simmer for 5 minutes.
4. Transfer the beans to a food mill or food processor and puree until creamy. Garnish with chopped parsley and serve.

Useful information:
Nutritionally, black soybeans are very similar to regular yellow soybeans, but without the classic "soybean-y" flavor, and many people find them more digestible. Black soybeans taste similar to regular black beans. High in fiber and complete proteins, in addition to being relatively low in carbohydrates, black soybeans are good for promoting mother's milk, especially when cooked with mochi. Black soybeans can also be made into a remedy tea that is useful for treating dry coughs, laryngitis, kidney/bladder issues, heavy menstruation/cramping and constipation from animal food intake. For less acute symptoms, it is generally taken 2 to 3 times per week. For acute ones, a cup may be taken daily.

The high fiber content of beans prevents blood sugar levels from rising too rapidly after a meal, making these beans an especially good choice for individuals with diabetes, insulin resistance or hypoglycemia. When combined with whole grains such as brown rice, beans provide high-quality protein that's virtually fat free.

Variation: This soup can also be made with black beans, such as black turtle, Mexican, or Spanish black beans.

brown rice
with Chestnuts

I love the sweet, distinct flavor of fresh chestnuts, which is especially enhanced when cooked with a combination of brown and sweet brown rice. Look for fresh chestnuts from September through February. Beneath their tough, porcupine needle-like exterior, chestnuts reveal a surprisingly smooth-skinned interior.

MAKES 4 SERVINGS

For the grains with chestnuts:
1 cup sweet brown rice
1 cup short-grain brown rice
½ cup fresh chestnuts, or dried chestnuts
   (see following page)
2 ½ to 3 cups purified water
2 pinches sea salt

To make the grains with chestnuts:
1. Wash and soak the rice according to the instructions listed in the sections titled "How to Wash and Soak Whole Grains," found on page 27.
2. In a pressure cooker over a medium-high flame, combine the soaked rice and the fresh peeled chestnuts or soaked dried chestnuts. Cook uncovered until it begins to boil.
3. Add sea salt, secure lid on the pressure cooker and allow pan to come to pressure.
4. Place a flame deflector over the flame, reduce heat to low and simmer for 45 to 50 minutes.
5. Remove the cooker from heat and allow pan to sit until the pressure comes down naturally.
6. Wait an additional 5 to 10 minutes and remove lid. Using a bamboo rice paddle or wooden spoon that has been moistened in water (to prevent sticking), gently stir the grains and chestnuts. Serve.

Useful information:
Chestnuts, as opposed to most other nuts, have a high water content and are very low in fat (less than 2% while other nuts can contain over 50% fat). They are high in complex carbohydrates, contain high quality protein comparable to eggs, and are an excellent source of trace minerals. Nutritionally, they are similar to brown rice and have been called "the grain that grows on a tree." Chestnuts can be used as a fresh vegetable, mashed into a purée or ground into flour. Treat yourself to a chestnut knife available at most kitchen supply stores, or select a sharp paring knife for removing the exterior and interior shells. In a crispy, fresh condition, chestnuts will keep for up to two months in the refrigerator. For long-term storage they should be stored in a thin plastic bag. Before they are at their best for eating, however, they need to dry slightly — either for a few days at room temperature or for a week or so in a mesh bag in the refrigerator. Always select plump and firm nuts. One pound serves 3 to 4 people.

How to Peel Fresh Chestnuts:

Boiling method:

1. Place a chestnut on a thick towel that is lying flat on a cutting board or on the countertop. This will allow the chestnut to "sink" into the towel and keep it from rolling while you make the cuts in the next step.
2. Cut an "X" on the flat side of each chestnut with a small knife all the way through the outer hull.
3. Drop them into a pot of water, bring to a boil, and cook for 2–3 minutes. Turn the heat to low and remove several nuts at a time using a slotted spoon.
4. Insert your knife—or fingernail into the cut "X" and peel away the outer shell.
5. Use the knife and your fingers to peel away the inner shell. If you have problems removing it, return the nut to the hot water to loosen it.

Roasting method:

1. Preheat oven to 425° F.
2. Place a chestnut on a thick towel that is lying flat on a cutting board or on the countertop. This will allow the chestnut to "sink" into the towel and keep it from rolling while you make the cuts in the next step.
3. Cut an "X" on the flat side of each chestnut with a small knife all the way through the outer hull.
4. Place each chestnut with the cuts facing up onto the cookie sheet.
5. Roast 10 to 15 minutes or until chestnuts are easy to peel, and the shells are beginning to open. Remove from cookie sheet using an oven mitt.
6. Peel nuts when they are cool enough to handle. Hot chestnuts peel easier than cold ones.
7. If the inner skins do not come off easily, the chestnut is either undercooked or overcooked.

How to Handle Dried Chestnuts:
(available year round)

1. They are already peeled, but sometimes the inner skin, called the pellicle, still needs to be removed with a toothpick after soaking.
2. Sort out any discolored and damaged dried chestnuts.
3. Wash and soak chestnuts in purified water for 4 to 8 hours or overnight to soften them and make them more digestible.

furofuki daikon

with Miso Sauce

Believe it or not, as a youngster I used to dislike the large white radish root known as daikon. Daikon literally means "large root," and in Japanese the expression "daikon-ashi" means big legs. It's a silly reason, but in high school I was called "daikon ashi," so I disliked daikon even more. My mom, in her infinite wisdom, said I will eventually grow to like it, and yet again, she was absolutely right.

MAKES 4 SERVINGS

For the daikon:
1 medium daikon radish
2 7-inch strips kombu
4 to 5 cups purified water
4 to 5 tablespoons soy sauce

For the sauce:
2 tablespoons barley miso
2 to 3 tablespoons cooking liquid (from daikon
    preparation)
yuzu vinegar, to taste (optional)
Ginger Pickles, as condiment
    (recipe on next page)

To make the daikon:
1. Using a sharp knife, slice the daikon into about 8 rounds about ¾-inch thick.
2. In a large pot over medium-high heat, place the kombu in the bottom of the pot and layer the daikon on top.
3. Add enough purified water to cover the daikon halfway. Bring to a boil.
4. Add 1 to 2 tablespoons of the soy sauce for each cup of water added. Cover, reduce heat to low and simmer until daikon is tender, about 30 to 40 minutes or more. Reserve cooking liquid for use in making the sauce.

To make the sauce:
1. In a suribachi, thoroughly combine the miso with the daikon cooking liquid.
2. Add yuzu vinegar, to taste.
3. Serve sauce with the daikon and ginger pickles (see recipe below).

Useful information:
Daikon helps eliminate excess water and animal fats from the body and has a wide range of uses for healing. It also aids in the digestion of whole grains and vegetables. Daikon is extremely low in calories, with only about 10 per ½ cup, and contains vitamin C and trace minerals. It is available in the U.S. year-round, but I find the autumn roots to be the most flavorful. The bottom part of the root tastes more bitter and pungent, while the top part is sweeter and juicier. I use the bottom part for slow cooking and the top part for grating raw. Try to find daikon with the greens still attached, as this will reveal how recently the root was pulled, and also can be prepared into the healthful Daikon Greens Ohitashi recipe found on page 174. If you cannot find the root with greens still attached, then choose roots with smooth, firm, unblemished skins. The size of the root does not have any bearing on the taste, so you can choose based on the size you need for your recipe.

ginger pickles

MAKES 4 SERVINGS

For the pickles:
2-inch long piece of fresh ginger, peeled
1 tablespoon soy sauce
⅛ cup purified water

To make the pickles:

1. Using a sharp knife, slice ginger into 1 ½-inch matchsticks.
2. In a small pan over medium-high heat, combine the soy sauce and purified water. Bring to a boil and immediately remove from heat.
3. Transfer liquid mixture to a small glass jar or container. Add ginger to the container while liquid is still hot and allow to marinate for anywhere from 3 to 8 hours at room temperature.
4. Rinse pickles with water if they taste too salty and serve. Pickles will keep for up to 3 days in the refrigerator.

Useful information:
Fresh ginger is available year round and adds zest to many Asian dishes, including fruit and vegetable dishes. Look for tubers with smooth skins that feel firm and heavy. Length is a sign of maturity, and mature ginger will be spicier and more fibrous. Avoid roots with wrinkled skins or flesh. Ginger has potent anti-inflammatory properties and is very useful for treating nausea and other gastrointestinal issues.

three-color layered vegetables

I came up with this colorful recipe early on during my macrobiotic studies. Onion (white color) brings out the squash's (orange color) natural sweetness, and collard greens (green color) offer freshness to the taste. This is still one of my favorite quick dishes in autumn.

MAKES 4 SERVINGS

For the layered vegetables:

1 medium acorn, butternut, or kabocha squash
2 to 3 collard green leaves, whole
1 yellow onion, thinly sliced into half-moons
1 cup or more purified water
1 pinch sea salt
½ to 1 tablespoon soy sauce

To make the layered vegetables:

1. Rinse the squash in cold water and wash it gently with a tawashi (see information on page 62). Using a sharp knife, remove the hard stalk, cut the squash in half and remove the seeds. Slice the squash into ½-inch crescents. (Be extra careful since the knife can easily slip on the hard skin of the squash.) Set aside.
2. Separate the collard leaves from their stems. Slice the stems diagonally into small bite-sized pieces. Slice remaining leaves into 1- to 1 ½-inch wide strips or squares. Set aside.
3. In a large pan over a medium-high flame, combine onions and just enough purified water to cover. Water-sauté until the onion aroma comes forth. Add sea salt and layer the squash slices on top of the onion. Pour in additional water to submerge the squash half way. Bring to a boil, reduce heat to low, cover and simmer for about 10 to 15 minutes.
4. Season with soy sauce. Layer the greens stems first and simmer about 1 to 2 minutes. Add leafy parts and simmer for another 1 to 2 minutes. (Note: It is important not to overcook greens in order to keep their bright green color.) Remove from heat.
5. Arrange the vegetables gracefully on a plate or in a shallow bowl, and serve warm or at room temperature.

continued on next page...

Useful information:

The traditional layered cooking technique is an excellent way for us to feel the balance between yin & yang vegetables in the beginning of macrobiotic cooking and to explore different layering combinations to reach a balanced state. It's a very simple and easy process that brings out the natural flavor of vegetables. The trick is to not mix the vegetables, and instead to allow the layers to naturally interact with one another during the cooking process, thereby allowing the individual flavors of each vegetable to be retained. In this recipe, I created very simple combinations based on the traditional layered cooking-style typically conducted in the following order:

Top layer: sea salt for seasoning

Middle layers: grains (brown rice, barley, millet, etc.); root vegetables (daikon, carrot, burdock, lotus root, etc.); round vegetables (squash, onion, cabbage, etc.); leafy greens (collard, kale, cabbage, leeks, etc.); beans (azuki, chick pea, black soy beans, etc.)

Bottom layer: sea vegetables/mushrooms (kombu, wakame, hijiki, shiitake, etc.)

Using a ceramic nabe pot is recommended; however, be sure to use a lid without holes (or use a chopstick to seal the hole). Add water only if necessary, to prevent burning.

negi hige
Fried Scallion Root

People often wonder if the white squiggly root tendrils of scallions are edible. Macrobiotic cooking always makes use of the whole vegetable, and scallion roots happen to be one of my favorites. They are very tender and taste great. Farmers markets are the best place to buy very fresh, long scallion roots that often have been picked that very morning.

MAKES 4 SERVINGS

For the scallion roots:
8 fresh scallion roots, 1- to 2-inches long
sesame oil
soy sauce

To make the scallion roots:

1. Selecting good-looking scallion roots is key. When you find long, vibrant scallion roots, then it's the perfect time for you to make this dish.
2. Thoroughly wash scallion roots to remove any trace of grit and soil.
3. Slice off the roots just above where the roots begin so that they are still attached to the base of the scallion. Thoroughly dry them with a towel to remove as much water as possible.
4. In a sauté pan over a medium-high flame, warm the sesame oil. Arrange the roots in the pan one by one so they don't touch each other.
5. Sauté until one side is crispy brown and repeat on the other side, adding a small amount of additional oil, if necessary. The roots cook quickly, so take care to not burn them.
6. When the other side is crispy brown, reduce heat to low, and add one drop of soy sauce to each root.
7. Serve individually, as shown in photo, or chop and combine with other vegetable dishes.

Useful information:
Scallions, also known as green onions, are one of our staple vegetables. Their smooth, yet pungent taste and gentle, warm energy create a perfect balance with almost any dish: soup, grains, noodles and beans. Scallions stimulate the appetite and have mild diuretic properties. Finely chopped scallion roots can be added, along with kombu, to any of the bean recipes in this book.

poached pear flowers

with Persimmon & Ginger

It was not pleasant for me to receive the advice that I should avoid fresh raw fruits during my healing process and recovery. Loving raw fruits since I was a child, I wasn't sure how to deal with this restriction. Since I was very determined to heal myself, however, I learned how to cook fruits and enjoy them when my condition allowed.

MAKES 4 SERVINGS

For the pears:
4 pears
1-inch piece of ginger
4 cups purified water
1 pinch sea salt
fuyu persimmon, cooked (see below) and puréed

To make the pears:
1. Peel the pears, slice them into quarter moons and remove seeds. Transfer pears to a medium saucepan, add ginger and cover with water.
2. Over medium-high flame, bring mixture to a boil. Reduce heat to medium-low, add sea salt, cover and simmer for 15 to 25 minutes.
3. Transfer pears to a plate and allow to cool. Remove ginger and slice into thin matchsticks.
4. Arrange the pear on the plate like a flower with persimmon purée and ginger matchsticks (as shown in photo).

For the persimmon:
1 ripe persimmon, chopped (about 1 cup)
⅛ cup purified water
1 pinch sea salt

To make persimmon:
1. In a saucepan over a medium flame, combine the persimmon, water and sea salt. Cook for 1 to 2 minutes.
2. When the persimmon changes color to a lighter shade of orange, remove from the heat.

Useful information:
Pears contain more soluble fiber than apples, and are a good source of vitamin C, copper and potassium. Pears are hypoallergenic and are good for toning the intestines.

Persimmons are an excellent source of potassium, as well as vitamins A and C. Persimmons have a cooling property, so avoid eating them raw if you are healing. There are two kinds of persimmons, both bright orange in color: Fuyu and Hachiya. Fuyus are easy to recognize by their squat shape and flat bottom, close to the appearance of a medium-sized tomato. They are a non-astringent variety of persimmon and are commonly eaten when crunchy, firm and sweet, just like an apple, or you can allow them to soften a bit at room temperature. The skin is edible, although most people prefer to peel them. Hachiyas, by contrast, have a more elongated shape with a pointed bottom. Hachiyas possess a rich, sweet, slightly spicy flavor when soft and fully ripe. Unripened, however, they have a highly astringent bitter taste, causing the mouth to pucker. Very soft hachiyas can be messy to bite into, and are easier to handle if halved lengthwise and eaten from the skin with a spoon.

193

The Story of Winter

A Time To Rest And Restore Ourselves
When I was younger I didn't appreciate winter. I simply did not like the cold weather or the short days. Many people get depressed in the winter and are even diagnosed with seasonal affective disorder (SAD — an appropriate acronym). I may even have suffered from it myself. Now I enjoy winter because I know and appreciate why winter is supposed to be cold, and the days short.

Each winter I wondered why I felt tired, sleepy, depressed, and experienced pain in my joints. After going non-stop since spring, I was bound to feel tired. Again, I had forgotten that I needed time to concentrate on being and to have a break—a hibernation, so to speak. In the winter I would stay inside and rest. I would focus on restoring myself, enjoying hot meals, like stew, reading good books, writing letters to family and friends, painting, knitting and playing music. I created art and light from within myself. Now I have many ways to appreciate winter, and I spend the winter solstice night with my hand-made soy candles to celebrate the joy of the season. I even embrace the winter blues. Every season has its place in the year.

TRANSFORMATION OF

winter

Remedy drinks:
Azuki Tea
Kombu Tea

Breakfast:
Miso Soup with Root Vegetables
Creamy Buckwheat with Tekka
Water-sautéed Radish Greens
Nuka Red Radish Pickles

Lunch:
Miso Nikomi Udon with Tofu
Steamed Chrysanthemum Greens
Kabu Turnip and Green Top Amazake Pickles

Dinner:
Azuki Kabocha Stew
Sweet Brown Rice and Almonds with Kombu Condiment
Nishime-style Dried Daikon with Shiitake and Carrots
Black Kale with Walnut Sauce
Burdock Miso Pickles

Dessert:
Apple Filet with Azuki Glaze

azuki tea

Remedy Drink

Because I always loved azuki beans, this was my favorite remedy drink to regulate my kidneys whenever they got constricted from overwork, stress and being concerned about too many things in my life.

MAKES 2 CUPS

For the tea:
1 cup azuki beans, dried
2-inch kombu strip, soaked and finely chopped
4 cups purified water

To make the tea:
1. Wash, sort and soak the beans according to the instructions listed in the section titled "How to Wash and Soak Beans," found on page 55.
2. In a medium saucepan over medium-high flame, combine the beans, kombu and water.
3. Bring to a boil, lower the heat, cover and simmer for 45 minutes to 1 hour.
4. Strain out the beans and drink the liquid while hot. (See variations below.)

Useful information:
For additional variety, try adding any of the following to the strained bean liquid and simmer for a few additional minutes: ½ cup freshly grated daikon or lotus root, ½ cup of fresh chopped greens, or one teaspoon of barley malt or rice syrup. Azuki beans are a small dark red bean variety with a distinctive white ridge along one side. Azuki tea is good for balancing kidney and urinary functions, as well as regulating bowel movements.

kombu tea

Remedy Drink

This light tea makes me feel very calm and clear-minded. It gives me a sense of harmony and neutralization.

MAKES 4 CUPS

For the tea:
3-inch strip of kombu, cleaned with a towel
1 quart purified water

To make the tea:
1. In a large pot over a medium-high flame, combine the kombu and the water.
2. Bring to a boil, reduce the heat to low, cover and simmer until the quantity of water is reduced by half, about 15 to 20 minutes.
3. Drink while hot. You can reheat any remaining tea and drink up to 2 to 3 cups per day.

Useful information:
Traditionally, kombu is used in daily cooking. This mineral-rich sea vegetable strengthens the blood and aids in restoring function to the nervous system. Kombu is a good source of folate, calcium, iodine, magnesium and fiber.

197

miso Soup
with Root Vegetables

Root vegetables inherently contain an abundance of energy to generate strength and warmth. In the cold of winter mornings, miso soup with root vegetables stabilizes and balances the downward energy, and helps to prepare the body for the upward energy signified by the advent of spring.

MAKES 4 SERVINGS

For the soup:

4 to 5 cups of kombu dashi
½ cup burdock, julienned (see next page
    for important information)
½ cup daikon, julienned
½ cup carrot, julienned
½ cup lotus root, thinly sliced into quarter moons
1 cup broccoli, cut into smaller flowerets
4 teaspoons barley miso

To make the soup:

1. In a soup pot over a medium flame, add the kombu dashi.
2. When it starts to boil, add the burdock. When it starts to boil again, add the daikon. When it starts to boil again, add the carrots.
3. When it starts to boil again, reduce heat to low and simmer for 3 to 5 minutes (depending on how crispy you prefer the texture of the vegetables).
4. While vegetables are cooking, in a suribachi or bowl, thoroughly combine the miso and ¼ cup of the soup broth from the pot. Set aside.
5. Add lotus root to the pot and simmer for 2 minutes. Add broccoli and simmer for 1 minute (taking care to not overcook broccoli).
6. Gently stir in the miso mixture and simmer for 2 minutes. Taste, adding more miso if needed, but not so much that the soup becomes too salty. Miso should mingle with the flavor of the soup and enhance but not overpower it. Never boil miso, as the beneficial bacteria and enzymes will be destroyed by intense heat.
7. Transfer soup to individual bowls and serve. Add your favorite garnish vegetables (not pictured).

continued on next page...

Useful information:

For more information on miso and miso soup, see pages 49 and 50. Root vegetables are incredibly versatile and especially good from October to March when our bodies crave hearty fare. I remember my grandmother cooking root vegetables often in the winter, but today they are not popular vegetables, mainly due to unfamiliarity with the many ways to enjoy them. They are a hearty addition to almost any dish, including soups, stews and casseroles, in addition to baked goods, snacks, cereals and a host of other dishes. Low in calories, with little if any fat and high in fiber, many root vegetables also provide vitamin C, potassium and iron. The deeper the root vegetable's color, the more it contains antioxidant-loaded phytonutrients. Since many nutrients are in the skin of root vegetables, don't peel the skin unless they are produced chemically (non-organic). Commonly found root vegetables in the U.S. include: beets, burdock, carrots, daikon, lotus root, rutabagas, turnips, parsnips and ginger.

I have used burdock, daikon, carrot and lotus root for this miso soup, each packed with nutrients and flavor. Burdock also works well in broths or in stir-fries.

Burdock root has a brown-colored, tissue-paper-thin skin that can easily be scrubbed away revealing the white flesh underneath. Be extra gentle when scrubbing burdock root with the tawashi vegetable brush (see page 62 for more information) so as to retain as much of the skin as possible.

creamy buckwheat

with Tekka

The cold winter season is a perfect backdrop for this rich, creamy and soothing cereal.

MAKES 4 SERVINGS

For the buckwheat:

1 cup buckwheat groats
4 to 5 cups purified water
1 pinch sea salt
Tekka, condiment (recipe on next page)

To make the buckwheat:

1. Wash and dry roast the buckwheat according to the instructions listed in the sections titled "How to Wash and Soak Whole Grains," found on page 27, and "How to Dry Roast Whole Grains or Seeds," found on page 29.
2. In a medium saucepan over a medium-high flame, bring water to a boil. Add the dry-roasted buckwheat and sea salt. Reduce heat to medium-low, cover and simmer for 20 to 30 minutes.
3. When cooking is complete, fluff grains with a wooden spoon and serve garnished with Tekka.

Useful information:

Energizing, nutritious, and high in fiber, buckwheat is a good alternative to rice during the winter season. Technically, buckwheat is not a grain, but a high-quality protein seed that contains all 8 essential amino acids (eight proteins that the body cannot manufacture). For people who struggle with wheat allergies, as well as those seeking to lower their cholesterol or blood pressure, buckwheat is ideal. In addition to being a good-quality protein source, buckwheat is also high in magnesium, pantothenic acid and the flavonoids rutin and quercetin.

tekka

Miso & Root Vegetable Condiment

This condiment takes a few hours to make, but is well worth the effort. It is available pre-made in natural food stores that sell macrobiotic items or from macrobiotic food companies online, but if you're adventuresome, try this recipe.

MAKES ABOUT 1 TO 2 CUPS

For the condiment:

½ cup dark sesame oil
⅔ cup onion, very finely minced*
⅔ cup burdock, very finely minced (or substitute with dandelion root)
⅔ cup carrots, very finely minced
⅔ cup lotus root, very finely minced
½ teaspoon grated fresh ginger
½ cup hatcho miso

To make the condiment:

1. In a cast-iron skillet over a medium-high flame, warm the oil.
2. Add onion and sauté for two minutes. Add burdock and sauté for several minutes. Add carrots and sauté for 1 to 2 minutes. Add lotus root and sauté for 2 more minutes.
3. Add ginger and miso, reduce heat to low and slow cook (about 3 to 4 hours), stirring frequently until all the liquid has evaporated and the tekka is dry and dark brown in color.
4. Cool tekka completely before storing in a glass jar with tight-fitting lid. Serve tekka as a condiment for whole grains and vegetables, 1 teaspoon per serving.

Useful information:

"Tekka" 鉄火 comes from characters meaning "Iron" and "Fire." Traditionally, tekka is cooked over low heat in a cast-iron pot for about 16 hours, or until it is dry and a very dark brown powder. It is an amalgam of strong root vegetables that provides energy for strong blood, especially when you are weak and need to heal. Frequent stirring during cooking will reduce the quantity of the final product and create a stronger flavor and more contracted/yang energy. See the Useful Information section on page 205 for interesting information about hatcho miso.

*Although tekka commonly does not have onion, I like to add it for a little sweetness.

water-sautéed radish greens

Sometimes I like to play around with new vegetable combinations. This dish "re-connects" the root and green tops of the red radish that have been prepared in different mediums. They still re-combine for a perfect match.

MAKES 4 SERVINGS

For the greens:
8 red radish green tops, thoroughly washed
purified water
1 pinch sea salt

To make the greens:
1. Thoroughly wash the green tops to remove all traces of grit or soil.
2. Transfer greens to a medium sauté pan over a medium flame. Add about ¼-inch of water and bring to a boil.
3. Add sea salt and cook for 45 seconds to 1 minute (do not overcook!!!)
4. Strain the water and serve with Nuka Red Radish Pickles (see recipe below).

nuka red radish pickles

MAKES 4 SERVINGS

For the pickles:
8 red radish roots, whole
nuka doko, (brown rice bran pickling bed)*

To make the pickles:
1. Thoroughly wash the radish roots. Transfer them to a bamboo tray and dry them outside, in a secluded shady spot, for about 12 to 24 hours.
2. Transfer dried radishes into a prepared nuka doko (brown rice bran bed) and pickle for 12 to 24 hours.

3. Serve one or two radishes per person with green tops on the side.

Useful information:
Making red radish nuka pickles is easy. When the red radish turns pink, it's ready to eat! Pickles promote lactic acid bacteria, which is essential to the digestive process and promotes better assimilation of food.

*See page 81 for instructions on how to prepare, store and maintain a nuka doko.

miso nikomi udon

with Tofu

This recipe is based on my hometown Nagoya's famous noodle dish. Using a ceramic pot to cook noodles with vegetables in a rich miso broth, you can enjoy this piping hot, steaming dish.

MAKES 4 SERVINGS

For the noodle soup:

purified water, for cooking udon

4 to 5 cups kombu dashi

1 onion, sliced thinly into half moons

7 ounces firm tofu, pressed to remove excess water and cut into ½ to 1-inch cubes

1 to 2 carrots, sliced into 1-inch rounds

1 8-ounce package udon noodles

4 leaves Chinese cabbage, sliced diagonally into ½-inch wide strips

2 tablespoons kuzu, mixed with 2 tablespoons purified water

2 tablespoons miso (hatcho miso and barley miso)

scallion, thinly sliced diagonal cuts

mirin, to taste (optional)

To make the noodle soup:

1. In a large pot over a medium-high flame, bring a pot of water to a boil.
2. While you are waiting for the water to boil, in a separate large pot over a medium-high flame, combine the kombu dashi and onion. Bring to a boil and continue cooking until the onion's strong aroma emerges.
3. Add tofu to the dashi pot and cook for about 2 minutes. Add carrots and cook for one minute. Add Chinese cabbage and cook for one more minute.
4. In the meantime, cook the udon according to package directions, drain the water and immediately transfer to the dashi pot.
5. In a suribachi or bowl, thoroughly combine the kuzu water mixture, miso and ¼ cup of the dashi broth until creamy. Gently stir mixture into the pot and reduce heat to low (to avoid boiling). Add mirin, if desired, and simmer for 2 to 3 minutes.
6. Add the scallion just before turning heat off and serve hot.

Useful information:

Hatcho miso's name came from central Japan's Aichi Province, in the town of Okazaki (near my home town Nagoya), on Hatcho (8th) Street. It is made with only soybeans, sea salt and water. The first hatcho miso was made around 1645, and it is one of Japan's true living treasures, the most revered miso in all of Japan. Aged at least two summers and two winters until it is very dark and strong in taste, Hatcho miso is thought to be high in salt content, but actually has less salt than miso that is aged in less time. Unpasteurized, traditionally-prepared miso paste is a live, fermented condiment rich in protein and digestion-enhancing enzymes (like lactobacillus). It is also a good source of iron, zinc, manganese, phosphorus and some B vitamins. Miso is a highly regarded whole food with healing properties that range from protection against air pollution and cancer to removal of heavy metals from the body (even radioactive ones—as was documented in studies conducted after the atomic bombing of Nagasaki). Boiling or excessively cooking even good quality miso can also destroy these enzymes, so miso is best added towards the tail end of cooking times. See page 49 and 50 for more information about miso.

Steamed chrysanthemum greens

Steaming is quick and one of the best ways to cook vegetables. It leaves more of the vegetable's natural taste, texture and color than other means of cooking. Steaming has both uplifting and downward energy since steam rises and falls, expanding to fill the inside of the pot.

MAKES 4 SERVINGS

For the greens:

2 to 3 cups chrysanthemum greens, sliced into 2-inch pieces
purified water
1 teaspoon roasted sesame seeds

To make the greens:

1. Separate the sliced stems from the sliced leaves, and set aside.
2. In a large pot over a high flame, add 1 to 2 inches of water. Cover and bring to a boil. Place a bamboo steamer (or steamer basket) in the pot.
3. Add sliced stems to the bottom of the steamer. Layer the sliced leaves on top, cover, and steam until bright green, about 30 seconds. (Do not overcook.)
4. Transfer to a serving dish and garnish with roasted sesame seeds.

Useful information:

A bamboo steamer is preferred to metal steamers because the wood inhibits water condensation. Choose bamboo steamers that are 100 percent bamboo, since some contain metal linings or racks that allow condensation, which can lead to soggy vegetables. Bamboo steamers are best used in a wok for easy fitting. Always use high heat to steam vegetables. Since steam is hotter than boiling water, vegetables will cook faster and will absorb less water. The most important tip is not to overcook steamed vegetables. Because they cook so quickly, cut vegetables are easy to overcook. So watch them carefully!

Dark leafy chrysanthemum greens, one of the most popular Japanese greens in the late autumn and winter seasons, are rich in B vitamins and minerals. The greens are available in most Asian markets and many farmers' markets. Overcooked chrysanthemum leaves can have a bitter taste, so quick cooking is best. If you find fresh baby leaves, use them as garnish or in salads. The flowers are also edible and can be used to garnish soups or float in drinks.

kabu turnip and green top amazake pickles

Amazake makes sweet-tasting pickles out of the refreshingly white flesh and gorgeous green tops of the turnip.

MAKES 4 SERVINGS

For the pickles:
4 Japanese turnips, washed
4 Japanese turnip green tops
2 cups plain/original flavor amazake, store bought, or homemade (see recipe on page 79)
1 pinch sea salt

To make the pickles:
1. In a large bowl, thoroughly combine the turnips, green tops, amazake and sea salt.
2. Transfer the mixture into a pickle press and apply pressure. (Note: If you don't have a pickle press, lay a plate over the radish mixture and place a heavy weight on top of the plate. See below for more information.) Allow to sit at least one hour to create a light crispy pickle
3. Arrange attractively in a serving dish.

Useful information:
Pickles can be pressed up to 3 days in a cool, dry place (not in a refrigerator). After pickling, store in a tightly sealed glass jar, refrigerated, for freshness.

Kabu, also known as the "Japanese turnip," is not as woody or fibrous as other turnips. It is fresh tasting with no earthiness or bitterness, with a slightly sweet, almost fruity flavor. Japanese turnips are similar to daikon radishes, but less watery. Many people think of turnips as woody, colorless, leaden spheres, without much culinary appeal. In fact, turnips are available in a wide array of beautiful colors: red-skinned, purple-tipped, pearl-white, golden-yellow. With more and more varieties available, it is possible to eat tender young turnips very lightly cooked, pickled or even raw. (Note: During healing, raw foods should be limited.) Turnip roots are high in fiber, vitamin C, folic acid, potassium and copper. Turnip greens contain even higher levels of these nutrients, along with calcium and beta carotene.

207

azuki kabocha stew

This stew is a thick, rich, and hearty combination of azuki, winter squash and root vegetables. Perfect for a cozy winter night!

MAKES 4 SERVINGS

For the stew:

1 cup azuki beans
purified water for soaking
4 1-inch strips of kombu
4 cups purified water
¼ cup burdock, diced into 1-inch pieces
½ cup lotus root, quartered and sliced
⅛-inch thick
1 cup kabocha, buttercup squash, or other winter
squash, cubed into 2-inch pieces
1 to 2 teaspoons soy sauce
dry-roasted pumpkin seeds, for garnish,
(see sections titled "How to Dry Roast
Whole Grains or Seeds," found on page 29,
and "Condiments & Garnishes," found on
page 242)
scallion or parsley, for garnish (optional)

To make the stew:

1. Wash and soak the azuki beans.
2. In a large pot over a medium-high flame, add the kombu strips. Layer with the beans on top, add the water and bring to a boil.
3. Layer the burdock on top of the beans, cover, reduce heat to low and simmer for 45 minutes.
4. Layer the lotus and kabocha on top of the burdock. Increase heat to medium-high and bring to a boil. Cover, reduce heat back to low and simmer for 15 minutes.
5. Add soy sauce, stirring gently and continue to simmer for five more minutes.
6. Remove from heat and serve garnished with roasted pumpkin seeds and/or green garnish.

Useful information:

The difference between stews and soups is that the ingredients of a stew are usually cut into larger pieces than those of a soup and retain more of their individual flavors. Stews may also have a thicker liquid than a soup and is more likely to be eaten as a main course than as a starter, unlike soup. Slow cooked stews provide more lasting warmth and calmness to the body, as well as a steady energy, in order to keep the body going during the cold winter.

sweet brown rice and almonds

with Kombu Condiment

Whenever people taste this grain recipe they are surprised by how almonds and brown rice are so compatible. I trust you will also love this pairing, as well as its perfect texture.

MAKES 4 SERVINGS

For the rice and almonds:

1 ⅓ cups sweet brown rice
4 cups purified water
⅔ cup almonds, raw
2 pinches sea salt
Kombu Condiment (recipe on next page)

To make the rice and almonds:

1. Wash and soak the rice according to the instructions listed in the section titled "How to Wash and Soak Whole Grains," found on page 27.
2. In a medium saucepan over a high flame, bring 1 cup of the purified water to a boil. Add the almonds and boil for 1 minute. Drain water and peel almonds (they are so easy to peel and so tasty, so don't be tempted to eat them while you are peeling, like I do!). Set aside.
3. In a pressure cooker over a high flame, combine the soaked rice, boiled almonds and 3 cups of the purified water.
4. Bring to a boil, add sea salt, cover and allow pressure to build. Place a flame deflector over the flame, reduce heat to low and cook for 45 to 50 minutes.
5. Remove the cooker from the stove and allow to sit until the pressure reduces naturally.
6. Wait another 5 to 10 minutes before removing the cover. Using a bamboo rice paddle or wooden spoon moistened with water, gently stir by lifting and turning the rice and almonds. (This step allows the rice and almonds to "breathe" and become fluffy, tasty rice.)
7. Serve with Kombu Condiment (recipe below). If not serving right away, cover the pot with a clean dishtowel or a bamboo sushi mat, instead of the lid, for better circulation of air.

Useful information:

Sweet brown rice is a whole grain that has not been processed, and has only the husk removed to ensure full flavor and purity. It has a naturally sweet taste and is high in fiber, protein and iron. Cooked sweet brown rice grains cling together, creating a delightfully chewy, sticky texture, making it ideal for use in Asian recipes and rice puddings.

Almonds are a rich source of heart-healthy monosaturated fats, as well as calcium, magnesium, protein and vitamin E.

kombu condiment

Shio Kombu

After using kombu to make dashi broth, this tasty sea vegetable can be "re-used" to make a condiment for rice balls, sprinkled on vegetables, or served with grains.

For the condiment:

½ ounce kombu (see below)*
½ cup purified water
1 tablespoon soy sauce

To make the condiment:

1. Slice the cooked kombu into ½-inch squares.
2. In a small saucepan over a medium-high flame, combine the kombu and water. Cover and cook until kombu is soft, about 30 minutes (or longer if using dried kombu).
3. Add soy sauce and continue cooking until all the liquid has evaporated.

This recipe uses the pre-cooked kombu reserved from making the kombu dashi (broth) recipes on page 52, 130 and 215. If you are using an un-cooked dried strip of kombu, cook the kombu for an additional 30 minutes, adding additional water if necessary. The flavor can be made stronger by adding more soy sauce.

nishime-style dried daikon

with Shiitake & Carrots

This naturally sweet country-style cooking was my mom's favorite. When I first started cooking this during my healing process, I appreciated her love more than ever.

MAKES 4 SERVINGS

For the daikon:

2 dried shiitake mushrooms
purified water for soaking
1 cup dried daikon
1 cup carrots, sliced diagonally
soy sauce, to taste

To make the daikon:

1. In a small bowl, soak the shiitake in purified water for about 30 minutes or until soft. Slice softened mushrooms into quarters.
2. In a separate bowl, soak the dried daikon in purified water for about 10 minutes or until soft. (Note: Dried daikon should be light beige in color. If you notice that the dried daikon is very dark brown, do not use it — especially during healing.)
3. In a pot, combine the daikon and shiitake along with the soaking water.
4. Add enough additional water to just cover the daikon and the shiitake. Add the carrots and bring to a boil over a medium-high flame.
5. Lower the heat, cover and simmer for about 25 minutes, or until the vegetables become tender.
6. Towards the end of cooking, add a small amount of soy sauce and continue to cook until excess liquid has evaporated. Serve hot or at room temperature.

Useful information:

Nishime-style refers to a cooking process that usually involves a very heavy iron or thick ceramic pot that imparts a warming, calming, yet strengthening property to the vegetables within.

Variation: There are many combinations of vegetables that can be used: carrots, daikon, turnips, lotus root, onions, kabocha (or other winter squash) and cabbage. Burdock root can also be used by slicing the root into smaller pieces first.

213

black kale

with Walnut Sauce

Beautifully deep, dark green, black kale has a slightly firm texture and lively flavor that combines well with the savory Walnut Sauce.

MAKES 4 SERVINGS

For the kale:

8 black kale leaves
purified water, for blanching
½ cup walnuts
2 tablespoons soy sauce
4 tablespoons Simple Kombu Dashi Broth (recipe on next page) or purified water

To make the kale:

1. Thoroughly wash the kale and trim off a small amount of stem ends.
2. In a large pot over a medium-high flame, bring water to a boil. Blanch the kale leaves for 1 to 2 minutes. (Do not overcook.) Drain in a colander, set aside and allow to cool.
3. In a suribachi or blender, grind the walnuts. Add the soy sauce and kombu broth. Blend until creamy.
4. Serve sauce drizzled on top of the cooked kale leaves.

Useful information:

Black kale, also known as Lacinato kale, is a variety of Italian heirloom kale with long, spiky, ruffled dark green leaves and peppery flavor, that is often served as a side dish of greens, a garnish, or as an ingredient in soups, pasta sauces, and stews. Related to the cabbage-family of vegetables, kale is chock-full of vitamins and minerals, including ample amounts of beta carotene, calcium, copper and iron, as well as potent cancer-fighting compounds.

Walnuts are another highly nutrient-dense food with a full complement of antioxidants, beneficial fats, such as omega-3 fatty acids, and they even boast the highest non-fish source of alpha-linolenic acid. Walnuts are rich in protein, fiber and vitamin E. Walnuts are a delicious way to add flavor and crunch to a meal, as well as providing an anticancer and cholesterol-lowering boost. While walnuts are harvested in December, they are available year round.

simple kombu dashi broth

For the dashi:
purified water
kombu, dried (use one ½-inch square piece per
cup of water)

To make the dashi:
1. Wipe kombu clean with a dry cloth.
2. *No-cook method:* In a bowl, combine the kombu
   and water and soak for at least 2 to 3 hours.
   Stovetop method: In a saucepan over medium-
   high flame, combine the kombu and water.
   Bring to a boil, reduce heat and simmer (either
   covered or uncovered) for about 20 to 30
   minutes.

3. Strain out and reserve the kombu strip to make
   Kombu Condiment (see recipe on page 212).
   Dashi is now ready for use in soups and stews.
   Dashi will keep for 2 or 3 days in the
   refrigerator.

Useful information:
An uncovered or covered pot can affect the yin/
yang energy of the broth. Depending on the
nature of your condition, you may choose to keep
the pot uncovered while the dashi simmers to
cultivate a more yin energy, or cover the pot for a
more yang energy.

burdock miso pickles

*These strong-tasting pickles are good for the cold winter.
It's easy to make and delicious.*

MAKES 4 SERVINGS

For the pickles:
1 burdock root, 10 to 20 inches long*
½ cup barley miso

To make the pickles:
1. Slice burdock into pieces about 3 to 4 inches
   long. Transfer to a bamboo tray.
2. Place tray of burdock outside to dry in a shady
   area for about one day.
3. In an 8- or 10-ounce glass jar, add the miso.
   Add the burdock, pushing the pieces into the
   miso so that they are completely covered.
4. Cover the jar and store in a cool place for
   about three days.

5. Remove the burdock and wipe or rinse off the
   miso. Slice burdock into very thin diagonal cuts
   before serving.

Useful information:
Due to the strong nature of these pickles, refrain
from overeating, more so than other pickles.
See page 78 for more information on pickling
with miso.

**Burdock root has a brown-colored, tissue-paper-thin
skin that can easily be scrubbed away revealing the
white flesh underneath. Be extra gentle when
scrubbing burdock root with the tawashi vegetable
brush (see page 62 for more information) so as to
retain as much of the skin as possible.*

215

apple filet

with Azuki Glaze

Being Japanese, I really love sweet azuki beans, as well as desserts, so I had to make something that fulfilled my ancestral craving. Just having a plain stewed apple was dull, but adding the Azuki Glaze really made that apple come alive.

MAKES 4 SERVINGS

For the apples:

4 cups purified water
1 to 2 organic red apples (depending on the size)
1 pinch sea salt
Azuki Glaze (recipe on next page)

To make the apples:

1. In a large pot, bring the water to a boil. In the meantime, slice the apples in half and remove the cores. Slice apple again from top to bottom into half-moon wedges, about ¼ inches thick. Set aside.

2. Add sea salt to the boiling water and sliced apples. Cook for 2 minutes.

3. Drain the water and allow the apples to cool off.

4. Transfer slices to serving plates and drizzle with Azuki Glaze.

Useful information:

Apples are one of the oldest and most well-known fruits grown in the temperate regions throughout the world. Their round shape, crispy texture and fresh taste appeal to just about everybody. In macrobiotics, we adore apples and frequently use them for desserts, as in this recipe. In fact, the process of learning to make macrobiotic desserts with apples often marks the beginning of one's macrobiotic journey. Apples are rich in soluble fiber, potassium and vitamin C, and are useful for reducing cholesterol, as well as for alleviating diarrhea and constipation.

azuki glaze

Sweet azuki beans bring back fond memories of my mom's elderly housekeeper, Mrs. Kato. She loved to take a snack break at around 3pm and always generously offered me some of her sweet azuki bean dessert. Although I was only 5 years old at the time, I quickly learned to enjoy this grown-up dessert, just like she did!

For the glaze:
1 cup azuki beans
purified water
1-inch piece of kombu
pinch of sea salt
2 tablespoons rice syrup

To make the glaze:

1. Wash and sort the azuki beans according to the instructions listed in the section titled "How to Wash and Sort Beans," found on page 55.
2. Place kombu on the bottom of a pot (preferably made of ceramic), layer washed beans on top, and add enough water to cover the beans.
3. Bring to a boil over a medium-high flame. Place a flame deflector under the pot, and add ½ cup of additional water (this process is called "bikkuri mizu," or "shocking water," which helps to soften the beans faster).

4. Bring to a boil again and add another ½ cup of water. You can repeat this process one more time. Cover, reduce the heat to low and simmer for 1-½ hours or until beans are soft and have not lost their shape.
5. Add the sea salt and simmer for another ½-hour.
6. Add the rice syrup to sweeten. Cook off the remaining liquid until the desired thickness is achieved and serve drizzled over the Apple Filet.

Variations: In addition to garnishing the Apple Filet, this delicious glaze can be eaten by itself, or served with Amazake Cream (recipe on page 141) or Pan Fried Mochi (recipe on page 45).

holidays & social occasions

A Time to Compromise and Adapt

Winter in the United States is a time to be with family and friends and often traditionally involves cooking loads of heavy, rich foods. When I first started cooking and eating macrobiotic foods, the holiday season was coming up, and I worried I would feel left out and have nothing to eat. It's not an easy time to heal during holiday gatherings, when the food is rich and lavish, straying from healthful habits. Shortly after I was diagnosed with cancer, I was invited to go to a friend's house for Thanksgiving. I told my hosts that I couldn't eat most of their food, but they still insisted that I come anyway; and so I did. I brought brown rice with me and was able to eat some of the vegetable dishes. At first, this seemed acceptable, but soon I found myself having to answer many questions about my special "diet." I quickly became exhausted and regretted going there at all. Thankfully, people are more accepting of alternate ways of preparing and enjoying foods nowadays, and I find that I am also more accepting of their curiosity and interest. The following recipes are proof that macrobiotic foods can be just as sumptuous and satisfying as they are healing. I have enjoyed these recipes many times during the holiday season, and I hope you will too.

Holiday Menu

Kabocha Squash with Brown Rice Stuffing
Mashed Parsnips
Shiitake Kuzu Gravy
Crispy Emerald Broccoli
Carrot Nuka Pickles
Chestnut Mousse with Cranberry Chutney

kabocha squash

with Brown Rice Stuffing

The first time I tried making this dish, I thought, "Wow, this is so simple, yet so tasty!" This recipe is truly dynamic — not only is stuffing an entire squash fun and enjoyable, but it perfectly embodies the macrobiotic principle of using the whole food. I always have great success serving this dish to people who don't follow vegan macrobiotic lifestyles. This is truly a dish everyone can enjoy!

MAKES 4 SERVINGS

For the squash and stuffing:

1 cup short-grain brown rice
1 cup sweet brown rice
½ cup wild rice, washed
1 kabocha/winter squash, about 2 to 4 pounds
4 ½ cups water
2 pinches sea salt
1 teaspoon sesame oil or ⅛ cup kombu dashi
   (recipes on page 52 and 215), for water-
   sautéeing
1 cup onion, diced small
¼ cup burdock, diced small
½ cup celery, diced small
½ cup carrots, diced small
½ cup parsley, chopped
1 tablespoon dried sage or 2 tablespoons fresh
   sage, finely chopped (optional)
1 tablespoon dried rosemary or 2 tablespoons
   fresh rosemary, finely chopped (optional)
½ cup roasted almonds or roasted pine nuts
   (optional)
½ cup fresh cranberries
1 tablespoon sesame oil, for baking squash

To make the squash and stuffing:

1. Wash and soak the brown rice according to the instructions listed in the section titled "How to Wash and Soak Whole Grains," found on page 27. Wash wild rice according to the same instructions, but skip the soaking process.

2. Using a sharp knife, carefully cut a round section out around the stem of the top of the squash. (This is a good time to ask for help from someone stronger than you since the skin can be tough.) Scoop out all the seeds, and reserve the cut-out top to use as a lid later.

3. In a large pot over a medium-high flame, combine the wild rice, soaked brown rice and the 4 cups of water. Bring to a boil, add sea salt and cover. Reduce heat to low and cook for about 50 minutes, or until rice is soft.

4. While rice is cooking, preheat the oven to 325° F. In a medium saucepan over a medium flame, heat the oil or dashi and sauté the onion for 1 to 2 minutes. Add burdock and sauté for one minute. Add celery and carrots and continue sautéing for 3 to 5 minutes, or until celery is soft.

continued on next page...

5. Add the herbs, stir to combine and remove from heat. Add roasted nuts and cranberries.

6. When rice is done, add it to the pan of vegetables and stir to combine.

7. Fill the hollowed-out squash with the vegetable/rice mixture, all the way to the top. There should be enough of the vegetable/rice mixture to stuff the squash and have extra for a side dish. Cover the squash with the cut-out lid and brush the skin of the entire squash with oil. Transfer the stuffed squash to a baking tray and bake for about 1 ½ to 2 hours.

8. Remove the lid and bake another 5 to 10 minutes. The squash is ready to eat when a skewer impales the skin easily.

9. Serve the squash whole on a large plate. Slice squash into individual servings at the table, add gravy, and enjoy a festive holiday with family and friends.

Useful information:
Winter squash, especially the orange-fleshed varieties like kabocha, are rich in beta carotene, folic acid and potassium.

Variation: The stuffing can also be used to stuff cabbage, or as a side dish for any occasion. Dried cranberries or dried cherries are also a good substitute instead of fresh cranberries, but look for ones without added sugar.

mashed parsnips

I had never tasted parsnips until I came to the U.S. and learned how to cook macrobiotically. Parsnips have a naturally sweet and earthy, yet light flavor. Friends are often surprised by how much they enjoy them as a substitute for mashed potatoes.

MAKES 4 SERVINGS

For the parsnips:
4 cups purified water
pinch of sea salt
7 cups parsnips, diced (about 2 pounds)
1 cup onion, diced
½ to 1 teaspoon umeboshi paste (optional)
½ cup parsley (optional)

To make the parsnips:

1. In a large pot over a medium-high flame, add the water and cover. Bring water to a boil and remove lid. Add sea salt, parsnips and onion.
2. Bring to a boil again, reduce heat to low and cook until parsnips are very soft and onions very clear, about 10 to 15 minutes.
3. Using a strainer, remove the vegetables and reserve the water.
4. Transfer vegetables to a food mill with a small-holed disk, adding additional cooking water, as needed.
5. After all the vegetables are milled, add umeboshi paste to taste and stir well to combine.
6. Serve garnished with parsley and Shiitake Kuzu Gravy (see recipe below).

Useful information:
Parsnips are a root vegetable, related to carrots, but with a creamy-white color and stronger flavor. Parsnips are also good for soups and stews, and also delicious when roasted. They are high in vitamin C and have healing properties for the middle to lower part of the body.

Variation: If you prefer a grain-based substitute for mashed potatoes, you can also substitute with mashed millet and cauliflower.

shiitake kuzu gravy
with Parsley

When I moved to the U.S., I noticed that most of the food was flavorless and covered by different sauces, gravies and sugary condiments. I always felt an oily and greasy aftertaste. My stomach would also swell up from the excessive amounts of oil and starch. When I first discovered that kuzu can be used to make gravy, I thought it was a brilliant idea. Kuzu-based gravies give all the satisfaction, without the oily side effects later.

MAKES 4 SERVINGS

For the gravy:
3 to 4 dried shiitake mushrooms
2 cups purified water, for soaking
2 tablespoons kuzu, dissolved in 4 tablespoons
    of purified water
1 tablespoon soy sauce, or to taste
chopped parsley, for garnish

To make the gravy:
1. In a small bowl, combine the shiitake and water, and soak for 30 minutes.
2. Chop the soaked mushrooms, reserving the soaking water for the next step.
3. In a medium stainless steel saucepan over medium heat, combine the chopped mushrooms and 1 ½ cups of the soaking water, and cook for five minutes.
4. Add dissolved kuzu, stirring constantly. Flavor with soy sauce.
5. Serve over mashed parsnips and garnish with chopped parsley.

Useful information:
For thicker gravy use more kuzu. Both shiitake and kuzu have very strong healing properties. Shiitake helps to reduce cholesterol and is also used to detox excess intake of animal foods. Kuzu is very useful for soothing the stomach and intestines.

Variation: This gravy is also excellent when served over mashed millet-cauliflower or grain burgers.

crispy emerald broccoli

Many people like broccoli and know that it's very nutritionally good for us, but almost everybody cooks it for far too long. Many also mistakenly think that macrobiotic vegetable dishes are cooked for a long time. This quick-boiled dish should prove otherwise. This method retains the broccoli's crispness, emerald-green color and natural sweetness; and makes a perfect complement to the baked stuffed squash and mashed parsnips for a festive holiday meal.

MAKES 4 SERVINGS

For the broccoli:

4 cups purified water
4 cups broccoli (about 2 heads), sliced into 3-inch long pieces, including flowerets and ½ inches of stalk
pinch sea salt

To make the broccoli:

1. In a large pot over a medium-high flame, bring the water to a boil.
2. Add the sea salt and broccoli and boil for about 1 to 2 minutes depending on the size of the broccoli pieces. Using a strainer spoon, immediately scoop out the broccoli and transfer to a metal strainer.
3. Serve warm or at room temperature; or if a crispier texture is desired, position strainer over the sink and pour cold water over the just-cooked broccoli.

Useful information:

This is a simple dish, but one needs to be especially attentive during preparation to avoid overly-cooked, mushy broccoli! Broccoli contains ample amounts of folic acid, beta carotene, as well as vitamins K and C. A compound found in broccoli appears to be more effective than modern antibiotics against Helicobacter pylori, the bacteria that causes peptic ulcers, and contains many anticancer compounds linked to a reduction in cancers of the breast, stomach, prostate and cervix.

carrot nuka pickles

In general, nuka pickles can be strong, but this version is pickled only overnight, thereby allowing the sweet taste of the carrots to be retained, while at the same time benefiting our digestion. One taste of these, and you'll know that pickles can be sweet and refreshing.

MAKES 4 SERVINGS

For the pickles:
2 baby carrots, or one small carrot
nuka bed*
purified water, for rinsing

To make the pickles:
1. Dry the carrot(s) in a shady area outside for a half-day or one day (see photo on next page).
2. Use the whole baby carrots or coarsely cut the small carrot to a size that will easily fit into your nuka jar.
3. With clean, dry hands, transfer carrots to the nuka jar and completely cover them with nuka paste. Allow jar to sit undisturbed for at least one night.
4. With clean, dry hands, remove desired amount of pickled carrots. Rinse carrots with purified water, slice thinly and serve.

Useful information:
Nuka pickles contain enzymes that are beneficial for intestinal flora. Eating a small amount of pickles every day towards the end of a meal is ideal. Please see page 77 for more information about pickles.

*See page 81 for recipe and instructions on how to prepare, store and maintain a nuka doko.

chestnut mousse

with Cranberry Chutney

This recipe comes from an image I had in my mind of mountains and a small tree. The smooth taste of chestnuts is the perfect complement to the sweet and sour cranberries.

MAKES 4 SERVINGS

For the mousse:

2 cups cooked chestnuts (about 300g)
1 tablespoon brown rice syrup
1 tablespoon barley malt
¼ cup purified water
fresh mint, cypress or other herb sprigs, for garnish

To make the mousse:

1. In a food processor, purée the chestnuts into a creamy smooth paste.
2. Add the rice syrup, barley malt and water. Pulse again until well blended. Transfer to a container and refrigerate.

For the chutney:

6 ounces fresh cranberries
1 pinch sea salt
2 tablespoons brown rice syrup
⅛ teaspoon cinnamon (optional)
¼ cup purified water

To make the chutney:

1. In a medium saucepan over medium-high heat, combine all the ingredients.
2. Bring to a boil, cover and simmer for 6 to 8 minutes, gently stirring to combine.
3. Remove from heat and transfer chutney to a glass container and refrigerate.

To assemble mousse and chutney:

1. Using a spoon, divide the chutney evenly across 4 serving plates and spread it around.
2. Using a clean tablespoon, scoop about 2 heaping tablespoons of chestnut mousse per serving. Garnish with a sprig of fresh herb (cypress sprig, shown in photo) and serve.

Useful information:

I never saw or tasted cranberries until I came to the U.S., and I wondered how many people eat cranberries outside of a Thanksgiving meal. Cranberries and their unsweetened juices are well known to combat urinary tract infections. These tart berries are closely related to blueberries and have high levels of vitamin C, fiber and cancer-fighting antioxidants.

macrobiotic essentials for healing

Many questions come up at the beginning of a macrobiotic practice. The methods and amount of time it takes people to use their new skills vary for each person's constitution and condition. In an effort to address these issues, I have provided this section to enable you to understand the macrobiotic essentials in greater depth. It took me a long time to get to this point, and I feel honored to share my understanding of macrobiotics with you. May this knowledge support you in whatever it is that you seek in life, and may our practice of the macrobiotic essentials flourish together...

SERVING & EATING PRINCIPLES

When I first started to delve into macrobiotic cooking, I learned not only how to properly prepare food, I also learned how to serve and eat it. It wasn't about grabbing a plate or bowl and digging in; it was a careful, tender, rhythmic and Zen manner in which the food really came alive. Living a fast-paced life like most of us do, we can get trapped in an oblivious existence. When I am too busy and distracted with my daily routines, I realize that I am not following the macrobiotic way at all.

Sometimes we feel great suffering and hopelessness before we begin to realize there's much more to life. After I experienced the pain of my illness and injuries, I came face-to-face with my deepest thoughts and acquired a deep appreciation of quality leisure time when I sat quietly, was in the present, and enjoyed my food the macrobiotic way, carefully chewing fifty to one hundred times. This simple act created a profound peace inside of me that I soon realized no amount of money could buy.

Serving

Presentation of food on our plates is the next step after preparation. Whole grains are the staple food, which are placed in the center or to the right side of the dinner plate. Beans are set next, in the lower right position. In clockwise order, sea vegetables are placed beside the beans, followed by root vegetables, round vegetables and leafy greens. Pickles are placed last, usually at the top of the plate.

Zen Prayer Before Meal

Innumerable labors have brought us this food.
We should know how it comes to us.
In receiving this offering,
we should consider whether our practice
and virtue deserve it.
Desiring the natural order of mind,
we should be free from hate, greed and delusion.
We eat to support life and practice
the way of the Universe (God).

(This prayer was given to me by my first macrobiotic teacher, Cecile Tovah Levin, at my first macrobiotic cooking class.)

Eating & Chewing

The manner of eating follows a clockwise direction, first taking a bite of whole grains, followed by beans or vegetables. Pickles should be eaten toward the end of the meal to best aid digestion. A quiet, peaceful area is preferable. Eat calmly, fully aware of how the food makes you feel, chewing each bite slowly and thoughtfully.

Have you ever heard that chewing each mouthful one hundred times (or at least fifty times) is very good for your health?

During times when I was very sick, I chewed slowly and well, and I indeed felt that I did not need anything else in the world, and the simple act of chewing was not something to be taken for granted. Herman Aihara sensei said that the word "chew" in Japanese is *Kami* (噛み), which is homonymous with *Kami* (神), which means "God." I felt I was close to God, who made me, as well as the food bestowed upon me.

Chewing one's food fifty to one hundred times per mouthful is a standard macrobiotic recommendation on how to eat for better health. As you can imagine, some people think this is crazy. Who would have the patience? But chewing our food well (until it's in a liquefied state) is vitally important since the process of digestion begins with the enzymes present in the saliva in our mouths. Saliva is one of the most important fluids in our body and thorough chewing increases this enzyme-rich saliva, thereby giving our stomach, small and large intestines less work to do. Whole grains, especially, have to be digested in the mouth for optimal absorption of nutrients. It is easy to mindlessly guzzle our food when we are hungry, but when we thoroughly chew we produce enough saliva to exceed the quantity of food in our mouth, turning our food into fluid. The act of chewing so thoroughly also allows us time to consider and feel gratitude for the food we are eating, as well as for those who prepared it. My teacher, Cecile Tovah Levin, once told me that Gandhi said, "Chew your liquids and drink your foods." I think Gandhi was macrobiotic!

Chewing takes consciousness, practice and time. To be honest, this is one of the most challenging recommendations for me to follow since I enjoy talking with my dining companions while I eat. I also have a hard time thoroughly chewing my food because I am simply not well practiced with it and I often do not take sufficient time for myself to enjoy my food, but when I make a conscious effort to chew it gets easier.

If I get really sick and I need to eat slowly and chew my food one hundred times per bite, I will do it again. I am sure many others would find chewing as challenging a practice as I have, so together, let's make a habit of regularly engaging in a silent eating ritual at home; just eating and chewing, focused and in the present, like meditation. (Hint: practice savoring each moment and feel grateful and happy. Saying "thank you," or in my case, "arigatou," is also key to good health and karma.)

WHAT IS MACROBIOTICS?

Many people are surprised to discover that the word "macrobiotics" originated from Greek. Most Americans I have talked to about it have scrunched their faces and asked "macro-what?" When you break apart the word — "macro" (meaning large, long), "bios" (meaning life), and "tics" (meaning skill) — it begins to make sense.

Usually macrobiotics is described as a dietary regimen that involves eating grains as a staple food, supplemented with other local organically grown foods, such as vegetables and beans, and prepared with traditional methods of cooking. The diet also avoids the use of highly processed, refined foods and sugar. This is all vitally true and important, but it's also very incomplete.

In fact, macrobiotics is a philosophy of life, following the Chinese principle of "yin" and "yang." This principle guides us in creating a balance, by choosing the right combinations of foods at the right time, when those foods are at their best. The major food groups include: whole grains, like brown rice, barley, and millet; whole grain products, such as buckwheat pasta (soba noodles); a variety of land and sea vegetables; soups; beans; soy products, such as tofu, tempeh and miso; supplemental foods, such as fruit from the organic local environment; nuts and seeds; mild natural seasonings; mild (non-stimulant) beverages, such as bancha, twig tea (kukicha) and barley tea.

As the seasons change and my physical condition changes, so does my energy level, cooking style and food choices. I do this in order to maintain balance and harmony within my natural environment. Macrobiotics explains how nature significantly and dynamically affects one's health, well-being, and happiness.

Is Macrobiotics Japanese?

This is the most common question I have been asked over the last fifteen years, perhaps partly because I am Japanese. And, in fact, it is true that a lot of what we study and practice in macrobiotics is based on the traditional cuisine that our ancestors in Japan were eating. With today's modern transportation methods and high-volume trade, however, we have lost much of our consciousness of traditional and seasonal foods. We can eat anything at any time and any place. Despite this, Japanese culture has managed to retain some of the traditional-style cuisine that has proven its benefits in terms of well-being and longevity. Most of the original macrobiotic teachers, Sagen Ishizuka (1850 - 1909), George Ohsawa (1893 -1966), and Michio Kushi (1926~) are Japanese, and their recommendation was simply to include more Japanese staple foods to start. Japanese food preparation—in its traditional method—is delicate and natural, low in fat and moderate in the use of oil. It is the closest to macrobiotic cooking, although as I continue to study macrobiotic food, I discover many other cultures also share the principles of macrobiotics in their food selection and preparation.

The philosophy of macrobiotics aligns closely with the uniquely Japanese concept of "wabi-sabi" (侘び寂び). Acceptance of transience, impermanence, and of the passing of time are at the core of wabi-sabi. By finding beauty in the imperfect and the incomplete, and bowing to the inevitability of change, a richer and deeper life experience naturally unfolds, leading to greater sensory perception and emotional intelligence. Wabi-sabi is a type of yin/yang energy that's very macrobiotic.

NATURAL FOODS

I find it so strange that we have to refer to certain foods as being "natural." Don't you agree? I often wonder why we even have the choice of chemically-grown vegetables and non-chemically-grown (organically-grown) vegetables. When you walk into a large natural foods market and see the word "conventional," what does this communicate? Some of my cooking class students have expressed that the presence of "conventional" food products in a "natural" foods market seems contradictory.

How did food become "un-" natural in the first place? Modern convenience, cosmetics, and pure and competitive business practices have made us consumers of unnatural foods. As a result, we find ourselves having to read signs, labels, and disclaimers before we know which foods are genuinely real and safe to eat.

Sea Salt

In my macrobiotic studies I discovered that we came from the oceans about 250 million years ago, and our body still carries the same proportion of minerals in our blood as the ancient seas. The salt most people use today is refined table salt, which is nutritionally-deficient sodium chloride (a chemical compound with the formula NaCl). Macrobiotically, we use only high-quality natural sea salt, which contains many trace minerals and has a damp texture. Using moderate amounts of natural sea salt in our cooking supports the nutrients of our foods. I like to keep sea salt by the stove in an attractive box, like one that holds jewelry, since it is such an important resource for our body.

Oil and Other Seasonings

High-quality vegetable oils and natural seasonings are not just good sources of flavor, but also help to strengthen our bodies. For healing purposes, it is best to use them in moderation. I did not use much oil in the beginning of my healing process, but I enjoyed using cold-pressed sesame oil on occasion. Now, I use a little olive oil from time to time, especially on warm days. The seasonings I used most were simple, naturally processed miso, tamari or soy sauce, and umeboshi vinegar. And, once in a while I used whole-grain sweeteners such as brown rice syrup, barley malt and amazake.

Soy Sauce

Soy sauce, the foundation of Japanese cuisine, is found in two types — shoyu and tamari. Shoyu is made with soybeans, wheat, and sea salt; while traditional tamari, a by-product of miso production, is made only from soybeans and sea salt. It is vitally important to purchase naturally-brewed and fermented soy sauce since commercially-made soy sauce contains preservatives, colorings, sugar and/or alcohol. Natural shoyu and tamari, found in health food stores, is used during cooking and can be stored at room temperature for up to one year.

Condiments & Garnishes

If you're like me, you enjoy watching a good movie. Sometimes I like to think of a good macrobiotic meal as a metaphor for a good film. The main characters and most important roles would be played by whole grains. Then we'd have the supporting roles of beans, land and sea vegetables — all very important. But what about the background characters? Without the extras in those background scenes, I think our macrobiotic movie would be boring, empty and tasteless. That's where the condiments and garnishes come in — to add variety, balance and to complete our macrobiotic movie meal.

When people come to study at our "studio mugen" (mugen translates to "infinity" in Japanese — the place where I believe we came from and are going back to), I have noticed that many students learn very quickly about the main and supporting characters because they are attractive, with a strong appearance (just like movie stars) and yet they forget all about the extras. The extra characters of condiments and garnishes may play small roles, yet their importance cannot be understated.

Good quality macrobiotic condiments add flavor, nutrition, nuance and complexity to whole grains, soups and salads. It is much better to use condiments rather than plain salt on foods. I recommend using condiments like Gomashio (Sesame Salt; see recipe on page 127), shiso powder (as used in recipe on page 135), green nori (aonori; see recipe on page 101), wakame (see recipe on page 113), Tekka (see recipe and information on page 202), kombu (Shio Kombu; see recipe on page 212), Ginger Pickles (see recipe on page 188), and sweet condiments, like my Homemade Amazake (see recipe on page 79).

Sesame seed and sea vegetable condiments contain calcium, iron, minerals and vitamins. Along with their sour and tart flavors, shiso powder and umeboshi condiments add alkalinizing minerals to your food, as well as aid in digestion.

Garnishes are the extra characters that lend a touch of fresh taste, eye-pleasing color and variety, adding a small, yet vibrant energy. To me, garnishes are similar to when I am getting dressed and I finish off my outfit with a colorful scarf, a belt, or maybe a hat. They are the bright little accents, that even when I am wearing a typical American casual get-up of blue jeans and a t-shirt, simply adding my favorite hat brings me pleasure and greater appeal to the whole me, just like garnishes on whole foods.

I recommend garnishes like: thinly sliced scallion (as used in the recipes on pages 40, 129 and 160), chopped or minced parsley (as used in the recipes on pages 69, 157, 159, 183, and 226), a sprig of oregano (as used in the recipe on page 75), minced carrot tops (as used in the recipes on pages 49 and 138), chopped greens (like watercress), sliced shiitake or finely shredded carrot (as used in the recipe on page 129), a sprinkling of 1 to 2 teaspoons of roasted sesame, pumpkin or sunflower seeds (as used in the recipes on pages 129, 133, 173, 206, and 209), $\frac{1}{2}$ to 1 sheet of nori (as used in the recipes on pages 40 and 135), 1 tablespoon freshly grated daikon (as used in the recipes on page 129), or a sprinkling of $\frac{1}{2}$ teaspoon lemon zest (as used in the recipes on page 117).

Oversalting/undersalting and Seasoning

It is easy, particularly at the beginning of your macrobiotic practice, to overuse salty seasonings such as miso, shoyu/soy sauce, sea salt, umeboshi plums, paste and vinegar, condiments and sea vegetables. It also happens that out of fear or unfamiliarity, people underuse these ingredients. However, overuse is the most common error in beginning macrobiotic practice. It arises from a desire to make the food tastier or because we are unfamiliar with proper seasoning amounts and techniques. Also, many people make the mistaken assumption that "if some is good, more is better." For these reasons, it is essential to study macrobiotic cooking with an experienced, well-trained and qualified macrobiotic cook in order to learn proper cooking techniques and to taste well-prepared, balanced food. It is also helpful to follow recipes and seasoning outlined in macrobiotic cookbooks which are designed for health recovery. Below is a list of common overuse errors:

Adding too much miso or shoyu/soy sauce to your soup:

Miso soup is best when it has a light, refreshing, mildly salty flavor. Michio Kushi's apt and poetic description for the ideal broth is "fresh as a spring breeze." You should still be able to taste the vegetables in it, see the bottom of the bowl, and not want to take a beverage or sweets after drinking it. Keep in mind, however, that it should taste like soup and not tea. Soup relaxes us before the meal, stimulates our appetite and digestion, and helps make good, strong blood. Learn to make elegant, delicate (and sometimes hearty, but not salty) soups, and you will enjoy your meals to the utmost.

Not simmering in the miso, shoyu, soy sauce or sea salt:

Miso needs to simmer in the soup over a low flame for three to four minutes before eating. Shoyu/soy sauce needs to simmer over a low flame for five minutes. Sea salt needs to simmer for 10 minutes or longer over a low flame. When the sea salt from these seasonings are properly blended in the broth, it not only tastes better and smoother, it is far more digestible and nourishing.

Using too much sea vegetable in soup:

Follow the recipe guidelines for wakame/kombu use in soup (below). Keep in mind that soup is seasoned with miso, shoyu/soy sauce or sea salt, not by the sea vegetable. A graceful leaf or two of wakame or a small piece of kombu floating in the bowl is the appropriate amount. On average, about ½- to 1-inch piece of dry wakame or ⅛- to ¼-inch piece of kombu per cup of miso is appropriate.

Overuse of sea vegetables in general:

Sea vegetables are a delicious part of natural foods diet. Not only do they supply important minerals, including iodine and complex sodium, they help to clean our blood, cells and tissues, keeping them strong and flexible. If we overeat them, we may become quite the opposite, however; stiff, inflexible, tired, and craving oily foods, or sweets. Please follow recipe suggestions and enjoy moderate amounts throughout the day and week. Just a note: when cooking rice with kombu we generally use almost a 1-inch square (U.S. postage stamp size) dry piece instead of sea salt to mineralize the rice.

Too many condiments or pickles:

Condiments are the spark plugs of macrobiotic eating. They supply vitamins and minerals, while improving the taste and digestibility of grains and vegetables. They should enhance, not overpower, the dish on which you sprinkle them. ¼ to 1 level teaspoon of condiment once or twice a day is an appropriate amount for most people. Some may need a bit more, many will do better to take a bit less. Consult an experienced macrobiotic teacher for guidance in other areas. Also, through studying cooking and through private counseling you can learn which condiments are the best for you to emphasize. In order to get the most benefit out of condiments, use just enough in a meal to taste it in several mouthfuls; rather than creating unidentifiable mounds by burying your food in a salty power, keep in mind that you should be able to fully see the food beneath the condiment. The same goes for pickles; a little goes a long way. The average consumption is one tablespoon per day. You may eat them with or following any meal. They are not the most ideal snack, as they may make you hungrier, thirstier, or crave sweets. Also, please remember to rinse or soak them well in cold water (including store bought pickles) before eating. This will remove any strong salty taste.

Using shoyu/soy sauce at the table:

Shoyu/soy sauce, while available as a table condiment in Japanese and Chinese restaurants, is really designed for use in cooking. Only when it is well blended into food over a low flame does the best, sweetest taste result and is proper digestibility assured. Pouring it on rice, noodles, beans, or other foods like popcorn, toasted nuts or seeds can make us feel stiff, irritable, thirsty and crave sweets.

Using the leftover water from cooking noodles/pasta:

This practice can make us feel tight, experience water retention and other symptoms of excess salt consumption. Discard noodle cooking water while healing and thoroughly rinse off noodles/pastas after cooking as these are usually made with salt.

Using miso as a spread like jam on bread or rice cakes:

Use miso only in cooking and only in modest amounts. While it is delicious right out of the container it is not easily absorbed by the body and is generally too salty for this type of use.

Adding salty condiments to already salty foods:

Snacking on salty umeboshi plums, adding condiments to already well-seasoned soups, and generally overdoing it is hard on the system. If you find yourself consistently craving a salty taste, please contact a qualified macrobiotic teacher for assistance in distinguishing what imbalance could be causing such cravings.

How to Handle Sugar Cravings:

1. Reduce your salt intake & animal foods
2. Eat more frequently throughout the day
3. Do not eat for two to three hours prior to sleep
4. Control your food volume
5. Exercise moderately, but consistently
6. Don't eat when upset
7. Eat a variety of good foods to balance your nutritional profile

---

Guidelines for mild to average use of sea salt, seasoning, condiments and sea vegetables:

Miso for soup:
⅛ to 1 level teaspoon per cup of broth, simmer in broth for 3 to 4 minutes

Shoyu/soy sauce for soup:
¼ to ¾ teaspoon per cup of broth, simmer in broth for 5 to 7 minutes

Sea salt for soup:
⅛ teaspoon per 2 cups liquid, simmer for at least 7 to 10 minutes

Umeboshi vinegar for soup:
½ level teaspoon per cup of soup, simmer in broth 5 to 7 minutes

Dry wakame sea vegetables for miso soup:
1 square inch per cup of soup stock

Kombu sea vegetable for soup:
1 ½-inch square per cup of water

Sea salt for beans:
¼ to ⅛ teaspoon per cup of dry beans, ¼ teaspoon per cup of black soybeans

Shoyu/soy sauce for beans:
1 ½ teaspoons per cup of dry beans (if used instead of sea salt)

Miso for beans:
1 ¼ teaspoon per cup of dry beans (if used instead of sea salt)

Sea salt for rice:
1 pinch (using thumb and index finger) per full cup of dry rice
(3 pinches equal about ¼ teaspoon)

Kombu sea vegetable for rice:
1 square inch dry kombu per cup of dry rice (for use instead of sea salt)

Sea salt when making pressed salad:
1 teaspoon per 2 cups of chopped, packed vegetables (rinse very well after pressing)

Umeboshi vinegar when making pressed salad:
3 teaspoons per 2 cups of chopped, packed vegetables (rinse well after pressing)

Gomashio condiment:
¼ to 1 level of teaspoon, 4 to 7 times per week

Shiso powder condiment:
⅛ to ¼ teaspoon, 3 times per week

Umeboshi plum condiment:
2 to 3 whole plums per week

Sea vegetable condiments:
Roasted sea vegetable powder — ½ level teaspoon, 2 to 5 times per week
Green nori flakes — 1 teaspoon, 3 times per week
Nori paste condiment — 2 to 3 round teaspoons, 2 times per week
Nori sheets — ½ to 1 sheet per day

Pickled condiments:
1 tablespoon per day

Usually only one kind of condiment is used every 1 or 2 days.

Organic Produce

"Organic produce is expensive!" is what I hear far too often. But when you stop to really think about it in a relative and reasonable way, you may realize organic foods don't really cost that much after all. Most fresh organic fruits and vegetables purchased in season only cost slightly more than their non-organic counterparts. Aren't we worth the difference? We splurge on clothes, shoes or anything else, whether or not we can afford it, and without giving it too much thought. Many times I have done just that, convincing myself that, "I'm worth it!" So, I am certainly worth the few extra dollars for organically-grown produce. Not only am I worth it, but also I am choosing organic for the benefit of the planet.

I also hear people say, "But even if it says organic on the label, is it really organic?" Certainly there is nothing that is purely 100% organic, since the soil and air are continuous, connected to neighboring farms which may not be organic, and so on. But is this a real reason for not buying organic, or is it just an excuse? I recommend shopping at a local farmers' market that features fresh, locally- and organically-grown foods at a reasonable price.

Pure Water

Not until I experienced fresh spring water in North Fork, California, where our macrobiotic retreat is located, did I realize how the quality of water is so vitally important. When we are in North Fork, not only does our food and tea taste much better, but our skin and hair is especially soft and shiny. Water is absorbed from the foods we cook and eat, as well as through our skin. Most city tap water contains chlorine, detergent residues, and trace amounts of toxins and pharmaceuticals. At our home in Santa Monica, we installed a whole-house water purification system and also at our organic vegan macrobiotic café, "seed" (www.seedkitchen.com) in Venice, California. (More information about our water purification system can be found at: www.loveericinc.com/special_en.html)

I understand that it may not be affordable to install a whole-house system, and many of us can only buy bottled water (which may not be any better than tap). However, by making an effort and doing a little research, we may be able to find an affordable way to filter water in order to avoid using toxic tap water and to be more environmentally friendly and bypass the plastic.

Supplements

I have seen many people eat poorly and take supplements regularly, but I don't really understand why. "Supplements" are meant to help or support, right? When we are not getting enough nutrients from food, we need help and support. For example, I sometimes take vitamins C and B-12, or other natural supplements while I am traveling or unable to cook, if I have too much work to do, or have visitors who want to eat out more often than I usually would. Supplements should be taken temporarily, in uncommon circumstances. Even if their sources are natural, they are processed into supplemental products that are not an adequate substitute for a good healthy diet.

MACROBIOTICS IS GREEN

In 2008, I lectured at a conference called LOHAS (Lifestyles Of Health And Sustainability) that drew over four hundred people. I took the opportunity to speak about the connection between macrobiotics and green living.

The macrobiotic way is genuinely and inherently ecologically sensitive. Eating locally - and organically - grown foods and minimizing kitchen waste are some of the more obvious ways that macrobiotics honors the connection between our health and that of the planet. Additionally, macrobiotics is a life-enriching experience that cultivates awareness of our actions and honors the seasonal and cyclical changes of the Earth.

During the conference, I had a chance to talk with people who are actively involved in green living. I was surprised to learn that many attendees were not eating organically-grown or natural foods. One man in particular happened to have a cold and was complaining about feeling the drowsy side effects of conventional medication. I asked him, "Don't you think taking care of your own body is as basic as taking care of our mother Earth?" With a puzzled look he asked, "What do you mean?" "I believe our body is our temple and that we are inseparable from Earth," I replied. At that point, more people clustered around as I went on to explain that by not taking care of our bodies—by eating processed foods, living un-naturally, and using synthetic chemicals—we were essentially treating the planet in the same terrible way. We have so many problems with our beautiful Earth, and so many people are sick. By taking care of ourselves—eating and living naturally—we are also taking care of the planet and truly embracing the change this world so desperately needs. We can't change Los Angeles' air overnight, but we can change *what* we eat and

how we eat at our very next meal. Even if we only do so in tiny incremental steps, we are embracing positive change. Most of us eat several times a day, so the importance of our decisions and the opportunity to choose the right foods are magnified. Some people might choose to start simply by avoiding processed, sugary, and artificially-colored junk foods, and begin to build a better world from there. Eating natural foods is so powerful because we quickly start to feel better, our mind becomes clear, and we notice that we don't get sick as frequently.

By this time, the group's eyes were wide open with amazement. One woman said, "Wow, I never thought about it that way before, but it makes sense! Our body is like the Earth and if we want to change our food choices, we really can start right away." I was happy to speak at the conference and to have the opportunity to enlighten others about this vital connection. Living consciously and sustainably is what we need *now* and for the future.

Eric and I also embraced a green business model when we decided to open our first organic vegan macrobiotic café, "seed." We were intent on making the café as eco-friendly as possible, and we were delighted that people very quickly began to notice and appreciate our efforts. A mere three months after opening, we were chosen as one of the top 10 vegan & vegetarian restaurants in Los Angeles by Black Book:
"Seed Kitchen (Venice, CA) - Along with vegan and macrobiotic fare, this restaurant is all about ecological sustainability — no microwaves or even nonstick pans here." (See http://www.seedkitchen.com/ seed_press.html). Wow, sustainable cooking works!

Following are additional examples of what I do as part of embracing a green way of living:

I make my own compost from vegetable scraps and grow organic herbs, greens and flowers on the rooftop of our home in Santa Monica, California; I use energy efficient light bulbs and turn off the lights whenever I leave a room; I plug small appliances and electronics into a power strip and turn off the switch when not in use; I carry my own chopsticks and spoon to restaurants; I re-use scraps of paper and purchase post-consumer recycled paper as much as I can; I use clean-burning soy candles; I wear organic cotton undergarments; I created a rock garden with native Californian drought-tolerant plants instead of having a water-wasting lawn; I reserve the water I use to wash beans and grains to water my plants; I clean our home and wash our clothes with natural cleaners, detergents, and dish soap; I use truly natural skin and bodycare products; I hang my clothes outside on a line to dry when the weather is warm; I installed a water purification system in our home to avoid plastic water bottles; I carry refillable stainless steel water bottles and containers for water and food; I take off my shoes inside the house to avoid bringing in toxins from outside; I have furnished our home with reclaimed wood furniture; and our future goal is to install a solar panel for hot water and electricity!

Handmade soy wax candle with brown rice.

MY HEALING

People have often asked me to define macrobiotics in my own words. My answer changes every time they ask, because everything changes, even macrobiotics.

What Macrobiotics Means to Me

In the beginning it meant eating the proper foods, like whole grains and vegetables, in the correct balance in order to heal myself from a physical problem. Knowing what and how much I ate, how to prepare it, as well as how I ate, were very important considerations for me since I had only a rudimentary understanding to begin with. I was learning the principles of macrobiotic cooking in order to heal myself.

Later, I made the connection between what I ate and the effects it had on my body. Whenever I take medication, for instance, my liver and kidneys react and suffer; so instead, I learned to relieve my symptoms with dandelion greens, azuki beans, and kabocha squash; or a hot ginger compress, and a healing remedy drink. Additionally, I learned that macrobiotic cooking changes according to an individual's needs, as well as according to a particular counselor's advice.

I also started to notice that food in and of itself was not enough. Having knowledge of how I lived with the food I ate, as well as how I interacted with the people I met and spent time with, became part of the whole macrobiotic way of life. Having practiced macrobiotics for over fifteen years now, I have observed various people incorporating macrobiotic principles in many different and creative ways, adjusting to the capriciousness of their lives with all of the knowledge and tools inherent to the macrobiotic way. Others were not as flexible, insisting on following a rigid regimen. I don't feel I have to eat the same food at the same time every day. More importantly, I feel macrobiotics is about cultivating a kindhearted and flexible attitude toward oneself, practicing better communication with loved ones and others who seek a healthy and happy life, and learning to speak up for oneself more freely when experiencing pain or sorrow.

In essence, practicing macrobiotics and living macrobiotically is about maintaining a healthy body and elevating the mind and spirit in order to find our real destiny and to ultimately make a dream come true. A healthy body, mind and spirit starts from eating healthy, living in accordance with nature and connecting to real happiness for a peaceful world.

My Most Challenging Moments

Because I had to make some big changes in the beginning, I often felt overwhelmed and perceived every little thing as a big challenge. Eventually, I learned that I had to take it one day at a time. Other challenging moments included:

Feeling left out and alone
For me, I think feeling lonely was harder than being sick. I felt so detached from my friends, whom I so enjoyed inviting or going out with, where food was an essential part of our sharing time.

Taking too much time
Everything from cooking to shopping seemed to take so much more time. I eventually had to learn that nature also takes its time, and so must I. When I went through my detox/discharge period, time seemed to have stopped, but each minute was an indispensable part of the process.

Thinking too much
I was already feeling shocked and miserable from being sick, and on top of that, I didn't know how I would be able to survive from day to day. What was I going to do next? How was I going to pay the bills? What was I going to tell my boss? Excessively thinking about my not knowing what to do started to consume my mind, and all that thinking didn't seem to get me any closer to a resolution.

Financial fear
Learning macrobiotics was not convenient when I started out, since everything was not easily accessible and it cost more money. Also, macrobiotic classes and counseling were not covered by my medical insurance.

Lack of support
There was no one around me who knew about macrobiotics, and again I felt hugely disconnected from the world.

SURVIVING & THRIVING

Eventually, I was able to deal with these challenges one by one, and they no longer became challenges. Here are my tips on surviving and thriving in the face of adversity:

Look at the Big Picture

Macrobiotic food is about something greater than the sum of its parts; it is also about the energy that flows from it. Macrobiotics is the practice of eating healthy and living in harmony. Take a moment to consider what this means to you. There are so many things I learned and experienced throughout my healing process. I now realize how very important and meaningful every aspect of that process was, and to actually be here now. My healing, however, is not over. I am continuously healing myself, and the process is happening even as I write this cookbook. I am happy to see myself for who I really am, whether I am up or down, and I am finally able to love myself – which has proven to be a critical component of my healing journey.

Awareness and Acceptance

I was feeling weak and tired before I became really sick, but for a long time I was not aware of my body sending messages. I was too busy doing things and not taking the responsibility of caring for my body. I was more worried about not making enough money to pay the bills, and as a result, I was not able to see the necessity to change. Not until I became really sick did I begin to change my way of thinking and lifestyle. If we do not know that we are making a mistake, how can we change? Having awareness was my first lesson. I needed awareness in order to realize that something needed changing.

The first time I met someone who was a vegetarian, I was a college student in San Francisco. I had no understanding as to why this person chose not to eat meat, and I dismissed him as an oddball. Now, when I meet new people who are into something different, I want to research it and incorporate any beneficial elements into my own life. I alone have responsibility for the body, mind and spirit that I have received. I have learned to be more aware and accepting, to want to grow, and not take for granted my humble beginnings.

Asking Myself:
What Do I Need in Order to Heal?

Many people habitually deprive themselves of improvement by saying, "I don't know what to do," "I can't do it," or "It's too difficult." They say it automatically, without truly thinking about it. I was one of those people who didn't pay attention to my words. Now, however, I know that words have vibrations and deeper meanings. Many times throughout my learning process, I caught myself uttering self-deprecating words. Of course, even now, I can experience fear, and my first impulse might be to say, "I can't;" but I also recognize that these feelings will come and go, no matter what I do. The more I pay attention to the origins of these destructive feelings, the more I come to the realization that it is only I who is clinging to them. It's as though I'm watching a show called "Fear," and I need to turn it off, but I think that I can't. It turns out, however, that I do have a choice after all, and I can switch to a show called "Happiness." I don't need to pay attention to the feelings that bring me down because in the long run, it's an exercise in futility that's not worth my time and energy.

Another pivotal learning experience happened during a 10-day Vipassana meditation course. This involved not talking, writing, reading or looking into other people's eyes, and mostly meditating during the entire course. Going deep inside means taking the time to be ourselves, to experience "being human" and to begin seeing everything as it truly is. I became aware of how my mind was so busy, constantly changing direction, and how feelings—both good and bad—were fighting for my attention. I realized how effortless it was to dwell on negative feelings. Even though I instinctively knew I needed to eat organically grown natural food instead of junk food, and that living naturally is better than chemically, when I was younger I was not thinking about consequences or contemplating my mission in this lifetime. I was too busy deciding which boyfriend I should have, or where my next thrill would come from. Eventually I got sick, and I needed to learn about life and macrobiotics by talking to someone, reading and taking classes. I don't know how you are going to find your way, but I know one thing: we all have only this lifetime to live and only this body to live it. You may be interested in a past life or the next life, but what about what we have right now? We need to be here in the now and take care of ourselves to the best of our ability in order to start the healing.

Cooking for Myself and/or Finding the Right Person to Cook for Me

If we really want to get well, we need to cook for ourselves. This is because we are the only ones who know what we truly need in order to heal. When I was able to cook for myself, I sincerely believed in what I was doing and in what I was eating. I also understood what our bodies are meant to receive from wholesome, natural foods. What if we don't take the time to cook for ourselves, or are unable to find the time? I have noticed that if I am always eating out or eating someone else's food, eventually I won't feel very well and I will have a sense that something isn't "quite right." If I am frequently unable to find the time to cook, I take that as a sign of how I am not taking good care of myself. It is very important to re-evaluate our lives and our priorities when we say we are "too busy," unable to cook and eat our own food at home.

I have noticed that people who cook for themselves heal and recover much faster than those who don't. When we are sick, who wants to get well more than anybody else? Who better to know our pain than ourselves? Now, if we are not physically able to cook for ourselves, we need to find the right person to cook for us. The natural foods movement is expanding, and more and more people are available to cook for others. However, macrobiotics is not just about what we are eating, but also about the energy we get from our food, as well as the energy we get from the person who is cooking it for us.

Getting (or Creating) Support

Human beings are not solitary creatures, and we can't really do much alone. We need to ask for help and learn to be patient, because the help we get may not be exactly what we are expecting. However, we must learn to receive whatever assistance we can get when we are sick and helpless.

When we claim to be independent, it is a frame of mind, not a literal reality. For example, I am sitting here and writing this now, but I bought the chair and the desk that was made by somebody else. Even if I could make them myself, I probably would want to depend on others. We need other people. The most important are family, friends, and others who understand and support us. If you are not getting support from your family and/or friends, find a support group, or contact a macrobiotic school. The Internet allows us to find anything anytime. Go to a library or an Internet café (unfortunately there are no macrobiotic Internet cafés… yet!) If you can't find a support group, make one yourself. Invite a friend or neighbor who is interested in healthy cooking, or maybe host a potluck. Exchange information and thoughts of the upsides and/or downsides (yin & yang), and see how it grows. I am planning to start my own support group called "Ruška," in memory of my best macrobiotic friend. I hope by the time this book is published, the group will be active.

When I first started macrobiotics, none of my friends knew the first thing about it, and they were nervous and apprehensive about what they were going to eat at our house. Slowly, but surely, however, their attitudes changed as they tasted and loved our food, and their interest grew. I remember a time when Eric and I made tofu French toast at a camp we used to frequent. People gathered around because of the delightful smell, and those who tasted it couldn't believe how delicious it was. I felt at that time, and still do, that being an inspiration to other people is one of macrobiotics' precious discoveries and perks in this fascinating adventure of life.

Knowing and Treating Side Effects

Practicing macrobiotics is not about ignoring modern western medicine. In my case, modern medicine did not play a significant part in my recovery from cancer, but modern medicine did bring me back to life and helped to control pain after my near-fatal car accident. What I learned from being a macrobian (person practicing macrobiotics) is that finding out what the side effects are, and preparing for them, can be very helpful.

Recently, I needed to use some over-the-counter pain medications and antibiotics. Six years after my car accident, I found out that I had sustained a cracked tooth. The tooth eventually became infected and I experienced tremendous pain. I tried a few herbal remedies, but experienced no relief, so I moved on to homeopathic medicine. The homeopathy worked for about two weeks, but the infection was very deep, and the more I took the liquid remedy, the more my tongue and mouth burned. I made an appointment for a root canal, but a few days prior, at three o'clock in the morning, I had to make an emergency trip to my dentist. I also had to ask my husband to go to a 24-hour pharmacy to pick up something to ease my pain. I was madly in pain, and the entire left side of my face was very swollen. I took the medication and was able to sleep for a few hours. After three nights of little to no sleep, this was indeed a welcome relief. Not being able to eat much for a while, in addition to taking the pain medication, amounted to an upset stomach and mild diarrhea. Of course, the dentist prescribed antibiotics. I asked him how long I would have to take it, how it would help me, and what the side effects were. I knew I had to take the medication for at least one week, so I set my mind to it, told myself that this will be part of the healing equation, but certainly not the end in itself. The antibiotics were healing my infected tooth, but not without severely intensifying my stomach discomfort, and I also developed an ear infection. To combat these side effects, I took a probiotic for my stomach and used a ginger-sesame oil remedy for my ear. Still, I was grateful that something was given to me to jump-start the healing process, even if it came at a price. As I healed, I nourished myself with very simple foods like miso soup and porridge. Shortly after surviving this ordeal, I went on a macrobiotic cruise to teach classes and had a wonderful time with many people. "Thank you" to the people who made the medicine, and to the doctor who put an end to my pain, which allowed me to move on to bigger and better things!

"Just Do It!"

Whatever we may learn, the key is to actually apply it to our own life. If we don't act on it, eventually we forget, and then we may never know what it really feels like. I'm not one for ad slogans, but Nike's "Just do it!" is an exception. We humans are very adept at making excuses and coming up with various reasons to put off or not do many beneficial things. We also tend to make assumptions and place limitations on ourselves. There are many books about meditation, but if you don't actually practice sitting and meditating, you will never reap the rewards. You may want to play music, or learn to swim, but if you never actually set your mind and body in motion, you'll never know what you're missing. With macrobiotics, you can start by talking to people, reading about it, or taking classes, and see where it leads from there. We really need to experience something with our own senses and bodies and just do it for ourselves.

Rest Therapy

On the flip side of "doing" is the simple act of not doing, and knowing when it's appropriate to balance the two out. As I was finishing this cookbook I had a major detox episode ("discharging" in macrobiotics). It was the first major detox I had experienced in ten years. It started with swelling in my right ear and a fever of 102° F. This lasted about three days, and then the swelling moved to the right side of my face, over the temples, then to the forehead and cheek bones, and finally to my eye. It took many days to heal completely.

What caused this to happen? When I eat something that is not agreeable to my body it shows up as fever, rash, sore throat, aches, and swelling. I also had been working very hard, perhaps too hard. People invariably ask me why I eat so well and take care of myself, yet my body is so sensitive and weak. In contrast, they claim that they can eat anything and don't get sick. Illnesses and their symptoms are a manifestation of the body's detoxing process, which is not necessarily a sign of being weak or prone to illness. I try to explain by using the "bucket of clear water" analogy. If your body is like a bucket of clear water, even one drop of ink will show on the surface. If your body is a bucket of dirty water, a drop of ink will not show. My body is constantly adjusting to the choices I made in my lifestyle and diet before macrobiotics, as well as those I make, whether intentional or not, after macrobiotics.

How did I heal myself? I utilized all of the macrobiotic remedies I had learned, including applying a tofu plaster and ginger compress on the swollen areas, and drinking azuki tea and ume sho kuzu to soothe my kidneys. At first my high fever kept me from eating, so I had a little watermelon at room temperature, but I was practically semi-fasting for a few days, just drinking whatever I could taste — water with lemon juice, then kukicha with lemon juice and rice syrup, azuki tea, and dandelion tea. Later, I started on a mild and simple healing diet.

The best and perhaps most underrated remedy, however, was "rest," or what some might call "vegging." I am a workaholic. When I felt better I worked on my computer in bed, but I made a conscious effort to rest without working, even for a few minutes here and there. I watched movies, the Olympics in Beijing, Martha Stewart, Oprah, or just looked outside my window, taking in the sky and cloud formations and earth movements, like an ever-changing canvas. Many people get tired but feel they cannot afford to stop doing everything they feel they must do. Some take

drugs or stimulants to keep going. Or they may go see a doctor to try to "fix" their tiredness. What may be a natural and appropriate reaction in our body cycle is treated as a "condition" that should be suppressed or overwritten. We have just enough time to do what we are supposed to do in our lifetime, but without honoring the need for proper rest and relaxation, we may inadvertently cut that time short.

PRINCIPLES & PRACTICALITY

As I have practiced and lived a macrobiotic way of life, I truly feel we are intended to live in a most natural way. Unfortunately, however, our modern lives are everything but natural. The resulting inconvenience of living in a more natural way discourages many people from living macrobiotically because they believe it's just too difficult to apply to their own lives. I know from my own experience that no matter how good living macrobiotically is, if it's not practical and adoptable, it's not a useful philosophy and lifestyle to circulate out into the world. Principles are important, but if they are not practical for many people to learn and apply to their own lives, it just becomes information that's not applicable to a vital and doable way of living.

Eric and I apply macrobiotics to our lives as much as we can, but our efforts are in no way perfect. Perfection is not our goal—practicality is. A state of perfection is an idealistic and unattainable goal. Macrobiotics is, after all, about finding balance; so with this in mind, we have learned to apply macrobiotic principles to our lives while simultaneously embracing practicality as much as possible. We simply do our best, as often as we can, and accept the final results; and this has become the practicing mantra for our lives.

Basic principles are very important, especially during the beginning stages of learning something new. At the same time, however, I personally feel that basic principles also need to be practical so that we can adapt them to our modern contemporary lives. I have observed many macrobiotic teachers and practitioners who faithfully practiced the principles, yet they were unable to adapt them to contemporary life. As a result, they were not able to live freely and without excessive struggle. Just as important as the basic principles are themselves, adaptability is equally important. My belief is that principles must sometimes change, just as anything else in life changes.

Awareness and Consciousness

Most people are not even aware of their sickness, and are not able to change their lives consciously. I was once just like that. When I was diagnosed with cancer, I didn't want to change my life much until I was so sick that I could barely move. Awareness is the first step towards living a natural life. By cultivating awareness we can then move towards change, by way of learning and practicing a more conscious way of living. In the early stages of my sickness, I wanted to know what I was putting in my mouth and applying to my body and mind, but I was not conscious enough to understand and know the effects of medication, junk food or unpurified water. Now I am aware of many things and live a more richly conscious life. When I know there is no purified water available, but I'm thirsty, I simply remedy the water (by boiling the water, adding a touch of sea salt or a flower essence rescue remedy). The ways in which we can adapt are not difficult things to do if we are aware. However, if we are not aware of the possibility of change, the results can be harmful.

Smile and Have Fun

Do you take things too seriously sometimes, forgetting to have fun and smile? I did, and sometimes, I still do! When I first got really sick, I focused too much on my sickness, my pain and suffering. I found myself dwelling on my illness and endlessly asking the unanswerable. Why did I get sick? Why me? I was unable to let go of anything until I changed my point of focus

261

towards something I could enjoy, and to finally see a different view. I remembered that I liked art since I was a child, but I never thought I was good enough or had the time to pursue it. When I was diagnosed with cancer, however, I really wanted to get well, and I knew I had to change my ways and preconceptions, so I decided to enroll in an art class. Through the simple act of not thinking about my sickness, and just drawing and coloring, I learned to have fun and to start smiling again. I believe this transformation is possible for everyone and that it's just a matter of doing something... anything. It could be watching a fun movie, reading a funny story, writing down your thoughts in a journal, or listening to uplifting music. If you like animals, it could be playing with dogs or cats, or simply closing your eyes and remembering all the fun times you've had. Most of us have had some fun times, even if it might have only happened once in our lives. Our mind is so powerful that we can imagine having a fun time and experience positive physiological changes. This is our one life to live, so it's totally up to us how we choose to think and how we choose to live it. Let's have fun and remember to smile; good things are coming. Actually, good things are already here. We need only to look right in front of us in order to see them. When you find yourself in an especially challenging situation, this is the best time for us to be, to smile and to remember!

"Thank You" Therapy

A friend once told me that just saying "arigatou" (thank you) will help me to heal myself. I could say "arigatou" about 3500 times in an hour! My friend also said it is obviously better to say it when you mean it, with gratitude, but it is not humanly possible to feel gratitude when you are suffering. So what do I do? When I feel lousy, I say "arigatou" anyway. Sometimes I repeat the words to the tune of "Santa Claus is coming to town" or another catchy melody. Words have vibrations that are recognized in the Universe, and they possess a power to heal. This very simple method appealed to me, so I have made it my mantra.

The possibilities are endless. Because of residual issues related to my car accident, I am usually not able to walk for more than 15 minutes at a time. If I do, I pay the price later with tremendous pain in my legs, and my feet become numb. On July 4, 2006, I was able to walk in the Mount Shasta area for almost one hour. By chanting the word "arigatou," I was able to walk much longer and farther than I ever had since the accident — without pain.

Whether or not you believe in the power of "thank you therapy," there certainly is no harm in trying. Whenever I encounter people who claim that they can't change their food choices, or that they can't change their life, I tell them, "Just start saying 'thank you,' and soon you'll see how things change!" It's so simple that anyone can do it, and yet its effects are so profound. When I am going through a challenging time, when I am feeling sad, when I have anxiety and when I am in pain, I just say the word. Then, sooner or later, I no longer feel as though I must linger in difficult situations.

My sad feelings have lifted, my anxiety is gone, and my pain has eased. Since I have been doing this for quite some time now, I am able to do it with a smile and find that I am able to have fun in the process. I can choose to say "thank you," no matter what, and I can choose to be happy, no matter what, for the benefit of myself, as well as everyone around me.

Wise Choices

At the beginning of my healing journey, I needed to eat macrobiotic food. Now, however, the reason for me to eat and live macrobiotically is not because I need to — it's because I want to. I choose to live this way. When I was not eating by choice, I felt as though I was losing my freedom to eat and live by my own will; but when I am eating by choice, then I create free expression of the truth of who I am and feel powerful enough to do all kinds of things, even achieving my dreams. Exercising one's choice is very powerful stuff!

Life is about choices. We make choices everyday and at every moment. Whether it's about where we live, what kind of food we eat, what material of clothes we wear, what kind of soap we use... so many choices! We are truly fortunate to have so many choices. If we are not making wise choices now, however, we may not have a choice later. Not only are we going to destroy our own health, we risk destroying our only home — our beautiful Earth. The benefits of making wise choices are tremendously broad and all encompassing; this positive energy resonates with the health of our body, the power of our mind, the radiance of our spirit, and by virtue of our interconnectedness, the vibrancy of our mother Earth. Let's start making wise choices today by cooking macrobiotic food and living macrobiotically for the benefit of all.

Flexibility and Adaptability

When I see a healthy baby trying to get up and walk for the first time, I'm always struck by how flexible and adaptable they are. They may fall, but they bounce right back up and try it again. They exercise a strong determination and willingness to try anything in order to adapt and learn how to stand, and eventually how to walk. These babies demonstrate amazing powers of courage and flexibility, and yet, in watching them I don't find myself getting discouraged. Flexibility and adaptability means having an open mind; essentially, being okay with anything that comes our way. As we grow older, however, we may find that we are attached to old ideas and routines that no longer serve us. There is a social stigma and seemingly ubiquitous negativity attached to the process of growing older, and this may feed distorted perceptions of ourselves, which in turn makes it difficult for us to even consider that we have the capacity to be flexible and adaptable people. Being flexible and adaptable in our thinking and being is an important consideration for many people now. Even macrobiotic people need to consider these ideas since we began our practice initially needing to change the way we lived; and now, we may need to continually adjust to a more practical way of macrobiotic living.

Change Your Clothes!

I often hear people say, "We eat macrobiotic food — brown rice, azuki beans and squash — but it's always the same old thing." To this I reply, "Change your clothes!"

Huh? Allow me to explain. Sometimes we become too attached to an old, narrow, or no longer useful eating pattern, including those of us who have gotten well by eating macrobiotic food, but continue to eat the same things. I like to compare our eating patterns to "changing our clothes." We change our clothes daily according to the weather, where we're going and what we're going to do. We also wear the same clothes, but in different combinations. When we wear a different variety of clothes we feel refreshed and revitalized. Otherwise we find ourselves in a rut. To say, "I have to eat this way," points to part of the problem, as the words "have to" are not really macrobiotic. While I was getting my health back on course, I needed to learn to eat in a way that honors the "universal order," or eating in a way that is in harmony with nature. This involved following a more strict approach, with lots of rules and repetition in order for me to learn the basics. After I learned to do so, however, I then needed to trust and nurture my intuition so that I could create my own universal order, and to cook according to my condition, as well as according to the current weather, season and environment. This is analogous to playing music. In order to learn how to play an instrument well, we first need to practice the basics, which can involve tedious and boring repetition of the musical scales. Once we master our instrument, however, we can then play whatever music may strike our fancy, even composing our own! Another example of this concept happened during my experience in massage school. Initially I had to follow their course and learn their specific techniques. In order to pass their test, I had to repeat exactly what they had taught me. After I graduated from massage school, I took what I had learned and improvised my own style of massage that honored what I believed was most appropriate for the people I worked with. Learn well, take what you've learned, and "change your clothes" by infusing your new skills and knowledge with fresh energy and make it your own.

Universal Foods

This book may be focused on food preparation, but there are equally important "universal foods," besides the foods that we eat. Food is energy, and there are many other forms of energy: Air, light/sun, sky, water/rain, color, sound, breath, vibration, wind, moons and stars, human communication, touch and words, and contact with other animals and nature — all equally and vitally important. So if you find yourself struggling to change your food choices from conventional to natural and organic, remember that these universal foods also may help you on your own personal healing journey. During your transition to a new way of eating, please remember to look at the sky, appreciate the sun that shines for us no matter what, or feel your own breath flowing in and out, feel your heartbeat, and enjoy this moment. That's right... this moment!

Shindo fuji 身土不二
   shin = human
   do = soil/earth
   fu = not separate
   ji = two
   Humans and the Earth are one.

身土不二とは、
「人と土は一体である。」
「人の命と健康は、
食べもので支えられ、
食べものは土が育てる。
人の命と健康は
その土と共にある。」
という捉え方です。

Ichimotu zentai 一物全体
   Whole food

WHAT ELSE HELPED ME?

Have faith in and believe in yourself.

When I go through very challenging times, I need to be by myself. I am not able to function well with other people when I have not sorted out my own feelings and taken care of myself first. I did not know this for a long time, and I put myself, and others, through suffering and stress, as a way of codependency. I am who I am, and I need to be with me and learn to have faith within myself. This may sound confusing since I had initially pointed out that we need to be open to receiving support from others. While this is still true, at the same time, we really need to understand ourselves and have faith in ourselves before asking others for help.

Understand that everything changes, every day.

Are we really aware and live as though we will never have the same day and same moment again? When I know that every moment goes by and every day changes, I live more consciously and try not to miss a thing. For example, we expanded and remodeled our bedroom window. I love the space so much that it has since become my very own personal sanctuary, my favorite space where I wrote this book. I look out every day at the plum tree that I planted 20 years ago. I distinctly remember that it was winter, and there was nothing on the tree; and as the weather got warmer, it started to have buds, and soon, it started to bloom. The flower petals slowly opened, and gradually the whole tree became a big white bouquet. The branches swayed in the wind, and the petals scattered like the first snow of the season. Its beauty is fleeting, as the scene is constantly changing. Soon all the flower petals

will fall, the tree will begin to bear fruit, and we will enjoy eating them and making jam. Watching the natural cycles of this plum tree reminds me that nothing in this world stays the same. While embracing each change, I would like to apply myself to live each passing day as the first—as well as possibly the last—day of my life.

Do what you can do and know what you can't.

I can't change the smog in Los Angeles today, but I can change what I eat right now. Changing what I eat is something I can change right away, and it is so powerful. When I find out there are things we can't do at the moment, and we need to wait for the right time, it's not easy to accept, but at the same time I am relieved. I used to think that if only I tried hard enough, I should be able to do anything. I put pressure on myself instead of realizing that everything has its proper moment. I believe we need to take responsibility for ourselves and do our homework, which is to find out what we truly want in our life and in the universe. We can do this by researching and obtaining information, and practicing the goodness of what we've learned. Sometimes things don't go smoothly, no matter how prepared we are, and we need to accept things we can't have or change right now. We can prioritize and find other things to do and change. In order for me to balance all of my needs, desires, and pressures, I need to take care of myself physically, mentally and spiritually. This three-way balance is achieved by eating macrobiotic foods, practicing meditation, as well as receiving and giving, good energy as often as possible. Take challenging incidents as they are, one step at a time, and practice what you've learned at your own speed.

Don't react.

When things don't go well, it is hard for me not to react reflexively and take everything personally. Deep down, however, I know that I did not create this universe and I am not to blame when things don't turn out well. When I react, usually things get worse, and this makes everyone involved uncomfortable. I have reacted too many times and have regretted doing so each and every time. When I was in the hospital after my near-fatal car accident, I thought I felt I had very little time left to live, and yet I felt calm. As morose as that may sound, each day should be lived that way. During that period, I was acutely aware of the aspects of life where we have no control, and I finally realized it was time to put my life in the hands of others and accept things as they were.

Remember that you have a choice.

We are faced with so many choices to make these days. Should I go out to a party, or stay home and read that book I've been meaning to read? Should I start thinking about eating healthy foods, or just eat anything fast and easy? Should I hug my husband and tell him I love him, or tell him what he forgot on our list of things to do? I am eating macrobiotics because I want to, not because I have to. This is a big difference. I believe that 30- to 40-percent of what we are is the food we eat, and we can choose from a vast array of products, diets and information nowadays. The rest is up to you, and I truly hope that how I choose to live will also help you.

HEALING CHECKLIST

I find it helpful to write in journals and to make lists. Here are a few examples of foods and healing work that I've written in my daily journals:

1. **Wake-up**
   Have a remedy drink & external remedy (if I need one). Having a remedy drink is akin to how others drink coffee in the morning.

2. **Breakfast**
   Have an uplifting breakfast of whole grains, soup, greens (some pickles), and drink (only if I'm thirsty).

3. **Mid-morning snack/drink**
   If I am hungry I'll eat a wholesome snack instead of pastries or donuts.

4. **Lunch**
   Have an energizing lunch of whole grains, side dishes, (some pickles) and drink (only if I'm thirsty).

5. **Afternoon remedy drink or snack**
   If I need one, a mid-afternoon snack helps me take a break and relax, but not crash.

6. **Dinner**
   Have a thoughtful, relaxed dinner of whole grains, soup, beans, vegetables/greens, sea vegetables, and drink (only if I'm thirsty).

7. **Desserts (optional)**
   Desserts are a precious treat, but keeping a record is good to track how much I eat, as well as when I should or shouldn't eat them (depending on my condition).

8. **Sit down and chew well**
   Sitting down and eating in a relaxed state is often forgotten in our busy life. It is a simple act, but it has changed me in profound ways, as I take my time and enjoy eating smaller portions.

9. **Check bowel movements (time/day)**
   Bowel movements are an important barometer of our health. I check for changes in color and odor, and I make a point of understanding the connections between my body and what I ate.

10. **Night remedy drink**
    This is an emergency drink that I may need after I've dined out and the food did not agree with my body. Night external remedy: when I go to sleep I use a hot water bottle (see Yutampo section on page 272) over my kidney or around my feet, especially in the winter season, and this helps me to sleep better.

11. **Check how I feel after waking up in the morning**
    Mentally/physically/spiritually.

12. **Check how I feel throughout the day**
    Mentally/physically/spiritually.

13. **Check what time I go to bed and what time I get up**
    I use my sleeping/waking patterns as a barometer of how I restore my energy.

14. **Hours of sleep**
    Sleeping a good amount of hours is a source of energy, but sleeping too much is not necessary for the body.

15. **Sleep quality**

I grade the quality in terms of poor/fair/good/dreaming and use this information as an indication of my health.

16. **Stressful incidents**

Even a good diet and a natural lifestyle do not make us immune to stressful situations. Having awareness and seeing these events and stimuli as they are helped me accept that nothing stays the same.

17. **Appreciation**

Finding something every moment of every day to appreciate in life is essential.

18. **Exercise**

Daily incorporation of Do-in exercise, yoga, or a walk outside for 30 minutes is vital. I don't need to do extreme sports, but making sure my body is flexible with daily stretches and going for walks are all it takes for me to feel good and happy.

19. **Meditation**

Most of us are accustomed to doing so much all the time, and I finally came to a point in my life where I just wanted to simply "be." This sounds easy, but it's one of the hardest things to achieve in daily life — to be able to sit and simply be.

20. **Body scrub**

After taking a bath or shower, scrub your body with a warm washcloth or a natural brush. This is an excellent way to activate your blood circulation and cleanse your skin. It also feels so refreshing and invigorating!

21. **Healing massage/shiatsu**

Massage/shiatsu stimulates the body's self-healing, but finding the right massage/shiatsu therapist is not easy. Receiving massage at least once a month is highly recommended.

22. **Time for myself**

Taking a bath, massaging my feet in the tub, and receiving a massage are truly bonding moments I take for myself and my body; and these are some of my most relaxing moments, next to meditation.

23. **Plants and water**

Having green plants in the house and workplace, and having a natural water filtration system to cook, brush my teeth and take my shower/bath, are essential!

24. **Breathe deeply and stay in touch with nature**

When I wake in the morning I take a moment to feel my breathing. I catch the light from the rising sun, and at dusk I linger by the sunset, marvel at the sky, the changing moon, and count the stars. I watch how the trees are moving and growing.

25. **Sing a happy song**

Because I am tone deaf, I just hum a tune, read books, or watch movies that entertain or inspire me, or simply make me laugh out loud. These are some of the best medicines.

NATURAL BODYCARE

Shortly after I started practicing macrobiotics, somebody asked me, "I don't know much about macrobiotics, but you care so much about what you eat, so what about what you use for your skin? Your face and lips? Maybe that lipstick you are using has chemicals in it? It's on your lips so aren't you 'eating' it too?"

It was kind of shocking to hear these questions, and especially from someone who didn't even know anything about macrobiotics! I got defensive and even a little upset, but this person made me realize that it's not just the food that I eat that can help me or hurt me. I quickly turned the realization into a fact-searching mission to find out just what was in my skin care, shampoo and soap, and what kinds of effects these ingredients have. I found out some pretty awful things. The most commonly used cosmetics and skin and bodycare products contained ingredients that pollute the Earth and cause…. cancer.

I read about conventional shampoo and conditioning products containing so many toxic chemicals that women have given birth to babies that smelled like shampoo. (And this resonated with other information I encountered about a connection between the uterus and the head.) I also discovered that so-called "natural" bodycare products may not be so natural after all. Currently, there is very little regulation of the words "natural" or "organic," especially in

bodycare products. Unfortunately this means we need to do a little homework. Just like for the foods we choose, we need to carefully read the labels of our bodycare products, ask ourselves some questions and do a little research. Which products contain truly natural ingredients? What percentage of these ingredients are truly organic? Which companies use 100% (or almost 100%) certified-organic ingredients in their products? When we combine the use of truly natural and organic bodycare products with the practice of eating natural and organic plant-based foods, we are likely to stay young for a long time, looking good and feeling happy knowing that we are doing the right thing for ourselves and for the planet.

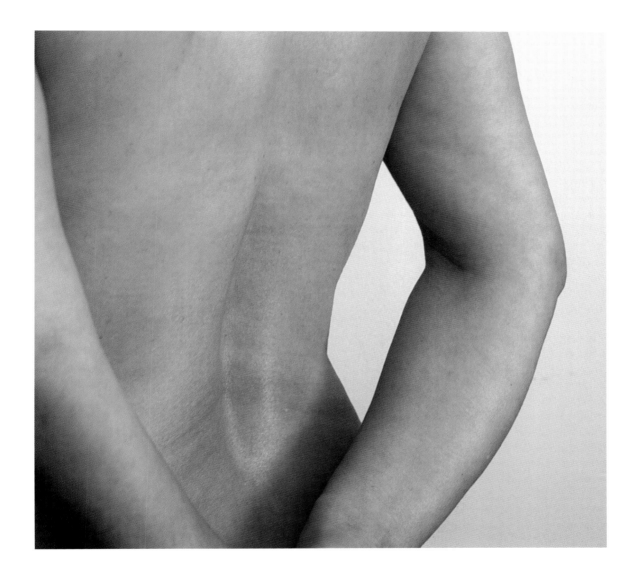

HYDROTHERAPY AND OTHER HEALING REMEDIES

Yutampo, Hot Baths & Compress

So simple and yet so powerful, hydrotherapy brought me great relief when I was healing. In addition to a good hot bath, a yutampo, or hot water bottle, can be deeply helpful.

Yutampo

When I was very ill, my kidney area felt very tense, stiff and cold, so I used a yutampo under my kidneys at night. This simple remedy had a tremendously relaxing effect on my kidneys, and this allowed me to have a much greater quality of sleep. The same held true when I suffered from menstrual cramps and had aches in my neck, back and legs.

Yutampo has come a long way, as it was used in China as early as the 9th century to heat the bed and aid sleep. I find that I feel much better using yutampo rather than electric heating pads or electric blankets. The heat generated by these devices is very drying on the skin, throat and body, and it also generates electromagnetic radiation that may be harmful. Yutampo is an ancient remedy that provides very soothing, non-drying heat. It's good old-fashioned wisdom that is enjoying a resurgence in these modern times. People interested in cutting back on their use of electricity are "rediscovering" the simplicity and warmth provided by a simple yutampo, as evidenced by the surge in even old-fashioned metal and ceramic ones, and coverings now

available in all shapes, colors and sizes, (see photo). I frequently use a yutampo for just warming myself up, especially if I'm up late working in the office. I also tuck one into my bed at night, so that when I'm ready to go to sleep, my bed is nice and toasty.

The modern yutampo made of rubber is a good choice, and I found it especially helpful to lay over when I had kidney issues. I also use a ceramic one and use the leftover water to wash my face in the morning. The water inside is still warm and it somehow feels good since it was sleeping with me! I also "recycle" the water from the yutampo by watering my plants or doing dishes.

I find that water heated on a gas stove stays warmer longer than water heated on an electric stove. Don't fill your yutampo with too much water, and try to get all the air out before securing the cap very tightly in order to prevent leakage.

In old literature, yutampo translates to "hot water wife." Must be that someone thought it was as good as holding a warm wife!

Hot bath

Soaking my body in a warm-hot bath brought me tremendous relief during my illness and allowed me to experience deeper, more restorative sleep. It is such a powerful, simple healing remedy, and yet, so many people don't ever take baths! Even now, if I have a particularly busy or stressful day, the more effort I make to be sure to take a hot bath later that day in order to thoroughly relax and take care of myself. Most of my clients complain that they feel tired after a bath, when in fact they are feeling truly relaxed, like a rubber band being unstretched. Sometimes, after a bath though, you may find it entirely appropriate to take a rest.

To enhance the experience and healing potential of a hot bath, there are a few important points to consider:

Most municipal water supplies contain chlorine and other contaminants, so installing a water filter is key.

Set the mood by lighting a naturally-scented soy candle. (Avoid paraffin candles, which emit toxic fumes.)

Instead of foaming bubble bath soaps and other commercial bathing products that contain toxic chemicals, synthetic fragrances and colorings that are harmful to your health, I add simple concoctions that come from the kitchen, instead of the drugstore:

Traditionally in Japan, taking a bath infused with pine needles in the New Year was considered auspicious and good for the spirit. It's also good for blood circulation and warming our body in the winter. For a stimulating bath, I sometimes add 1 tablespoon of freshly-squeezed ginger juice, or ½ cup of sliced ginger, to one regular-sized bath tub. To help cleanse my blood, I add a 2- by 3-inch strip of kombu (sea vegetable). Sometimes a handful of sea salt is a good addition to a bath, though this may be too strong for some people's condition. To help me sleep better and to relax my muscles, I also like to add a few drops of 100% pure essential oils, like lavender or clary sage (or a handful of the fresh herbs), though this may be too strong for some people's condition.

Slip into the hot water, breathe deeply and close your eyes. It's your own time to be with you!

Daikon hip bath

I have used a daikon hip bath to help my reproductive organ disorders and also to draw odors, excessive animal protein, fat and oil from my body. This is also a good external remedy to warm the body and to aid skin conditions. I also follow the bath with a kukicha douche.

For the bath:
3 to 5 bunches of fresh daikon leaves
    (or substitute with turnip leaves or red radish
    leaves)
1- to 1-½ gallons of water
large pot
1 cup or handful of sea salt
large towel

To prepare the ingredients for the bath, hang the fresh daikon leaves in the shade (not direct sunlight), until they become brittle and change to a brown color.

In the large pot, combine the dried daikon leaves and water over a medium-high flame. Bring to a boil, reduce the flame to medium and simmer until the water turns brown. Strain the leaves, add the sea salt and stir well to dissolve. Pour the hot liquid into a small tub or bath. Add hot water until the bath level is waist-high when sitting in the tub. Keep the temperature as hot as possible and cover your upper body with a large towel to induce perspiration. Stay in the bath for 10 to 20 minutes or until the hips become very red. Your body will get hot as sweating begins. Keep your body warm when emerging from the tub.

This bath is best and most effective just before bedtime, but at least 1 hour after eating. Repeat as needed, up to ten days.

Follow a bath with a kukicha douche which helps to eliminate excess mucus and fat in the uterine and vaginal region.

For the douche:
kukicha tea, warmed to body temperature
½ teaspoon sea salt
juice of half a lemon
douche bag

To prepare the douche, dissolve the sea salt and lemon juice in the kukicha tea and transfer to a douche bag.

Ginger compress

A ginger compress can be very helpful for dissolving tension and stimulating blood circulation and energy flow.

For the compress, you will need:
large pot
fresh ginger roots
stainless steel grater
cotton bag or cheesecloth
string
2 to 4 small towels
1 large towel
rubber gloves or long wooden cooking spoon

In the pot, heat up the water, but do not allow it to boil. While the water is heating, coarsely grate enough fresh ginger root to form a small tennis ball-sized mound. I recommend a regular stainless steel grater, rather than a ceramic one, since it's faster and you don't need the ginger to be finely grated.

When the water gets hot, reduce heat to low, and place the ginger into a cotton bag or a single layer of cheesecloth. Squeeze the bag or cheesecloth of the ginger to release the juices into the hot water. Attach a long string to the bag or cheesecloth and place bag or sack into the pot like a large tea bag. Allow it to steep in the water without boiling for about five minutes.

Keeping the pot over a low flame, dip a small towel into the ginger water. Using the gloves or wooden spoon, carefully remove and wring out the towel tightly, and apply it to the desired area

on the body. Cover area with a large dry towel to trap in the heat. Change the small towel every two to three minutes, replacing it with a fresh hot towel. Alternate towels quickly so that the skin does not cool off between applications. Continue the applications for 10 to 15 minutes, or until the area becomes pink. After applying the ginger compress, it is best to relax, sit quietly or sleep.

Special caution for applying a ginger compress: Ginger compresses are not recommended for use on babies or elderly persons, nor should it be used on the head. It should also be avoided over the abdominal area during pregnancy or appendicitis. Persons who have cancer should consult a macrobiotic counselor before applying a ginger compress.

DETOXING AND DISCHARGE

Our body is constantly discharging and detoxing from what we eat, breathe, put on our skin/hair/nails, wear, and smell, in addition to how we live, think and feel, every moment of every day. This manifests in the following ways:

A natural detox/discharge process through urine, stool, gas, sweat, hair shedding, changes in skin color/texture/quality, mucus from eyes, nose, mouth, coughing and sneezing, etc.

A secondary detox/discharge process is a sign of the body trying to adjust or send messages by way of colds, flu, fever, headache, diarrhea, and/or constipation.

A macrobiotic detox/discharge process, which can happen in different stages and manifestations:

1. When you first begin eating a natural diet, the body works hard to rid itself of toxic build-up. This may include having aches in parts of, or throughout the entire body, as well as excessive mucus, diarrhea, constipation, conditions like colds, flu and fever, skin peeling, rash, oily and/or shedding hair, eye mucus, coughing, and/or sneezing.

2. After you become accustomed to a natural diet, your body will continue to discharge as it adjusts to seasonal change. These adjustments may include mucus collecting in the lungs and sinuses, feeling tightness or muscle tension, or anything listed in the sections above.

3. Throughout the entire healing process you may experience emotional, mental and psychological detox and discharging: anger, frustration, worry, fear, anxiety, jealousy, isolation, insomnia and depression, etc.

MAGIC WORDS

1. Repeating the phrase, "I am getting better no matter what!"
2. Saying, "Thank you" to my body and my soul/ spirit.
3. To my cancer and pain I say "thank you for coming into my life. I have learned so much from you and I appreciate you, but your job is finished and I don't need you anymore."
4. Saying, "Hello" and "Goodbye," to my sickness
5. Telling myself, "I love you! You are doing so well. I appreciate you from the bottom of my heart."
6. Telling myself, "I am sorry for not taking care of you for so long. I will take care of you with the best of my ability from now on. So don't worry, let's be happy together."
7. Believing in myself, asking for help, seeing things as they are, and receiving blessings.
8. Having awareness, acceptance and determination.
9. Reminding myself that "it's all good in the end."
10. Repeating the mantra, "Follow your heart!"

LEARNING THE MACROBIOTIC WAY

These are examples of what helped me to learn the macrobiotic way:

1. Reading books to better understand what macrobiotics is all about.
2. Trying out recipes in macrobiotic cookbooks.
3. Seeking guidance from a professional macrobiotic counselor.
4. Attending macrobiotic cooking & lecture classes.
5. Seeking out and networking with the macrobiotic community.
6. Attending macrobiotic conferences.
7. Getting a therapist – to express fear, anger and frustrations.
8. Getting somebody to cook for me when I couldn't cook for myself.

The first time I read George Ohsawa's book, "Macrobiotic Guidebook for Living," about the order of the universe, I learned the "Seven Principles of the Order of the Universe." These principles helped me during my healing process:

1. All things are a differentiated apparatus of one infinity.
2. Everything changes.
3. All antagonisms are complementary.
4. There is nothing identical.
5. What has a front has a back.
6. The bigger the front, the bigger the back.
7. What has a beginning has an end.

277

PREPARING A VEGAN MACROBIOTIC KITCHEN

In order for me to start cooking in a vegan macrobiotic way, I needed to have a fully equipped vegan macrobiotic kitchen. The overhaul helped me to create delicious, healthy meals.

Before any cooking begins, it is essential to have high-quality cookware and utensils. These will help to improve the flavor and taste of food, as well as make for more nourishing and satisfying meals. Aluminum, plastic, or other synthetic materials should be avoided, as they can produce an unpleasant taste and impart synthetic or harmful compounds to your food. Natural materials, such as bamboo, ceramic, wood, earthenware, porcelain, glass and cast-iron should be the most sought-after utensils for your kitchen, as they do not interact negatively with the food. The finest quality stainless steel cookware is also an excellent second choice. Don't feel stressed out about the following list, just itemize and obtain each tool one at a time, some of which you may already have.

Apron
Hat/scarf, for your head & hair
Cheesecloth, unbleached and 100% cotton
Chopsticks, for cooking & eating
Colander
Stainless steel pots and pans, large, medium, small & extra small (for remedy drinks)
Stainless steel tea kettle & lunch box containers
Cast-iron pan, for roasting
Cast-iron (and/or stainless steel) sauté pan, with lid
Ceramic nabe pot
Cotton towels
Dish for pickles
Fine mesh strainer
Flame deflector
Gas stove
Glass jars for storage, large
Good quality knife, for cutting vegetables, & sharpening stone
Graters, flat ceramic & stainless steel
Hand food mill
Natural dish soap
Oil brush
Pickle press
Pots with heavy lids, cast-iron & stainless steel
Pressure cooker, stainless steel
Rice bowl
Rice container
Sea salt container
Serving plates, for vegetables
Shoyu sauce dispenser
Soup bowl
Suribachi & surikogi (pestle), shown at left
Sushi mat, bamboo
Steamer basket
Wooden cutting board
Wooden paddle, for turning rice/grains
Wooden spoons & spatula
Tawashi (vegetable cleaning brush)
Tea cups
Tea strainer
Trivets

THE THREE TYPES OF MACROBIOTIC FOOD

When I started macrobiotic cooking I was very sick. I learned how to cook and thrive on healing food, but the feelings of deprivation and cravings for my favorite foods — omelettes, cream gratin, crème brulee — had to be trumped by my desire to get healthy. After a year or so I was physically better, stronger, and focused on my macrobiotic path to recovery. However, brown rice every day had taken the joy and fun out of eating. I needed to graduate from healing food and work on my mental and emotional recovery.

At first, expanding my diet from healing foods to basic macrobiotic food gave me side effects such as headaches, muscle aches, and congestion. At the same time, I felt guilt and anxiety about my cancer coming back. A therapist helped me put those feelings into perspective and balance the needs of my body, mind and spirit. After many years of experience learning and evaluating this balancing act, I found a simple way to explain the process through three distinct but complementary types of macrobiotic foods.

1. Healing Macrobiotic Food is specifically prepared for the purpose of healing, recovery and treatment of different health conditions. This food is based on Basic Macrobiotic Food, but variations are prescribed or recommended for specific health conditions. It is very important to receive professional advice from a qualified counselor, complemented with private cooking classes, and if you are really sick, seek out a compatible person trained in macrobiotics to cook for you. This food helps for times of recuperating from illnesses, as well as for resting and cleansing our overworked bodies.

2. Basic Macrobiotic Food, or "standard macrobiotic food," as my teacher Michio Kushi called it, is based on whole grains, land and sea vegetables, and beans. It builds the foundation and reference point for guaging our health condition and shifting to healing and occasional foods. It is prepared at home for everyday consumption. I believe that cooking with your own hands and energy is important, as your condition is known best to yourself. Taking cooking and lecture classes is essential to learn this style of cooking.

3. Occasional / Transitional Macrobiotic Food is prepared for special occasions, such as for entertaining, parties and holidays, or consumed outside the home for work or social occasions, as well as when traveling. It is also consumed while gradually adapting and transitioning to Basic Macrobiotic Food. It is based on Basic Macrobiotic Food, but with richer, stronger tastes, with more oil, spices and seasoning. It is important to learn how to cook Basic Macrobiotic Food before expanding your repertoire to include this more "gourmet" style of cooking.

You may notice that even today's conventional foods can be similarly divided:

1. Bland and boring, but recommended while healing: chicken soup, oatmeal.

2. Basic food prepared at home often with canned, packaged, or frozen ingredients.

3. Food prepared at restaurants, fast-food joints, school cafeterias, on holidays, etc.

Further Understanding of the Three Types of Macrobiotic Food Circles

healing

These circles best represent how I ate when I was healing. The focus here is on Healing Macrobiotic Food for everyday, with occasional forays into eating from the Basic Macrobiotic Food category. Occasional food is only when you need to travel and have no choice.

basic

These circles represent the proportions of food that most healthy macrobiotic people should eat in daily life. Even if you eat Basic Macrobiotic Food regularly, you might lose balance by working too long or by experiencing relationship stress, in which case you may need to adjust by eating more Healing Macrobiotic Food. In the company of non-macrobiotic friends, you might occasionally end up eating foods that you don't usually eat. In this case, it is important to learn how to recognize better food choices wherever you go and at the very least choose foods that are more akin to a macrobiotic style, so that you can relax and enjoy yourself.

occasional

(or transitional)

These circles are representative of those transitioning their eating style from a more conventional approach to a more organic, natural and healthy way of eating. In this case you are training your palate to be more sensitive to the natural taste of whole, unadulterated and unprocessed foods. This is achieved by slowly but regularly introducing Basic Macrobiotic Food, as well as by eating Healing Food when you are not feeling well, so that you can avoid using prescription medications.

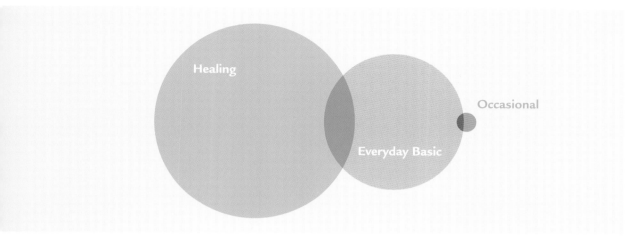

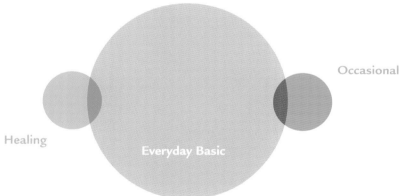

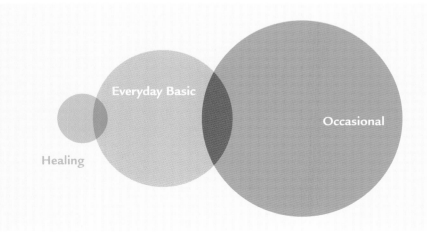

HEALING VEGAN MACROBIOTIC SHOPPING LIST

Having this shopping list helped me so much at the beginning of my macrobiotic journey (and I still use it today!)

Grains
- [ ] Brown rice (Short-grain)
- [ ] Brown rice (Long-grain)
- [ ] Sweet brown rice
- [ ] Millet
- [ ] Barley
- [ ] Pearl barley
- [ ] Quinoa
- [ ] Buckwheat
- [ ] Whole oats

Beans
- [ ] Azuki
- [ ] Black soy
- [ ] Chickpeas
- [ ] Lentils
- [ ] Navy
- [ ] Kidney
- [ ] Split pea

Noodles/Pasta
- [ ] Udon
- [ ] Soba
- [ ] Somen
- [ ] Whole wheat pasta
- [ ] Brown rice pasta

Seeds and Nuts
- [ ] Brown sesame
- [ ] Black sesame
- [ ] Pumpkin seeds
- [ ] Sunflower seeds
- [ ] Almonds
- [ ] Walnuts

Round Vegetables
- [ ] Onions
- [ ] Kabocha
- [ ] Butternut squash
- [ ] Broccoli
- [ ] Cauliflower
- [ ] Cabbage

Root Vegetables
- [ ] Carrots
- [ ] Daikon
- [ ] Lotus root
- [ ] Burdock
- [ ] Turnip
- [ ] Red radish
- [ ] Ginger
- [ ] Jinenjo
- [ ] Parsnip

Leafy Greens
- [ ] Collard
- [ ] Kale
- [ ] Bok choy
- [ ] Napa cabbage
- [ ] Dandelion greens
- [ ] Mustard greens
- [ ] Leek
- [ ] Scallions

Misc. Vegetables
- [ ] Cucumbers
- [ ] String beans
- [ ] Snap peas
- [ ] Snow peas
- [ ] Corn

Fridge Items
- [ ] Tofu
- [ ] Tempeh
- [ ] Seitan
- [ ] Mochi
- [ ] Amazake
- [ ] Rice milk

Pickles
- [ ] Sauerkraut
- [ ] Nuka pickles

Sea Vegetables
- [ ] Kombu
- [ ] Wakame
- [ ] Hijiki
- [ ] Arame
- [ ] Nori
- [ ] Agar

Dried Items
- [ ] Kuzu
- [ ] Dried shiitake
- [ ] Dried daikon

Fruit
- [ ] Apples
- [ ] Seasonal Fruit

Seasonings
- [ ] Barley miso
- [ ] White miso
- [ ] Soy sauce
- [ ] Sea salt
- [ ] Ume vinegar
- [ ] Brown rice vinegar
- [ ] Mirin

Condiments
- [ ] Umeboshi
- [ ] Ume paste
- [ ] Shiso powder
- [ ] Tekka
- [ ] Green nori flakes

Sweetener
- [ ] Brown rice syrup
- [ ] Barley malt
- [ ] Maple syrup
- [ ] Apple juice

Oils
- [ ] Sesame
- [ ] Toasted sesame
- [ ] Safflower
- [ ] Olive

Beverages
- [ ] Twig tea bags
- [ ] Twig tea (loose)
- [ ] Roasted barley tea

MACROBIOTIC DAILY FOOD CHART FOR THE TEMPERATE ZONE

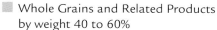 Whole Grains and Related Products
by weight 40 to 60%

Vegetables
by weight 20 to 30%

Soup
by weight 5 to 10%

Beans and Sea Vegetables
by weight 5 to 10%

Supplemental Foods
by weight 3 to 5%

*This chart is a general recommendation.
Percentages may change depending on a
person's health condition and lifestyle.
The chart, like this cookbook, adapts vegan
macrobiotic cooking, which excludes fish or
seafood.*

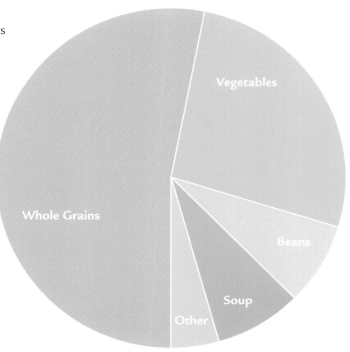

HOW TO WARM UP LEFTOVERS WITHOUT A MICROWAVE

If you are accustomed to using a microwave to warm up leftover food, and are wondering about all the trouble involved in functioning without it, I feel your pain. Before I started cooking in the macrobiotic way, I too used a microwave to warm up my food. I recall that I didn't even have the foggiest idea of where to begin warming something up without one! It's actually quite simple — just use a double boiler, and heat the food for a few minutes or so. If you don't have a double boiler, you can also make your own by setting a small ceramic bowl or container inside a large pot that has been filled with about ½ inch of purified water. Simply place your leftovers in the bowl, cover the pot and bring to boil for a few minutes.

For leftover rice, use the above methods, or try another, simpler method: Fill a pot with ¼ inch or less of water, add leftover rice to the pot and boil for a minute or so. Try not to put too much water in the pan or to boil for too long since the rice can get soggy. Leftover rice can keep in the refrigerator for a few days, so if you're busy, be sure to make a larger quantity and warm it up each time and eat as it is, or:

- Add to soups.
- Sauté with vegetables to make fried rice.
- Make sushi rolls with vegetables.
- Mix with blanched vegetables, nuts and seeds for making rice salad.
- Add with chopped vegetables and make croquettes.

FOOD & HEALING JOURNAL

I find it very useful to keep a journal of my daily food intake, sleep and exercise patterns, bowel movements, as well as my mental and spiritual states. This infomation allows me to keep track of my state of being and to discern patterns of cause and effect. I encourage you to start a journal of your own with the following information.

Date:
AM remedy drink External remedy

Breakfast:
    Whole grains
    Soup
    Greens
    Drink

Mid-morning:
    Snack
    Drink

Lunch:
    Whole grains
    Side dishes
    Drink

PM remedy drink External remedy

Dinner:
    Whole grains
    Soup
    Beans
    Greens/vegetables
    Sea vegetables
    Dessert
    Drink

Sleeping patterns:
    _____ hours of sleep
    Bed time/waking time
    Sleep quality:
        poor / fair / good / dreaming

Bowel movement:
    _____ times/day
    time / amount / color/ scent
    1.
    2.
    3.
    4.
    5.
    6.

Feeling at wake-up time   Mentally/physically/spiritually

Note throughout the day
    Mentally/physically/spiritually
    Stressful incident
    Appreciation

Exercise Meditation Body scrub Healing bodywork/massage/shiatsu
Time for myself In touch with nature

TRAVELING TIPS & STORIES

I thought it would be impossible for me to travel when I started to eat macrobiotically. I didn't have the confidence to travel by myself since I felt I would be unable to find anything to eat. I had to be well enough to travel and flexible wherever I went. With the ubiquity of junk food and fast food joints – on airplanes, trains, buses, terminals, and rest areas on highways – I really had to toughen up and be responsible for making choices with my best interests at heart.

Here is a list of items I have brought on trips:

1. My traveling food: Brown rice balls, pickles (usually umeboshi plum or red radish), and whole grain tortilla wrap sandwiches.
2. Twig tea in a thermos for car trips. Twig tea bags for air travel. (Just ask for a cup of hot water.)
3. Instant natural miso soup.
4. Instant oatmeal or other hot cereal.
5. Gomashio (sesame salt, preferably homemade).
6. Sea salt for seasoning, and to use as an oral rinse and body scrub.
7. A small amount of soy sauce (shoyu), kuzu, and nori.
8. Brown rice cakes with almond butter & brown rice syrup, for dessert.
9. Organic apples.
10. Flower remedy (liquid and cream), such as Rescue Remedy.
11. My wooden hashi (chopsticks) and spoon.
12. Organic cotton body washcloths.
13. Yutampo (see page 272).
14. Stainless steel thermos for tea and/or food.

Going to Tahiti with Brown Rice Balls

It was my first long solo trip after I started to recover from cancer. I was excited, but at the same time nervous. I made 12 brown rice balls with umeboshi plum inside, of which I ate two on the plane. As soon as I arrived in Tahiti, I put the remaining balls in an ice chest to keep them cold. Every day I took two out, waited until they reached room temperature, and ate them with vegetables and salad that I was able to purchase on the island. It was a seven-day trip and I was able to eat my brown rice balls for five days. I put nori seaweed in my salad everyday. I also made soy sauce and olive oil dressing with a touch of lemon juice. I appreciated my brown rice balls, nori and soy sauce so much.

Driving Across America: My Meal in Iowa (circa 1998)

After checking into a Motel 6 located in a small town outside of Des Moines, Iowa, I couldn't find any place to eat when I finally spotted a family-style restaurant. When I looked at the menu, I said to myself, "Oh no, there's nothing to eat," but I was hungry and saw a mushroom burger. I smiled and asked the server if the mushroom was canned or fresh, and how they prepared it. He had to go back to the kitchen and came back and told me "it's fresh and sautéed with butter," so I asked him "do you have sesame oil or olive oil?" He looked perplexed and had the "why are you asking these questions" look, but he went back again and told me they had olive oil. I felt it was my lucky night and told him "I would like to order a mushroom burger without the meat, and the mushrooms sautéed in olive oil, please." He did a double take and said to me, "can you repeat your order again?"

Of course, I said exactly the same thing. He could not believe what he heard and told me, "The price is going to be the same." So I said, "That's okay," and, "Can you hold the tomato and pickles, but put extra lettuce, please?" By then he decided that I was a freak, so it became easier for me to keep asking. The bun was dry and not fresh so I ate only half of it, but the mushrooms were very good. I had my organic soy sauce, so I used a little, and it made it taste even better. The server came back to ask if I wanted anything else. Guess what I told him! "It was great, so I would like to have the same thing once more." I am sure I made his evening interesting, and he had a story to tell his family and friends. I made sure that I left him a good tip before I headed back to the Motel 6 for a good night's sleep.

What Mistakes Did I Make at First?

What I didn't understand in the beginning was that I needed to practice macrobiotics as a whole lifestyle. If I considered macrobiotics to be simply a "diet," I would study nutrition and dietetics. Macrobiotics is the application of natural energies and common sense to cooking, as well as living. When first starting out, I felt I just had to follow a certain diet in order to avoid getting sicker. I had such a tremendous fear of dying, that I forgot that I would eventually die no matter what. I was not free from my emotional fear, sadness, and anger, which are natural feelings that can be balanced with other feelings. I was not able to feel, nor follow, my heart.

For example, I was very afraid to travel without my stainless steel pots and pans, and was afraid of not having access to a gas stove. As a result, I would carry my pans with me, even on flights. It was so stressful to travel that I often didn't feel good after the trip. Now I know that I don't need to feel that I have to make such a tremendous effort — I can adjust to the travel environment and circumstances, or choose to stay home and heal.

Another time, I was advised to eat pickles, so I made sea salt pickles and ate a lot of it. I got sick and had such a high fever at night that I was worried to death. I said to myself, "I did as my macrobiotic counselor instructed, but I got worse! Macrobiotics is not working for me!" But the truth was I forgot to ask my counselor how much I should eat. I thought if it was good for me, I could eat as much as I wanted. Taking in the excessive salt content of the pickles was too much yang or heat energy in my body, so naturally — I ran a fever.

How I Ate at Restaurants

At first I was too sick to go out and worried that I would get sicker if I did, so I didn't go out at all. Cooking for myself was not always easy when I was sick, but I learned to ask for help. I had been a very independent person, so it was not easy to ask for help. Slowly, however, I learned to accept that I am not living here alone in the universe, and that it's okay for me to ask for help. Going out to eat involved asking restaurant servers to make certain adjustments. I asked them what kind of seasoning was used in the food and if they were able to make adjustments. Some servers looked at me with disdain for asking such questions, but I really had no choice. Otherwise, I would feel sick after I came home. After a while, I found some restaurants that would accommodate such requests, and I eventually became friends with them. I greatly appreciate these people for helping me.

Examples of What I Have Asked the Restaurant Staff

1. If the "vegetarian" soups have any animal broth, because many times beef or chicken broth is used.
2. If they could replace the butter with sesame or olive oil.
3. Ask for salad without cheese.
4. Ask for pizza without cheese and tomato sauce, just vegetables.
5. If they could hold the salt or spicy seasoning.
6. Ask for vegetable sushi to be made with rice without added sugar and vinegar.
7. Ask for plain soy or rice milk (unsweetened) instead of cow's milk.
8. Ask what kind of sweetener was used in their vegan desserts.
9. Ask for water without ice.
10. Ask for vegetables to be steamed (instead of fried) even if this option is not listed on the menu.

YIN & YANG

Understanding yin and yang is key to macrobiotics. Initially, those words were very foreign to me. When actually, yin and yang are as common as day and night, men and women, right and left. They exist all around us, and we are experiencing the beauty of yin and yang in our lives all the time. As we understand yin and yang energy and learn to use these energies, we can properly prepare macrobiotic foods in order to maintain a balanced body, mind and spirit.

Everything is relative, and energy is either completed or balanced by an opposite energy. Fire is balanced by water; time is balanced by space; and days are balanced by nights. If we didn't have the darkness of night to contrast with the brightness of day (as is the case on certain parts of the Earth), our ability to get deep restorative sleep is compromised.

The first step in macrobiotics is to learn that the forces of yin and yang create balanced health within our environment and within ourselves. We are living within three simple principles of changing phenomena:

1. yin attracts yang and yang attracts yin
2. yin opposes yin and yang opposes yang
3. yin converts to yang and yang converts to yin

Example of Yin and Yang in Food Selection & Preparation

	More Yang	More Yin
Soup	warm, chunky, salty	cold, creamy, sweet
Grains	small, rounder and growing in cold climates; buckwheat, millet, short-grain brown rice	large, more elongated and growing in warm climates; barley, long-grain brown rice
Vegetables	root and round, less water; burdock, carrot, cabbage	leafy greens, more water; bok choy collard greens, napa cabbage, cucumber
Beans	small; azuki	large; soy beans
Nuts & seeds	small, less oily; almond, sesame	large, more oily; walnut, pumpkin
Fruits	small, hard, less sweet, less juicy, less aroma, growing in the ground or cold climate; strawberry, apple	large, soft, sweeter, more juicy, more aroma, growing on trees or warm climate; peaches, melons
Seasoning	more salt; miso, tamari, soy sauce; less or no oil; vinegar, herbs or spices	less salt; miso, tamari, soy sauce; more oil; vinegar, herbs or spices
Salt	refined	unrefined
Sugar	raw	refined
Beverages	warm, non-aromatic, non-stimulating	cold, aromatic, stimulating
Cooking style	pressure-cooking, long-time boiling, baking, pan-frying, tempura, deep-frying	raw or uncooked, steaming, light or medium boiling, water-sauté, quick sautéing
Time	long cooking	short cooking
Volume	small serving	large serving
Taste	salty, pungent	sweet, sour, bitter, hot and aromatic taste

THE FUTURE

I believe the future is bright. Why? Because more and more people are changing to an increasingly natural style of living, the environmental movement is growing and natural foods companies are flourishing.

Living a macrobiotic life is far more convenient than when I started 15 years ago. I can now buy organically grown brown rice almost anywhere, and I can fairly easily find miso, umeboshi plums, and even kuzu. People's reactions are changing, and they are listening. When I talk to almost anyone nowadays-from taxi drivers to plumbers, to the person behind the counter or the person sitting next to me on the plane—I find that organic, natural foods, and even macrobiotic foods, are a current and vibrant topic. This is all good. I am very happy all the seeds that have been planted for so many years are finally sprouting. I look forward to seeing them continue to grow, bloom, and be harvested.

WHERE ARE LOVE, REAL HEALTH & HAPPINESS?

I was seeking these things outside of myself and from someone else for a long time. By eating and living in a natural and macrobiotic way, I have found love inside myself. Yes, love is inside of me, and inside of you, and inside of everyone. I am free to choose how I eat and how I live. I have a choice to be healthy and be happy. To have this freedom is the foundation of real health and happiness.

Here are George Ohsawa's Seven Main Conditions of Health and Happiness excerpted from his book, "An Invitation to Health & Happiness..."

1. No fatigue
2. Good appetite
3. Deep and good sleep
4. Good memory
5. Good humor
6. Clarity in thinking and doing (quick in thoughts and decisions)
7. Never lie (the mood of justice)

THE HOUSE RULES

In closing, I would like to share my favorite house rules. Most of them are courtesy of my mother, who wrote on each door of our house, "If you open it, close it."

1. If I open it, close it.
2. If I turn it on, turn it off.
3. If I unlock it, lock it.
4. If I break it, repair it.
5. If I can't fix it, call in someone who can.
6. If I borrow it, return it.
7. If I use it, take care of it.
8. If I make a mess, clean it up.
9. If I move it, put it back.
10. If it belongs to someone else and I want to use it, get permission.
11. If I don't know how to operate it, leave it alone.
12. If it doesn't concern me, don't mess with it.
13. If I can't say nice things, don't say anything.
14. If I can't chew it well, don't eat it.
15. Sit down to eat, and chew well.
16. Take off my shoes when I come home.
17. Wash my hands when I come home.
18. Sing or hum a happy song.
19. Cry when I am sad.
20. Say "I am sorry" when I make others feel uncomfortable and/or make a mistake. (Making amends is as important as saying "Thank you!")
21. Say "thank you" and "my pleasure" frequently.

EPILOGUE

The year 2008 was a very auspicious year in my life, as well as in both Chinese and Japanese astrological traditions. In the Chinese tradition, 2008—the year of the rat—is the first of twelve different animals featured in the Zodiac. In the Japanese tradition of Nine Star Ki, a type of "astrology" used by macrobiotic practitioners that follows cyclical biorhythms, 2008 featured the first of the five elements (or five natural phenomena stages) known as a 1 Water Year. These events coincided to mark an incredible transition to a new year and a new beginning. I also began 2008 by writing and working on this cookbook. In order to face this "new beginning," change was an inevitable and important part of my process. And just like the principles inherent in yin and yang, some of these changes were ups and some were downs, with changes within changes, as well.

The most challenging of these changes was losing loved ones and being especially attached to physical connections I had with them. Learning from my grief was a necessary and important step that enabled me to grow. I also needed to remind myself that my loved ones are here with me in spirit any time I want them to be, and that it's possible they may come back to this earthly plane.

I eventually came to a place of acceptance after processing my feelings of losing so many dear companions in such a short time. There was Ruška, who called me every day while I was bedridden for an entire year after my car accident; Linda, who was an amazing client and friend who held onto hope until the very end; Susan, who was the most kind-spirited client I ever had; and Luchi,

my great spiritual teacher and friend. And who can forget Dore, the most cheerful dog I ever had, who made us all laugh so much; and my beloved Kin, the wonder dog who survived the near-fatal car accident with me, and was my pillar of moral support during the entire time we shared our lives together. And at the very end of 2008, my longest feline companion, Key-chain, had gone to heaven also. Her gentle love and kind manner supported my busy life for almost twenty years, and I am going to miss her forever. Throughout this grieving process, I also learned to cherish the memory of my father and mother more deeply.

With the exception of a major detoxification experience I had in the summer of 2008, I greatly appreciate that my health has been good. Through it all, I can honestly say that I am excited to wake up to the miracle of a new day and greet new beginnings. And this is no small feat considering that I used to regularly wake up in a bad mood (due to hypoglycemia) before I started macrobiotics. Now, however, I feel uplifted, healthy and positive.

Also, in November of 2008, my husband Eric and I opened an organic vegan macrobiotic café called "seed." We are thrilled that this long-held dream has finally come to fruition. Finishing this cookbook took much longer than I had expected, but somehow this book and the opening of the café all came together in the Universal Schedule. "Seed" and "love, sanae" marked the beginning of a new chapter in my life.

I will continue to do my best and learn to appreciate life—and loved ones—more in this lifetime. Thank you all for reading my book. Let's continue our path of healing together...

love, sanae
Spring, 2009

CONVERSIONS

Seasoning Equivalents

1 pinch sea salt	½ teaspoon soy sauce
	⅔ teaspoon miso
	⅓ umeboshi plum
¼ teaspoon sea salt	1 ½ teaspoon soy sauce
	1 ⅔ teaspoon miso
	1 umeboshi plum
½ teaspoon sea salt	1 tablespoon soy sauce
	1 tablespoon +
	1 teaspoon miso
	2 umeboshi plums
1 teaspoon grated ginger	¼ teaspoon squeezed ginger juice

Umeboshi

| 1 plum | 1 ½ teaspoons paste |
| 1 teaspoon vinegar (umesu) | ⅔ umeboshi plum |

Weights

1 pound	16 ounces
¾ pound	12 ounces
½ pound	8 ounces
¼ pound	4 ounces
¹⁄₁₆ pound	1 ounce

Length Measures

US	Metric
⅛ inch	3 millimeters
¼ inch	6 millimeters
½ inch	12 millimeters
1 inch	2.5 centimeters

Temperature

Fahrenheit to Celsius

°F	°C
200 – 205	95
229 – 225	105
245 – 250	120
275	135
300 – 305	150
325 – 330	165
345 – 350	175
370 – 375	190
400 – 405	205
425 – 430	220
445 – 450	230
470 – 475	245
500	260

Liquid / Dry Measures and Volumes

1 tablespoon	3 teaspoons
4 tablespoons	¼ cup
5 ⅓ tablespoons	⅓ cup
8 tablespoons	½ cup
16 tablespoons	1 cup
4 cups	1 quart

U.S.	Metric (1mL = 1 g)
¼ teaspoon	1.25 milliliters or grams
½ teaspoon	2.5 milliliters or grams
1 teaspoon	5 milliliters or grams
1 tablespoon	15 milliliters or grams
¼ cup	60 milliliters or grams
⅓ cup	80 milliliters or grams
1 cup	240 milliliters or grams
1 pint (2 cups)	480 milliliters or grams
1 quart (4 cups)	960 milliliters or grams
1 gallon (4 quarts)	3.84 liters
1 ounce (ounce)	28 grams
1 pound (16 ounces)	454 grams
2.2 pounds	1 kilogram

Measure Equivalents

cup	fluid ounce	tablespoons	teaspoons	milliliter
1 c	8 oz	16 Tbsp	48 tsp	237 mL
¾	6	12	36	177
⅔	5	11	32	158
½	4	8	24	118
⅓	3	5	16	79
¼	2	4	12	59
⅛	1	2	6	30
1⁄16	0.5	1	3	15

INDEX

GLOSSARY

Agar agar
A sea vegetable that comes in bar, powder or flake form. Used for making vegetable-based gelatins, aspics and kanten.

Aonori
See *Green nori flakes*.

Arame
A mildly-flavored sea vegetable in the form of many long, thin brown or black strands; a good choice for those new to sea vegetables.

Amazake
A thick, fermented liquid made from rice and koji starter. Used as a beverage or sweetener.

Bancha tea
A Japanese tea made from the leaves and stems of the mature tea plant. Good for digestion.

Barley malt
A dark brown, thick and sticky sweetener made from sprouted barley. Used for desserts, sauces and remedy drinks.

Black sesame seeds
Similar to the more common tan sesame seed, except black in color and richer in flavor. Used as a garnish and in black gomashio.

Brown rice syrup
A sweetener made from fermented brown rice that provides a steady source of energy after consumption for several hours. Used in desserts, sauces and remedy drinks.

Buckwheat
Not a grain but a high-protein seed that contains all 8 essential amino acids. Used in soba noodles. Available in flour, whole groats and kasha form. Good for those who have wheat or gluten allergies.

Burdock root (gobo)
A long, thick root vegetable with an earthy flavor, similar to an artichoke; used in soups, side dishes and salads. Highly valued in macrobiotics for its strengthening qualities.

Chives
Long, thin green vegetable related to the onion family. Used in garnishes, soups and sauces.

Chrysanthemum
A flowering, edible plant that is also used as an ornamental. The greens are more commonly found in Asian cuisine either steamed or boiled.

Corn silk
The thin thread-like strands found inside the husks of corn. Used for remedy drinks.

Dandelion tea
A tea made from the roasted root and/or leaves of the dandelion plant. Used in remedy drinks.

Daikon
A long, white Japanese radish, shaped like a very large carrot. Available fresh or dried. Used in soups, salads, side dishes or remedy drinks.

Dashi
A soup base or cooking stock fundamental to Japanese cuisine. In macrobiotics, the common form of dashi is made from kombu and/or shiitake mushrooms.

Dulse
A reddish-colored sea vegetable used in salads, vegetable dishes and soups. Also available in small flakes.

Gobo
See *Burdock root*.

Gomashio
A condiment made from roasted sesame seeds and roasted sea salt; typically served on steamed whole grains. Can be made with brown and/or black sesame seeds.

Green nori flakes (aonori)
A dry sea vegetable that is available in Japanese markets. It is high in calcium, iron, and other minerals and vitamins.

Hatomugi
An unpolished cereal grass, similar to barley, but more closely related to corn. Also called Job's Tears or Coixseed.

Hijiki
A brown-black, strong and wiry sea vegetable known for its richness in calcium; delicious when combined with strong seasonings.

Jinenjo potato
A wild yam-like potato, also known as nagaimo, yamaimo or mountain potato, with a stickier texture and higher nutritional content than white potatoes.

Kabocha
A Japanese variety of winter squash with a bright orange flesh.

Kabu
A Japanese variety of turnip.

Kanten
A plant-based gelatin made with agar and prepared in a sweet or savory fashion. See page 140 for additional information.

Kimpira
A Japanese cooking style that can be summarized as "sauté and simmer" and is commonly used with root vegetables such as carrots, burdock and lotus root.

Kombu
A sea vegetable related to kelp, and notable for its mild, salty flavor; typically used to flavor soups (especially dashi), beans, or as a condiment.

Kukicha (twig tea)
Japanese tea made from the twigs and stems of the mature tea plant; extremely low caffeine content.

Kuzu (kudzu)
A white starchlike extract made from the wild root of kuzu vines; used for thickening soups, beverages, desserts and sauces. Also used for medicinal purposes.

Lotus root
The hollow, multi-chambered root of the water lily, available whole, dried, or in powder form. Seeds found inside the root are also used in cooking. Macrobiotically used for the respiratory organs.

Mirin
A sweet cooking wine made from whole grain sweet rice. Commonly used in land and sea vegetable dishes.

Miso
A savory fermented paste made from soybeans, grains and/or beans; traditionally used to flavor soups. Available in several different varieties; see pages 49 and 50 for additional information.

Mochi
Pounded dumpling-like rice cake made from brown or white sweet rice.

Nabe
Pronounced "nah-bay," nabe translates to "pot" in Japanese. The pot is usually made of ceramic and is used for a popular Japanese dish. "Nabemono" means "things in pot."

Natto
A steamed, fermented soybean condiment with a strong flavor. See pages 110 and 111 for additional information.

Nishime
A Japanese cooking style of vegetables that have been slowly braised until all liquid has evaporated and browned. In Japanese, "ni" translates to "cook," and "shime" to "colored."

Nori
Paper-thin sheets of dried sea vegetable typically used in making sushi, or served with rice balls. Also available in flake form (aonori) and used as a garnish.

Nuka
The bran portion of brown rice. Used for making a "nuka doko" or brown rice bran pickling bed. See page 81 for additional information.

Ohitashi
Boiled or steamed greens with a sauce.

Ojiya
A slow-cooked Japanese rice porridge with miso or shoyu. Usually eaten for breakfast or as a winter dish.

Onigiri
Steamed rice formed into balls or other shapes. See pages 38 and 39 for additional information.

Seitan
Also called wheat gluten, wheat meat, or simply gluten. It is made from the protein (or gluten) of wheat. Used as a meat substitute in sandwiches, soups, sautés, or other dishes.

Shiso
Green shiso: The bright green, distinctly-flavored leaves of the beefsteak plant; served as a condiment, and with salad.
Red shiso: The purple-reddish colored leaves are used to colorize umeboshi and shiso powder condiment.

Shiitake mushroom
A large-capped, meaty-flavored mushroom native to East Asia. Usually dried shiitake mushrooms are used in macrobiotic cooking.

Shoyu
A traditional, naturally-brewed soy sauce made from whole soybeans, wheat and sea salt. Wheat-free versions are also available.

Suribachi
A ceramic bowl with a serrated interior for grinding, mashing or puréeing seeds, spreads, dressings, condiments, etc.

Surikogi
A wooden pestle used with a suribachi.

Tekka
A richly-flavored condiment made from dark hatcho miso, sesame oil, ginger and long-simmered vegetables. See page 202 for additional information.

Tempeh
A fermented, whole and minimally-processed cake made from soybeans; easy to digest.

Tofu
A curd made from boiled soybeans and a coagulant (usually the magnesium-rich nigari or calcium sulfate).

Twig tea
See *Kukicha*.

Umeboshi
Salty, pickled Japanese plums made with red shiso. Used to aid digestion due to their very alkaline nature. Also available in paste form, as well as the basis for umeboshi vinegar. See page 95 for additional information.

Yuzu vinegar
A vinegar with a lime-like fragrance made from a variety of bitter orange plants.

Wakame
A thin, deep green sea vegetable; rich in iodine and calcium and often used in miso soups and salads.